TAPPING INTO WIRELESS

The Savvy Investor's Guide to Profiting from the Wireless Wave

TOM TAULLI
DAVE MOCK

McGraw-Hill
New York   Chicago   San Francisco
Lisbon   London   Madrid   Mexico City
Milan   New Delhi   San Juan   Seoul
Singapore   Sydney   Toronto

Library of Congress Cataloging-in-Publication Data

Taulli, Tom.
   Tapping into wireless : the savvy investor's guide to
profiting from the wireless wave / Dave Mock.
     p. cm.
     Includes bibliographical references.
     ISBN 0-07-138419-7
   1. Telephone, Wireless. 2. Telecommunication.
3. Cellular telephone services industry. 4. Securities.

HE9713.T38 2002   12524506
  384.5/34 21   CIP

McGraw-Hill

A Division of The McGraw·Hill Companies

1 2 3 4 5 6 7 8 9 0 DOC/DOC 0 9 8 7 6 5 4 3 2

ISBN 0-07-138419-7

This book was set in Palatino by Hendrickson Creative Communications.
Printed and bound by R. R. Donnelley & Sons Company.

McGraw-Hill books are available at special quantity discounts to use as premiums and
sales promotions, or for use in corporate training programs. For more information, please
write to the Director of Special Sales, Professional Publishing, McGraw-Hill, Two Penn
Plaza, New York, NY 10121-2298. Or contact your local bookstore.

This publication is designed to provide accurate and authoritative information in regard to
the subject matter covered. It is sold with the understanding that neither the author nor
the publisher is engaged in rendering legal, accounting, futures/securities trading, or other
professional service. If legal advice or other expert assistance is required, the services of a
competent professional person should be sought.

> *—From a Declaration of Principles jointly adopted by a Committee*
> *of the American Bar Association and a Committee of Publishers*

 This book is printed on recycled, acid-free paper containing a
minimum of 50% recycled, de-inked fiber.

To Shauna
              T. T.

To Gina
              D. M.

CONTENTS

Foreword   ix

Acknowledgments   xi

Introduction   xiii

Chapter 1

Wireless History   1

Just How New Is Wireless?   2

Not When or Where, but Why and How   3

Where It All Began: The Electric Telegraph   4

The Telephone and Alexander Graham Bell   10

Wireless Radio   13

The Dawn of Commercial Cellular   21

Act II   23

We're Just Getting Started   25

Summary   26

Chapter 2

The Driving Forces for Wireless   29

Buy-In from Industry Leaders   30

The M&A Factor   34

Foreign M&A   36

Politics and Money Go Hand in Hand   38

Regulation   40

Standards Adoption   44

Consumer Tastes   51

Convergence   52

Summary   53

Chapter 3

Wireless Network Operators   55

Wireless Service Providers: Their Role in the Industry   57

The Technology   58
First- and Second-Generation (1G/2G) Cellular Networks   61
Circuits versus Packets   64
The Next-Generation (2.5G and 3G) Cellular Networks   67
Wireless Network Operator Metrics   73
Key Investment Themes   79
Summary   83

Chapter 4

Wireless Equipment/Component Suppliers   85

Role in the Industry   87
Wireless Component Manufacturers   89
Application/Baseband Processors   91
Digital Signal Processors   92
RF Components   94
Displays   94
Intellectual Property   95
Portable Equipment   98
Consumer Segment   100
Business Segment   104
Wireless Infrastructure Equipment   105
Wireless Equipment Manufacturer Metrics   108
Summary   111

Chapter 5

Wireless Enterprise Solutions   115

The Collaborative Economy   118
The Trends in the Enterprise   119
Finding the Right Companies   123
Signs of a Breakout   133
Summary   138

Chapter 6

Emerging Technologies and Markets   141

Emerging Technologies   145
Wireless Consumer Applications   155
Summary   160

Chapter 7

IPO Fever   163

What's an IPO?   165
On the Ground Floor   170
Risk Factors   172
Other Key Sections of the Prospectus   179
IPO Strategies   182
Slice 'Em and Dice 'Em   184
Good Investments   186
Tracking Stocks: On the Right Track for Investors?   187
Summary   189
Online Resources   190

Chapter 8

Red Flags: When to Sell Your Wireless Stock   191

Junk Bonds   192
Convertible Financing   194
Insider Selling   197
Building a Wireless Network   199
The Price Knows   200
Penny Stocks   201
Research Analysts   202
Bad News   205
Chat Boards   206
Hot Markets   206
Summary   207

Chapter 9

Foreign Investing   209

Emerging Markets   210
Privatization Boom   211
Risks   212
American Depositary Shares   215
United States: A Drop in the Bucket?   217
The Finland Factor   220
Asia   223
Summary   224

Chapter 10

Wireless Mutual Funds   225

Benefits   227
Some Background   227

Chapter 11

Private Equity   235

Risks versus Rewards   235
Protections   238
Thinking Like a Venture Capitalist   241
Dealflow   244
Summary   245

Conclusion   247

Appendix: Resources   249
Glossary   257
Sources   269
Index   273

FOREWORD

The biggest single issue for investors in the mobile telecommunications sector concerns the question of who will benefit most from the explosive growth of wireless communications. This is the hardest, most impenetrable enigma for investors—and it is remarkable how many people refuse even to acknowledge just how unpredictable the profitability issue is. A few years ago, most specialists thought that the dilemma was rather trivial—of course, it is the infrastructure vendors who will reap the real benefits. The year 2001 proved with devastating clarity that the conventional wisdom turned out to be wrong—the infrastructure sector became an almost entirely profit-free zone and led some major players to gruesome losses.

This reversal of the most important late-nineties telecom investing golden rule, "The network companies are more profitable than operators or handset manufacturers," is only one example of how the mobile telecommunications sector consistently has defeated prophets and pundits throughout its existence. Another example concerns the meteoric rise of Short Messaging Service (SMS) and how it is currently transforming the way people use their mobile phones—possibly offering us clues about how the mobile content business may mutate in surprising ways in the future.

One big mistake people consistently make when evaluating mobile telecom sector companies is drawing overt or unconscious parallels to the birth and maturation of the personal computer (PC) industry. These industries are fundamentally different, and they keep evolving into directions that do not seem to be converging—partly because the mobile telecom sector is not dominated by the "Wintel" duopoly that effectively took over the entire global PC market. As a result of current competition between various standards and philosophies concerning the future evolution of mobile services, the entire sector is in flux—moving toward some future equilibrium that we can only guess at.

Realizing the capricious and sometimes violently unpredictable nature of the industry is the first and most important lesson investors need to learn. Realizing the limits of our predictive ability is actually a lot harder than it sounds—which is why most people writing about the industry so easily don the cloak of foresight and try to pawn off guesswork as valid projections.

The value of this book is in the way it offers us an overall look at the complexity of the industry. The first step in getting a grip on the companies involved is reviewing their places in the history of the industry—how they fit into the intricate ecology of the sector. There are no easy shortcuts to gaining insights about the companies—you have to review them in the context of the industry history. Many of the standardization and technology issues here are so complex that the business press never really bothers to go into details. As a result, many individual investors focus on quarterly numbers and short-term trends that rarely reveal much about the slower, grander trends that eventually influence the companies far more than whether they beat the "Street" during the next 3 months.

It's vital for investors in this sector to pull back and think about the larger picture every now and then. Dave Mock and Tom Taulli have crafted their book specifically to aid this process. Not by offering hot tips or making deceptively confident claims about the unknowable future. Not by pretending to be a guide to instant riches and "ten-baggers." But by offering an intricate, absorbing look at the past and current states of the industry. We have all learned something about humility during the turbulent tech crash of recent years. Humility is not a guarantee of wisdom—but it is a requirement. Understanding how complex and unpredictable, how exciting and dynamic the mobile telecommunications industry is will help investors in the sector to make conscious decisions about the relative risks of different approaches.

Dave and Tom challenge investors to become conscious of their current assumptions. This awareness is a prerequisite for evaluating whether new trends support these investment assumptions in the future or not. There are no simple solutions or gimmicky rules in this book—the reality is far too baroque and complex, far more intriguing than that. And this is the key to the vitality and turbulence of mobile telecoms. We have some mind-boggling twists and turns ahead of us during this decade. It is time to take an in-depth look at the sector to get our bearings before the frenzied denouement of the mobile data evolution reaches one peak during 2002–2005.

Tero Kuittinen
Technology Advisor,
Opstock Investment Banking
Columnist, TheStreet.com

ACKNOWLEDGMENTS

I would like to recognize the countless colleagues, friends, and coworkers who deserve credit for helping me reach the point where I could write this book. Of all these, I think it is most important to thank Tom Farley for planting the seed and providing all his insights into telecommunications history. I would also like to thank all those who are my eyes and ears to the wireless world abroad when I can't be there to experience it firsthand—especially Oliver Thylmann, who put up with countless inquiries to keep me in tune with the latest European trends.

A great deal of gratitude also goes to those who took a risk with me starting out, notably The Motley Fool for publishing a no-name writer in a sophisticated community. Appreciation is also reserved for our editor, Kelli Christiansen, and her team, who championed the book from day one and brought it to fruition in an uncertain market.

Lastly, none of this would be worth it without the support of my close friends and family. Special thanks go to my wife, Gina, who never hesitated to make sacrifices for my benefit.

Dave Mock

I would like to thank my wife, who put up with me while writing this book. I also want to thank Kelli Christiansen for her work and diligence. The process was great!

Tom Taulli

INTRODUCTION

Radio has no future. Heavier-than-air flying machines are impossible. X-rays will prove to be a hoax.

British scientist William Thomson, 1899

This sentiment was not the minority opinion as the nineteenth century came to a close. Essentially, radio communications—which is, in effect, wireless—was thought to be a novelty by some and a complete hoax by others. Most thought it wouldn't amount to anything, let alone be a critical part of the world economy. Rather, most figured wireline communications would be the dominant system. With the introduction of the telegraph and the telephone, the United States and Europe became wired with millions of lines of copper. There also were undersea cables that linked the two continents. Wire was king.

Interestingly enough, the discoveries for wireless communications started in the early 1800s. A key breakthrough occurred in 1820, when Hans Christian Oersted discovered that if an electric current passed through a regular compass, the needle would move. At that point in history, this discovery was truly amazing. It meant that electricity could move through thin air. Wireless!

While this discovery tantalized the scientific community, few people saw any practical use for it. Only a select few visionaries realized that the transmission of electricity through the air could be used to communicate over long distances.

Many years later, in 1886, Heinrich Hertz developed a machine that generated high-voltage sparks between two metal balls. Again, it sounds simple, but it was revolutionary for the time. Hertz proved that electricity had, in fact, traveled through the air. However, he did not seem to grasp the importance of the discovery. After all, the charge only traveled 1 meter, which was clearly inadequate for communications.

Guglielmo Marconi was intrigued by these discoveries. He was only 19 when he looked at the discoveries of Hertz and Oersted. Unlike many before him, however, he was convinced that the signals could be used to communicate, even over long distances.

After much success at short distances, Marconi decided that he would build a device that would attempt to provide communications over a much longer distance between Newfoundland and England. Scientists thought it was impossible because of the curvature of the earth.

But it worked.

On December 12, 1901, after sending the first message, Marconi remarked:

> I had always held a belief, amounting almost to an intuition, that radio signals would some day be sent across the greatest distances. I now knew that all my anticipations had been justified. The electric waves sent out into space from Poldu had traversed the Atlantic, unimpeded by the curvature of the earth.

For the most part, however, Marconi's wireless technology was relegated to a niche—that is, it focused on ocean vessels. Much of it was for passengers who wanted access to information, such as stock quotes, news stories, and so on. Passengers also could send and receive messages (called *MarconiGrams*).

When stacked up against the wired telegraph and telephone networks on the mainland, wireless couldn't compete. The wired networks were well developed and efficient. Radio signals were problematic and sometimes unreliable due to interference. Operators still did not fully understand the nature of radio waves. Additionally, the equipment necessary to transmit radio signals, while relatively simple, was bulky.

However, as you will discover in Chapter 1, the current practical limitations of wireless technology were not enough to keep thousands of companies from springing up at the turn of the century to capitalize on the new discovery. Speculation in the stock market soon reached a fever pitch, and investors were clamoring to get into anything that had even a remote connection to wireless.

What led to this sudden love for wireless was visions of personal communications made possible through radio. The earliest ideas about the use of radio converged on the almost mystical idea of personal mobile communication. Even before Marconi's work, speculators hypothesized about radio devices that could be carried by any person or vehicle.

As each year passed, radio receivers were improved and made smaller, increasing speculation about the concept of a personal communicator. Even as early as 1919, the U.S. War Department speculated that the day of personal voice communications from anywhere on earth was not far off. It was widespread optimism like this that not only fueled rampant stock speculation but also supported some of the worst corporate stock scams in history.

The world was captivated. When would people see these portable devices? When could they put one in their new horseless carriage in order to signal for help when it broke down? When would the wireless communicators make the telegraph obsolete?

Many people waited their entire lives for these events to come to pass. For them, it never happened. It would take almost a century for these predictions to come true.

BABY STEPS

One event did a lot to make wireless a mainstream technology. It happened on April 14, 1912. It was on this date that the so-called unsinkable *Titanic* did, indeed, sink when it plowed into an iceberg.

An officer on board was able to send out a distress signal using a Marconi wireless device. The passenger ship *Carpathia* heard the signal and was able to rescue 711 passengers.

Another passenger ship, the *Californian*, was only 10 miles away. But the *Californian* did not have its wireless device on. If it had, perhaps all the passengers could have been saved. Instead, 1,500 passengers died. In fact, hours before the *Titanic* hit the iceberg, two wireless messages had been sent that warned of icebergs. The messages were ignored.

In light of these blunders, the United States and Great Britain set up a convention in 1912 and called for international regulations for the seas. Sixty-five countries attended. One of the regulations was establishment of the universal SOS distress signal. A year later, another convention was held, and the same 65 countries agreed to require wireless devices on all ocean vessels—whether motor-propelled or under sail. And the wireless device would need to be manned 24 hours a day.

No doubt, the new regulations were a boon for Marconi's wireless business. Soon the unique aspects of wireless communications began to show value. But it still didn't form into the type of wireless world that most people envisioned.

Rather than personal communications, radio found its place in broadcasting. Once audio information was transmitted successfully over radio signals, broadcasting boomed. In the early 1920s, after many early wireless companies went bust, a new wave of companies moved in to capitalize on a lucrative broadcast market.

Radio would go on to have a long, fruitful life as a medium for dispensing real-time information and entertainment to thousands, even millions of people at once. With a large, captive audience, radio broadcasters made a mint off paid advertising.

As the years passed and broadcasting grew in size and scope, people began to realize just how unrealistic the idea of personal communications was. Even with dramatic advances in vacuum-tube technology, the receivers would never be made compact enough to be practical.

The wave of wireless optimism soon died, replaced by interest in continuing advances in telephone systems. The wireless revolution had fallen somewhat short of expectations, and the radio industry was unable to deliver on promises glamorized in the media.

This was not the end, however. The personal communications revolution was only waiting to begin.

THE COMEBACK OF THE CENTURY

Jacques almost drops the recorder he is so excited. High up in the Andes mountain range, his testing confirms that he has indeed found the geologic site he has been hunting for. Pulling the satellite phone from his equipment pack, he calls back to the laboratory 9,500 miles away to share the good news. They've reached their milestone days ahead of schedule and could actually fly the next round of supplies to the rendezvous point to start the next phase. If they can quickly communicate the details, they can fit in the next expedition before the worst weather hits, saving them hundreds of thousands of dollars.

Jukka anxiously pulls his mobile from his hip pocket to answer the message. His opponent has taken the bait and moved into a precarious position. Undetected, the young Finn's character can now sneak in to capture the flag of his opponent and move on to the larger goal of facing the notorious Bucat—the screen name for the most notorious player in the world. Gamers only know that the player behind Bucat exists somewhere in southern China, although many have personally fallen to him or her many times.

Anthony quickly hands the cab driver the fare with a generous tip and heads toward the gate. Briefcase in hand, he walks by the counter lines because his mobile has already checked him in ahead of time. An SMS appears on his phone stating that the flight is 10 minutes behind, giving him a chance to take a breather. After grabbing a hot Danish, he heads for the wireless lounge to download the latest sales presentation on his Pocket PC. After only a few minutes, he has the updated presentation that includes their latest financials. As a bonus, he recalls the current inventory levels from his corporate Web site. He now has everything he needs to close the deal in Beijing on the spot.

At a shopping square in Germany, Klaus taps away on the phone keypad. His companion, Hiroshi, is in downtown Tokyo waiting for information about the antiquated items offered. Hiroshi has informed Klaus of the prices he's willing to pay for genuine aged Levi's, books, and other rare antiquities to resell there in Japan. Between the two of them, they've made almost a million dollars by quickly evaluating hidden gems in "junk sales" around the world. The items that Klaus snapped up for less than an hour's wage were quickly cataloged and shipped to Tokyo, tracked through Hiroshi's cellular phone, and already sold to eager buyers who were alerted to their pending arrival by SMS.

Yu Jie sits patiently at her mother's side, staring at the small screen. Soon, a bright color image fills in the pale background. The profile on the phone screen is her cousin, several hundred miles away in Zhejiang, whom they have not seen in years. Over the next few minutes, several images from her sixth birthday celebration come to the screen. A smile covers Yu Jie's face as she remembers the days playing with her cousin. They save the pictures to memory so that they can always feel close to their distant family.

For those of us fortunate enough to live in this day and age, the mobile revolution is finally here. After decades of refinement and progress, the concept of a portable wireless communications device is no longer a pondered idea—it is physical reality.

The twisted tale of wireless communications has never failed to amaze people. In the early days of scientific discoveries, people were fascinated with the magical nature of the technology. Today, people are equally awed at the rampant proliferation of wireless communications devices. Most industry followers are still underestimating the impact of wireless by drastic amounts.

In the 1980s, people finally began to see portable wireless devices that were practical. The time of personal mobile communications definitely was at hand. Many pondered just how pervasive the new technology would be.

In the early stages of cellular service in America, AT&T had predicted that the number of U.S. cellular subscribers would reach 1 million by 1999. Much to the surprise of AT&T, that number was surpassed only a few years later in 1987. By the time 1999 rolled around, there would be 70 million subscribers in the United States.

As late as 1995, most forecasts put forth in the industry stated that by the year 2005 there would be more than 100 million cellular subscribers around the world. While this figure dazzled many at the time, it was almost laughably inaccurate in its underestimation.

As you read this text, there will be more than a *billion* cellular subscribers around the world. And this does not even account for many types of wireless pagers, personal digital assistants (PDAs), and other portable devices.

What caught many off guard in predicting the cellular boom was the naiveté in assuming that mobile communications would be practical only for middle-class individuals in industrialized nations due to its prohibitive cost. However, wireless truly has become a technology for everyone, and it has reached just about every populated area on earth.

This rapid acceleration in the proliferation of wireless devices started in the late 1990s and has continued its upward trend. Soon many nations will have the vast majority of their population connected wirelessly.

It seems the predictions of "wireless everywhere" a century ago are finally coming true.

ONLY THE BEGINNING

The rapid growth of wireless communications around the world has set up the next phase of this exciting market. With billions of people now familiar with the concept of mobile communications, new ideas and creative uses of wireless devices are coming around every day. Many concepts only dreamed of in cartoons and fictional movies are filtering into society today.

Noted futurist Paul A. Ostendorf made this statement to the *Wall Street Journal* in June 2001:

> Now that it is smaller and more portable, the computer is coming to me. The Palm Pilot fits in my palm. Not long from now it will be in my shoe and the next step is in my body. Applied Digital Solutions just came out with a watch that has a chip on its backside sitting on one's skin, which is activated by a satellite code. It measures one's pulse. In case of a heart attack, emergency services are automatically warned and directed to the patient by a GPS system built into the watch.

In Finland, shoppers at the local supermarket have wireless devices that track the items removed from the store. They no longer have to wait in lines to itemize and pay for items.

Real-time traffic-monitoring systems are being installed in Europe and the United States to provide optimal travel routes for roadway commuters. Subscribers to a traffic service can have messages sent to them at specified times detailing the amount of time it would take to travel specific routes. If your normal route to work exceeds a certain time, for instance, an automatic request to find an alternate route with less traffic kicks in, and you receive the information on your mobile device.

It is safe to assume that there are many more wireless visions like these yet to be discovered as well. As the technology matures and more entrepreneurs start to develop novel products, the usefulness of wireless connectivity will continue to grow.

THE 100-YEAR R&D PROJECT

How could it take more than 100 years to get portable wireless communications from the concept stage into a working system? This is one question we hope to shed light on in this book.

In Chapter 1 of this book we will take a more detailed look at the history of wireless communications. Starting with the early experiments in electricity and moving through the era of the telegraph and telephone, we will examine the birth of wireless communications in the industrial age.

In this first chapter we hope to give you a solid perspective on some of the major events and issues that went into the development of telecommunications systems in the United States and abroad. It may surprise investors to see many events of the past that closely mimic events of today.

After laying out the "story" of wireless, in Chapter 2 we will discuss some of the major forces that drive the wireless industry today. Many of these driving forces have been in place from day one and will continue to influence the market long into the future. It is important to understand these market forces because they have a dramatic impact on investments.

Unfortunately, many investors believe that a company's success largely follows from simple market rules of supply and demand. While it is definitely important to have a good product that's in demand, ignoring other influences, such as government regulations and standards compliance, can leave investors shy of all the tools necessary for successful investing in the wireless market. The goal of this book is to provide you with a good grasp of the "big picture" of wireless, and the driving forces of the market are vital to this view.

In Chapter 3 we will start to break down the industry into major segments. The first, and probably most important, is the wireless network operator segment. These are the massive telecom companies that provide wireless services. They play a key role in the industry because they guide the development of new technologies and services for consumers and business users.

In this chapter we will look at various aspects of the network operators' business. As stated earlier, we first want you to get a good grasp of their role in the industry. This is essentially learning where they fall in the wireless "food chain." As you will see, their operations touch almost every aspect of the industry. Therefore, their role in the industry is important to understand no matter what segment of the wireless market you invest in.

We also will break down the common technologies that go into building wireless networks. There are myriad acronyms and technical terms used commonly when referring to wireless communications, so we want you to become comfortable with these terms. The goal of this section is not to provide you with an understanding of how wireless works in detail. Rather, it is to make you aware of the significance of the various technologies and how they fit into the big picture.

Once you have a handle on the operations of the service providers, we will take a look at some key metrics used in their evaluation. There are many unique measures that analysts and investors use to gauge the quality of an investment in this area. Again, there are many unusual terms here that actually refer to pretty simple concepts.

We finish Chapter 3 with a discussion about various investment themes in this segment. For example, service providers tend to have consistent risk profiles, corporate focuses, and other attributes. This section can help an investor decide if this is the area of the wireless market that is best suited for his or her financial goals.

After this review of network operators, we open Chapter 4 with a similar look at wireless equipment and component providers. These are the companies that make the "nuts and bolts" of the industry.

We will review their role in the industry to see how they collaborate with service providers and other companies. We want you to understand their sometimes-awkward relationships with other companies in the industry and look at what it takes to be successful at getting a company's product "designed into" an end product.

It is also important to determine what level of equipment a company builds. Knowing whether a company builds wireless components, portable equipment, or network infrastructure is important in determining the available market and key competitors. A short discussion of each of these areas will give you a firm footing in the opportunities of this segment.

As in Chapter 3, we will look at some of the key metrics used to evaluate companies in this segment of the wireless market. Since the overall goal of this book is to help investors pick good stocks in the wireless space, we will outline the various tips and tools that are important for thorough analysis.

In Chapter 5 we will explore a rapidly expanding area of the wireless sector: the enterprise segment. Since many of the early adopters of new technologies tend to be business users looking for a competitive advantage, this area is geared for growth.

We will look at some of the special needs for the enterprise and the wireless solutions offered to meet those needs. Looking at several examples from parallel industries in the past, we touch on many of the important factors guiding the growth in this nascent market segment.

In Chapter 6 we will go even farther out and look at emerging technologies and markets in wireless. This is a peek into the future and an attempt to see what new technologies could change mobile communications profoundly. While the investment opportunities in this area tend to be fewer, it nonetheless provides insight into the direction of the industry.

We also will explore the consumer applications market in this chapter. With the culture of personal communications only now beginning to take hold, the software and services segment of the market is also at an early stage. Looking at what drives consumer applications and where investors can look for opportunities will round out the topics in Chapter 6.

The discussion of emerging markets leads naturally into a look at initial public offerings (IPOs) in Chapter 7. With many young companies coming into the wireless market every day, they will play a big part in the IPO market for years to come. In this chapter we will discuss many of the aspects of IPOs and what tools exist for investors. We also will look at some recent examples of wireless IPOs to see what can be learned.

In Chapter 8 we will look at some effective strategies to determine when to sell a wireless stock. There are numerous red flags or advance warnings that investors can pick up in the course of business operations with any company. Through analysis of these events, investors can determine if a company's future is still bright or if its business is starting to decay.

In this chapter we will look at such issues as insider selling, debt offerings, and the capital costs to build out networks. Several areas we touch on in this section can give clues to the health of an organization and even foretell rough times ahead. While it is always preferable to invest in a stock that goes up forever, realistically, investors have to regularly assess when may be a good time to take profits and move on to a better opportunity.

Chapter 9 opens the discussion of investing in foreign wireless companies. Since this is another area that investors may want to consider, we will look at some of the options available today. Since many foreign markets are in the emerging stage, there is a large potential for growth in many regions. However, this growth comes with unique risks as well, and investors need to take the time to understand these risks before diving in.

One of the more popular ways to invest in foreign companies is through stock that is listed on an American exchange (these are called *American depositary shares*, or ADSs). We will take a brief look at several of these investments and their common attributes. While many of these stocks are larger blue-chip-type companies, they still can provide good returns.

Chapter 10 discusses another investment option in the wireless space: mutual funds. Investors who do not want to take the time and effort necessary to pick individual stocks may want to look into some of these funds. While many are relatively young, there also are many general telecommunications funds available that have some exposure to wireless companies.

Investors will find this chapter useful for explaining a number of the fees associated with mutual funds. It also will give some tips for buying into funds and explore some of the benefits in this area.

In Chapter 11 we will close the book with a brief look at private equity in the wireless market. Since investors may have an opportunity to buy into a venture at the pre-IPO stage, we will look at the important aspects of this process. For those who want to be "angel investors," a lot of information is available to help minimize the risk of investing early in ventures.

The Conclusion summarizes the major points of the text. While it is difficult to write a complete book for every type of reader, we will focus on capturing the most important aspects of the wireless market.

After the Conclusion, you will find plenty of additional sources of information in the Appendix. On top of dozens of useful Web sites, there are a number of good print publications that provide insight into the wireless market. We will list a few of the best ones for investors to continue their research. Also, we have included a handy glossary at the end of the book to help describe the many unusual terms used in this book.

EXCITING TIMES AHEAD

As you will see in this book, some of the best years for wireless technology are still ahead. With the coming third-generation (3G) cellular services, new doors will be opened to wireless data services that once again will change the way people view the world and each other.

For investors, advances in wireless technology translate into new opportunities for profit. Determining who will lead the future of the wireless market is not out of reach for the average investor either. There are a number of simple lessons from history that give good indications for future success stories—it is only a matter of realizing their significance.

Take the time to read this book at your leisure. Do not attempt to cram the information into your head so that you can make a stock decision tomorrow. Absorb the ideas and arguments made here and then continue your quest to stay informed about the industry and the companies in which you invest. If you keep an open mind and avoid the traps that many investors fall into, the wireless industry can provide financial returns beyond your expectations.

1

Wireless History

Arriving at work, you find a coworker has left you three voicemails to call him as soon as you get in. Before you can even dial, he calls again and quickly spills the beans—he's discovered a true gem of a stock. An unknown wireless company is developing a technology that is truly revolutionary, one that will make all current technologies obsolete. They have patented it and are sure to lock in massive profits—just buy now and retire early he says. Never in history has there been a company on the brink of success such as this one he remarks.

We've all heard stories like this one about a company in some indus-try, if not wireless. It seems like there is always someone out there with a small but vocal following that will revolutionize the world. It is tough as an investor simply to write off these promises, even if they are only partially achievable. What makes an objective evalu-ation of these types of scenarios difficult is that the company usually is going into uncharted territory, where there is no real standard or reference by which to judge them.

In reality, however, there is much perspective that can be added to these types of "pipe dream" stocks and the wireless industry as a whole. Understanding a little of the history of wireless communica-tions (and telecommunications as a whole) can give investors a leg

1

up in weeding out hype. You may be surprised to learn that there have been several events in history that closely mimic events today.

How do you know hype from the real deal? These stories aren't all hype—after all, Phone.com set out to change the world in the late 1990s when most people didn't even know what the wireless Internet was. To some extent, it did change the wireless world—and still does under the new company, Openwave. While it hasn't yet dominated the world as some hoped, it certainly has rewarded visionary share-holders—both inside the company and out. If your coworker was talking about Phone.com at its initial public offering (IPO) in 1999, a $10,000 investment in the vision would have had you sitting on over $70,000 a mere 6 months later.

JUST HOW NEW IS WIRELESS?

The explosive growth in wireless communications in the last few years has to be at least one of the reasons you've picked up this book. Looking at the growth of wireless subscribers in the United States over the years (Figure 1.1), you will see a sharp upward turn on the "hockey stick" in the late 1990s.

FIGURE 1.1

Estimated Wireless Subscribers in the United States

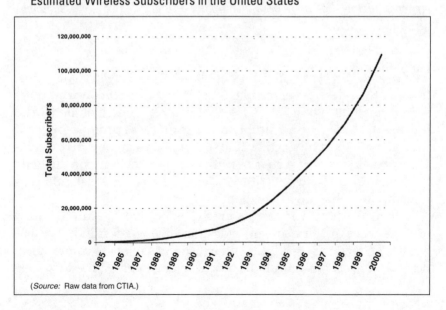

(*Source:* Raw data from CTIA.)

As of this writing in 2002, we continue to accelerate forward at a rapid pace, with almost a half billion cellular phones coming into the market each year. And this does not even factor in all the wireless personal digital assistants (PDAs), pagers, e-mail devices, tablet personal computers (PCs), and dozens of other types of portable communications products.

Looking back in history, though, personal wireless communications was not always such a high-flying market or fast-growing industry. As a matter of fact, there were decades of methodical progress and redundant experimentation leading to where we are today. There are several reasons why the wireless industry bumbled along for so long before finally moving into the mainstream. Not surprisingly, most of these reasons are tied intimately to the nature of wireless devices themselves.

As we'll see in this chapter's brief walk through wireless history, the principles necessary to carry the communication of information over the air were developed and well understood even before the 1900s. What made the implementation of these technologies impractical and expensive until recently was the size of the equipment and power necessary to convey information without wires.

The very nature of mobile communications dictates that a portable handheld device must be small enough to be carried comfortably. Even the esteemed Martin Cooper, who many claim to be the father of the first cellular phone, did not himself carry one until recently, when they became light and small. Until the 1980s, mobile phones were just too large and bulky to be carried on one's person. In addition, the battery life of the devices made constant recharges the norm.

For most of its early life, limitations still restricted wireless communications to fixed locations on land or in cars or ships, where large, heavy antennas and radio equipment could be mounted. It is only in the last 15 to 20 years that the concept of personal communications devices really has caught on with the general population. At this point, people are finally completely free to communicate at leisure without being tied to any particular point or locale, such as their car, office, or home. This is the point where the wireless culture began.

NOT WHEN OR WHERE, BUT WHY AND HOW

Why should an investor be subjected to a history lesson? It is not important for investors to remember names or dates of significant events to select good companies. However, it does help to understand some of the major events and achievements that helped shape the industry into what it is today. In other words, it is not important to remember the *when* or *where*, but it is important to know the *why* and *how*. The wireless industry today is still influenced dramatically by events that occurred decades ago, so at least a cursory review would be beneficial.

Along these lines, this chapter is not structured to be a comprehensive history of the developments in the wireless communications industry. It is designed to be a baseline, or reference, for investors to understand the industry today and how it came to be. For sure, certain inventors and events may be discussed in an unbalanced fashion, or several years of work may not be discussed at all. If you are looking for a lesson in history, you will find many holes here.

We will break down the last 200 years or so into several chunks and look at each of them chronologically to follow the "story" of wireless. In the end, we hope to have given you a collection of memorable tales that explain why wireless is where it is today and give hints as to where it is going tomorrow. Realize, though, that understanding where the industry is going is only half the battle. While history may tend to repeat itself, investors have an additional challenge to determine which companies are at the forefront when it does repeat.

WHERE IT ALL BEGAN: THE ELECTRIC TELEGRAPH

Many people are surprised at the concept of wireless technology being used in the nineteenth century, but it's true. Visionaries such as Michael Faraday and Joseph Henry discovered the principles that enable the transmission of information through the air in the early 1800s. Both these scientists and many others worked on discoveries in the area of electromagnetism that laid the groundwork for modern wireless communications. However, the theories were first applied to wired communications.

In the 1820s, both Faraday and Henry demonstrated how a changing magnetic field could induce current in a wire. This early discovery accompanied and supported a wave of research around the world as scientists sought to apply this new discovery in practical ways. These and countless other observations led to more advanced theories in electrical communications, although most of it was developed around communicating signals over wire by means of conduction.

The most notable development from decades of research in the early 1800s was the electric telegraph. Based on the discovery that electrical energy could be transformed into mechanical energy and vice versa, telegraph machines began to quickly replace other, slower forms of communication such as hand-carried mail and optical signaling systems. Wires were strung for miles on poles, often along railroad routes, so as to connect cities and rural towns. There were a number of variations of the telegraph. Some communicated letters of the alphabet over numerous wires, whereas others employed a coded scheme with fewer transmission wires.

Until the 1840s, while discoveries related to telegraphing information continued to excite inventors, most people outside the science community showed little interest in the new communications devices. In 1841, though, the usefulness of an early telegraph developed by Charles Wheatstone gained the public's attention in Europe when it was used to capture a suspected murderer, John Tawell.

As the story goes, a man was seen leaving the residence of Sarah Hart, who was later found dead inside, apparently poisoned with prussic acid. The police knew that John Tawell frequented the house, and they had information that Mr. Tawell had been noticed boarding a train for London only a short time earlier. Criminals and thieves often jumped aboard trains after committing crimes because trains were the fastest form of transportation (and communication) at the time. If a suspect could leave on a train before apprehension, he or she was almost assured of escape because the police could not notify authorities at the other end until the next train passed through.

The electric telegraph, however, changed all this. In this case, the police immediately telegraphed a message ahead to Paddington giving Tawell's description to authorities there and asking that he be detained. As he stepped off the train, John Tawell was captured and later confessed to the crime. Although Tawell was once a respected member of the community, the details of his "other life" came out, and he was executed for his crime. Word of the method of his capture spread quickly.

The publicity of the event boosted the credibility of the telegraph and helped legitimize its use in transferring information. With a practical use now demonstrated, it wasn't long before more telegraph wires were being strung between cities and along railways.

The next few decades that followed the 1840s were consumed with the proliferation of telegraph systems in the United States and abroad. Some of the most fascinating tales of this time center around accomplishing the profound goal of laying a trans-Atlantic cable for telegraph messages to travel between the United States and Europe.

Attempts at laying a trans-Atlantic cable were preceded by other submarine cables run across shorter lengths such as the English Channel. Even at these short distances, though, many of the early cables failed after a short time of operation. Improved cable designs were appearing rapidly in the late 1850s to make these connections more reliable.

Not convinced of the reliability of submerged cable, Western Union, a huge telegraph conglomerate in the United States, wanted to take the less direct route of running wires through Alaska and Siberia, leaving the water crossing to a mere 25 miles at the Bering Strait. While Western Union pursued this goal, several companies with eager backing in Europe pushed ahead to cross the Atlantic with improved cables.

Attempts to lay 2,300 miles of cable in the summer months of 1857 were frustrated from the very beginning. Two ships, the British battleship *Agamemnon* and the American frigate *Niagara*, set out to run the wire, starting in Valentia Bay, Ireland. After only 30 miles of laying out cable, it broke under its own weight, and the project was abandoned until the next year, when the Atlantic waters would be relatively calm again.

The expedition that began in June 1858 didn't start any better. The same two ships began laying the cable in the mid-Atlantic this time, with intentions of running half the line back to each shore. After weathering a furious storm and numerous failed attempts to maintain a spliced line, the ships returned to shore for repairs. A quick turnaround put the ships back out to sea for another attempt in late July. This time, it was successful.

By August 1858, a continuous cable finally had been laid between the United States and Europe. The first messages sent across the cable were extremely feeble and difficult to discern. After a few weeks of struggling with its operation, the fateful decision to increase the operating voltage from about 600 volts to roughly 2,000 volts was made in the belief that it would improve the signal, and the cable basically was fried (the insulation failed). After several weeks and only a few hundred garbled messages, the connection was now dead.

It wasn't until years later, in July 1866, that a new cable was laid across the Atlantic successfully. This cable proved much more reliable, and more cables were laid soon after. Western Union finally abandoned its attempt to cross Alaska and Siberia in 1867 after having the project delayed due to severe weather. The submerged cable finally did prove commercially feasible.

Like the first telegraph systems on land, though, use of the submarine cables was relegated to governments, businesses, and the wealthy due to the high costs of messages. Messages of only a handful of words cost upwards of $100. While the high costs kept most people from using the systems for anything but critical communications, telegraph companies still made enough business to pay for investments in their systems within several months. Major investors in the undersea Atlantic cables recouped their investments in little more than a year.

It is interesting to note here that it literally took decades before telegraph communications matured to a point where they were reliable. Early systems failed often and sometimes took days or weeks to get back online. It wasn't until later in its maturity that the real proliferation of devices began, spurred on by the reduction in costs for developing/installing systems, better technology, and the lower cost of service.

While wireless systems of today are developed faster, cutting-edge technologies still have to go through a "teething stage" where the kinks are ironed out. This is usually at least a few years in length and sometimes up to 5 years. Anyone expecting a new technology to work right out of the gate at a reasonable cost to consumers has been smoking funny stuff. Remember, it took nearly a decade to improve undersea cables to the point where they were reliable enough to provide continuous service. This is only one of the important lessons that history teaches investors.

A very familiar name working with telegraphs at the time in the United States was Samuel Morse. In the late 1830s, Morse developed and patented a telegraph that used a lever switch to make or break an electric circuit powered by a battery. A single insulated wire extended to another station that had a receiver that responded to the electrical impulses. The receiver made a clicking sound each time the key was pressed at the sending station. Since a single click didn't convey much information, an assistant named Alfred Vail helped Morse develop a code of short and long clicks that could be combined to spell out words.

The Morse alphabet (commonly referred to as *Morse code*) became a popular standard for communication not only in wired telegraphs but in early radio as well. It also was used in other communication media, such as when ships signal each other with high-powered lamps. It also has saved countless lives over the years.

In one notable incident, a U.S. submarine, the *USS Squalus*, unexpectedly sank in over 200 feet of cold water in May 1939 during routine dive tests. The submarine was partially flooded and came to rest on the bottom of the Atlantic near the Isles of Shoals. Amazingly, 33 of 59 men survived the sinking by moving to forward compartments that could be sealed. During an unprecedented rescue effort, the crew of the *Squalus* signaled messages in Morse code to their rescuers by banging on the hull with a hammer, giving details of their condition and location on the submarine. The messages were instrumental in eventually bringing the 33 men to the surface almost 39 hours after they sank.

While many inventors of this time delved into improving wired communications, Samuel Morse also played around with similar methods of communicating through different media. In one notable experiment, Morse attempted to demonstrate that he could telegraph signals through a wire submerged in the water rather than just lines strung on poles.

In October 1842, Morse laid about a mile of wire underwater between Governor's Island and Castle Garden in New York. Before he could fully demonstrate the telegraph, however, a ship pulled up the cable at its anchor and ended his demonstration. Realizing first-hand that wired communication had its weak points, Morse set out on a new path.

Morse decided to duplicate the intended result of this experiment with a different system. This new system would use the water itself to transmit the telegraph signals. In order to do this, Morse placed copper plates on each side of the river to serve as transmitters and receivers of the signal. The system worked, giving evidence that the passage of signals could be accomplished through other media besides metal conductors. This experiment and many other variations would be performed at ever-longer distances in the coming years.

This experiment and many others encouraged some inventors to look beyond communications over wires, although it would be quite a while before notable achievements would be made here. Most inventors and investors were working tirelessly to capitalize on telegraphy.

Thus at this point in history we have a brand-new method of communication coming into the world. Centuries had passed where communication was only as fast as a runner, horse, or ship. Suddenly, communications across great distances were almost instantaneous. The telegraph opened doors to speeding the passage of information and helping save lives in ways not possible before. A similar leap in communications has occurred with personal wireless devices. With the capability of people to call for police assistance immediately rather than running to payphones, wireless technology holds similar promises to improve the ability to communicate instantly today.

As one may expect, the invention of the telegraph and associated technologies not only advanced communications around the world but also generated profound wealth for smart investors in the industry. Like all young industries, the telegraph boom had its share of success stories as well as countless tales of missed opportunities. Just like emerging markets today, there were some real winners, lots of losers, and plenty of frauds.

By 1851, the telegraph industry was well established in the United States, and more than 50 companies operated telegraph lines in various areas of the country. Consolidation was eminent, and one company in particular, Western Union Telegraph Company, came to be the bigger fish eating up the small fish. As time wore on, Western Union gained a virtual monopoly in the telegraph business.

Throughout the following decade Western Union grew to tremendous size and scope. In 1867, the company was valued at over $41 million, some 11,000% above where it started only a little more than a decade previously. Early investors such as Ezra Cornell became fabulously rich. A $500,000 endowment in Western Union stock to the University that carries Cornell's name in 1868 helped establish a fund that still provides financial support to the school today.

Another prominent person who earned substantial wealth through the telegraph system was Edward Creighton. Considered by many to be instrumental in completing the transcontinental telegraph line connecting both coasts, Creighton and investors who followed his lead were rewarded handsomely. Stock in the Pacific Telegraph Company (for which Creighton was granted "options") that connected Omaha to Fort Churchill, Nevada, grew 20-fold in only 4 years.

While Creighton got an added boost of acquiring much of his stock for 15 cents on the dollar, the return for other investors was still nothing to sneeze at. Soon after his death, Creighton's widow carried out his desire to fund, among other things, a college from his vast wealth, which today is Creighton University in Omaha. The excitement of coast-to-coast communications also quickly pushed up the stock of Western Union, which had a controlling interest in the Pacific Telegraph Company. The Western Union Company and its investors continued to flourish.

As in most high-growth industries, however, countless young companies sprang up only to shut down soon thereafter. This led to many investors holding worthless shares. The telegraph and associated networks certainly were no guarantee of wealth. Investors still had to pick the very best companies to profit. Not unlike the recent dot-com era, the few businesses that survived the initial shakeout were shrewd and had competent, experienced management.

Despite the wild growth in the new era of telegraphy, there was more to come in the communications industry. The invention of the telegraph was soon to be only a stepping-stone to something greater: the telephone.

THE TELEPHONE AND ALEXANDER GRAHAM BELL

The history of the development of the telephone and telephone systems is a long and fascinating one. It is also one that is far too deep to cover in anything less than a full-length book, let alone a portion of a single chapter. For this reason, we will touch on only a few major events that help explain how voice communications developed at the turn of the century. We also will examine how these developments shaped the industry and the corporate giants that fought over the technology.

Alexander Graham Bell is probably only second to Thomas Alva Edison as the most remembered inventor of the nineteenth century. However, dozens of other inventors, such as Elisha Gray, played equally pivotal roles in the development of wired communications. To Bell goes the credit for invention of the telephone—but only by a scant 3 hours—and some still say that Gray developed it sooner. There's been a long-standing debate about who really invented the first telephone, but we won't get into that here.

Alexander Graham Bell's invention of a working telephone had a lot to do with knowledge he lacked rather than expertise he retained. In the beginning, Bell actually had little working knowledge of electricity. However, he was brilliant in another field—acoustics. Bell's family had a long history in the study of methods of vocal communication, with his father and grandfather both occupying much of their lives with a study of methods to help deaf people communicate and "hear." Bell's own mother, Eliza, became deaf as well, and Alexander learned much about sound through interaction with her.

As Bell developed into a resilient inventor, he began to apply his talents to the invention of the telephone after coming to the notion that voice could be carried over a wire. With financial backing from the fathers of two deaf students Bell was teaching, Bell teamed up with Thomas Watson to develop a working telephone. Some early successes in 1875 of transmitting tones through wires across rooms further fueled Bell's passion for this speaking machine.

Finally, on March 10, 1876, Bell and Watson were successful in the conduction of voice over a wire with the transmission of the infamous phrase, "Mr. Watson, come here. I want you." Watson raced into the other room where Bell sat to exclaim that he could indeed understand what Bell had said. The telephone was born.

From early on, the development of telephone systems exploded. As Bell and his associates were busy installing lines, interest in the new device began to take hold. This is not to say that everything was smooth sailing. Unfortunately, as with the early telegraph, many people had a hard time seeing the telephone as anything but a novelty item—one that had little use when compared with the reliable telegraph system in operation. There were times in these early months when Bell and his backers feared they couldn't make enough money to support the new system.

One of the biggest corporate gaffes in history relates to the perceived value of the early telephone inventions (and associated patents) in 1877. At the time, Bell and his partners were struggling to license Bell's invention and establish a profitable company. At the lowest point, the company trustee Gardiner Hubbard offered to sell all of Bell's patents to Western Union President William Orton for $100,000. This was much less than the group had invested in the venture, but it was viewed as better than the alternative—dissolution.

Western Union was highly profitable in the telegraph and associated businesses at the time. However, upper management at Western Union saw the telephone as more of a joke than a practical device. True, the Bell group was partially funding their venture by holding paid demonstrations reminiscent of street performers doing magic tricks. But Western Union did not share Bell's vision of the future, and ultimately it rejected the offer. It wouldn't be long before

Western Union realized the magnitude of its mistake, but it was too late by then.

One of Western Union's lines of business was stock tickers used to transmit data from the major exchanges. Within months of shunning the opportunity to own the Bell telephone patents, Western Union found many of the stockbrokers ordering telephone systems rather than tickers because they preferred the two-way voice communications provided by the telephone. As the weeks wore on, Western Union began to see a surge in demand for telephone equipment.

At this point, Western Union had another opportunity to capitalize on a budding industry, one that had equal potential to the telegraph to generate massive profits. Western Union quickly formed the American Speaking Telephone Company and licensed the telephone work of Elisha Gray to compete against the Bell system. The company also hired a great inventor of the time, Thomas Alva Edison, to improve telephone designs. Within a short period of time, Edison had improved the telephone transmitters substantially, and Western Union put Bell and his partners in a tight spot. Western Union literally was 100 times the size of the Bell Telephone Company, and it had vast resources in wired networks at its disposal.

When Bell Telephone Company fought back with an improved telephone design of its own, the competition between the two heated up. At one strenuous point, the tenacious general manager of the Bell Telephone Company, Theodore Vail, filed a patent infringement lawsuit against Western Union. Many thought that this was a battle that could not be won.

However, Bell Telephone Company was the unintended recipient of another stroke of good luck. Another financial tycoon at that time was Jay Gould, who had a reputation for influencing markets and stocks with unscrupulous tactics. Gould had his mind set on gaining control of Western Union from the Vanderbilts, who had control of the company at the time.

Gould patched together several telegraph companies and began to eat into Western Union's revenue. Hoping to force Western Union to buy him out at an outrageous valuation, Gould also began to put telephone and telegraph services together by buying some of Bell's telephone franchises in large markets. Faced with a patent lawsuit on one side and a hostile corporate attack on the other, Western Union was forced to settle with Bell Telephone Company.

This proved to be a wise move, for the settlement dictated that each company must stay out of the other's business. Part of this agreement meant that Western Union sold Bell all its telephone systems. It also dictated that Bell could not sell services to other telegraph companies. This settlement, while denying Western Union the telephone market until Bell's patents expired in 1893, effectively short-circuited Gould's attempt to take over Western Union (for the moment). It also essentially established two monopolies in the United States: Western Union with the telegraph and Bell with the telephone.

While Jay Gould still grappled with Western Union over control of the company, Bell Telephone Company went on to flourish almost unfettered for the next several years. It would go on to build a nation-wide network that is often simply referred to today as the *Bell system*. In the coming decades, numerous significant events would unfold to shape the U.S. telecommunications industry. Unfortunately, it would take far too many pages to discuss them all here. And our interest is in still yet another branch of telecommunications—wireless radio.

WIRELESS RADIO

When one looks at the history of wireless communications, one name is inescapable—Guglielmo Marconi, who often is considered the father of radio. In 1894, Marconi began experimenting with electro-magnetic waves described earlier by German Heinrich Hertz. Like many of the inventors working with wired telegraphy, Marconi believed that intelligence could be passed through other media besides metal wire. In his case, Marconi was consumed with demonstrating a method for sending signals over long distances through the air.

Marconi was successful in sending radio signals over short distances while he was still in his early twenties. Some of his earliest experiments involved attempts to wirelessly transmit a single letter *S* to a receiver a few hundred yards away. After successfully transmitting a signal along a line-of-sight path, Marconi wanted to show that radio waves could reach beyond obstacles. He positioned his receiver on the opposite side of a hill and instructed an assistant to attend to it with a gun in hand. When he had heard three distinct rings from the receiver—signifying the letter *S*—he would fire his gun to let Marconi know that the transmission was a success. That single gunshot started a third revolution in communications.

After obtaining a patent on the method in 1896, Marconi received a cold reception from the Italian government. This led him to embark on a trip to England, where he hoped to find influential backers that saw the value of his experiments. After several successful demonstrations, Marconi found himself overwhelmed with invitations from various governments and groups to demonstrate and build radio systems for them. This included his native Italy. Eventually, in 1909, Guglielmo Marconi would be awarded the Nobel Prize for physics.

As with the earlier inventions of the telegraph and telephone, the U.S. military showed great interest in the new developments in wireless communications as well. The most interested of the armed forces was, not surprisingly, the U.S. Navy, who foresaw great advantages to being able to communicate with ships at sea. In a few short years at the turn of the century, the Navy equipped its entire fleet with radio transmitters and also set up a coastal system. Radio communications became so important to the Navy that the government mandated closure of all stations it was not using in 1917 as the United States entered into World War I.

Once inventors and experimenters the world over learned of Marconi's achievements, the development of radio systems exploded. Many hobbyists and curious students replicated equipments and "tweaked" systems constantly to improve their range and clarity. It is in this early stage that a community of private, amateur radio operators was born. Since radio communications needed little investment compared with telephone and telegraph systems, just about anyone could set up an effective communications system.

The growth of amateur radio operators also went unchecked for several years due to the lack of regulation of the airwaves. As in many areas of new technology, practical working systems are developed and in use before operators even fully understand the principles by which the devices work. As more and more radio stations went up, the problem of congestion in the airwaves got worse. By the time the U.S. government had formulated methods for governing the use of radio devices, the New England region in particular was fraught with interference from multiple stations broadcasting messages on top of each other.

It is important to remember that radio communications systems developed within the first two decades of Marconi's discovery were designed simply for wireless telegraphy—not telephony. The technology necessary to transmit audio information did not come about until 1912, when the vacuum tube was advanced to the point of practical use in electronic circuits. Radiotelegraphy used spark transmitters and, later, arc transmitters to transmit codes, and neither of these technologies could be developed to send clear audio reliably. A properly constructed vacuum tube, however, made radio transmitters and receivers thousands of times more powerful than before.

The perceived value and eventual use of the telephone and wireless communications diverged substantially. While the telephone was seen initially as most useful as a broadcast device—where daily news or events could be distributed by voice—it didn't work out that way. With their simple operation and relatively low cost, people quickly adopted telephones as a personal communications device for business and leisure.

Wireless radio, on the other hand, was keenly promoted in the early 1900s as a device that everyone would one day carry so that they could speak with anyone in the world at any time. Indeed, many people also thought that every horseless carriage would contain a wireless phone in case the vehicle broke down in rural areas. It wasn't until the 1980s, though—nearly a century later—that this would be close to reality. In the 80 years since that time, wireless communications have served the role that was envisioned initially for the telephone—broadcast of information.

One of the main factors that held up the development of wireless as a method of personal communications was the technology. In order to be adopted by consumers in mass, wireless radio units had to be small and inexpensive. Even with vacuum tube technology, this was not possible. The discovery of the transistor in the late 1940s and the subsequent development of integrated circuits are what ultimately led to the explosion of personal wireless communications.

From the standpoint of entrepreneurs and capitalists in the early 1900s, though, the current limitations in mobile radio were just that—current. It seemed almost natural to conclude that wireless communications soon would overtake and obsolete the wired telegraph and telephone systems due to its lower cost and portability. Many people thought that it was only a short matter of time before refinements in the system would help wireless radio fulfill all the promises of the telegraph and telephone combined—and then some. After all, the biggest drawback—and concern to investors—of telegraph/telephone systems was the high cost of stringing wires to complete the systems. Radio simply eliminated this cost.

Unfortunately, unscrupulous stock promoters exaggerated this theoretical advantage of radio way beyond reason at the time. This widespread hyperbole took the U.S. stock market by storm in the early 1900s and led to what one notable writer termed the "wireless telegraph bubble." The problem boiled down to the fact that most early radio systems were not profitable, even with their vast potential. This didn't stop dozens of zealous stock promoters, though. Many of them continued to promise returns in excess of thousands of percent all the while the companies they created struggled to make their equipment function.

One of the most prominent scams of the time involved a company called United Wireless and a notorious stock promoter, Abraham White. It was formed from an endless stream of earlier wireless companies that were created to bait investors and then merged to hide losses. Millions of dollars were conned from hapless investors over several years. Many bought their stock at several dollars a share from local brokers to find it quoted at the same time in New York for pennies. The disparity in stock prices and the surrounding chaos were covered by more and more promises for astonishing wealth in new companies formed from assets of now worthless ones.

The situation eventually got so bad that the government finally raided the company and arrested the senior officers. United Wireless was found to be guilty not only of stock fraud but also of patent infringement (it was sued by Marconi Wireless). Eventually, the company would be dissolved and the assets sold off to Marconi Wireless, making its American subsidiary the largest radio operator in the United States at the time.

While this episode in history does not reflect well on the wireless industry, it does demonstrate what can happen when a revolutionary technology emerges in a capitalist society. Truly, there was a very real and promising industry in wireless telegraphy and telephony; it only needed more time to develop. The problems with stock scams at this time actually had more to do with corrupt financiers than with the radio industry (similar scams appeared in mining and oil stocks). It might as well have been the Internet boom of the 1990s.

American Marconi went on to dominate the radio industry for several years, but the U.S. government became uneasy with the notion of a foreign-controlled corporation having such dominion over international communications. Eventually, pressure put on American Marconi led to the sale of the company to none other than General Electric (GE). In 1919, the Radio Corporation of America (RCA) was created out of the assets of American Marconi. Virtually overnight, RCA was now the largest radio company in the United States.

For all the work and investment that went into radio during the early years, there was little payoff for those seeking to profit from it. Owen D. Young, a GE executive who carried out the purchase of American Marconi, phrased it this way: "Fifteen years is the average period of probation, and during that time the inventor, the promoter, and the investor, who see a great future, generally lose their shirts. . . . This is why the wise capitalist keeps out of exploiting new inventions and comes in only when the public is ready for mass demand."

By the early 1920s, this mass demand came in the form of broadcasting. Many of the failed businesses in the early stages of radio were being replaced by companies focusing in this area. With relatively inexpensive equipment made possible by the vacuum tube, major meeting areas and eventually households could be equipped with a receiver capable of picking up broadcasts of major events and sports highlights. Initially free, broadcasting soon would turn to paid advertising to support stations, much to the lament of many listeners. While public distaste for commercials was very strong initially, commercials quickly became a standard at all the major broadcasting companies.

Outside radio broadcasting efforts, many companies still were pursuing private communications through wireless devices. Throughout the next two decades in the United States following the war, radiotelephony systems were improved at a steady rate. While most radio transmissions were still telegraphed in code, voice transmissions could be done too. The problem was the quality of the voice and difficulties with interference. Because the industry was still emerging, there was no regulation yet, and many users could not predict what other radios were operating in the area.

Some order to the chaos obviously was needed. In an attempt to regulate the radio industry, the U.S. government created the Federal Radio Commission in 1927. A few years later, in 1934, this agency was superseded by the Federal Communications Commission

(FCC), which still exists today. The FCC was given sole power to oversee the allocation of frequencies to various radio groups, permitting only one organization at a time to use any given channel. This would help "clean up" the airwaves in the United States and improve radio broadcasts.

As a government agency, the FCC was directed to manage the frequency spectrum in a way that benefited the public at large. This led to the agency giving preference to emergency services agencies, utilities, and of course, the government. The FCC would not open up the airwaves for private commercial operation until after World War II. With a single radio call between two people taking up as much airspace as a radio broadcast reaching thousands of people, the FCC could not justify using valuable frequencies for such purposes.

As portable electronics became more practical with the development of the vacuum tube, the possibility of wireless communications occurring while moving became a reality. Some early mobile telephone systems were developed in the late 1920s. One notable system was set up for the Detroit police department. One-way communications could be sent to squad cars around the city, dramatically improving dispatch capabilities and speed of service.

None of the early radio systems was connected with the extensive telephone network, though. Most of them were only capable of communicating one way, just like a radio broadcast. Whoever received a wireless message had to find a telephone to call back to the sender if they needed more information. In this way, it was very much like pagers, whose use boomed through the 1980s and 1990s.

It took decades to advance radiotelephony systems to a point where they were reliable and affordable. Most systems used before World War II were experimental in nature and designed for use by government agencies or emergency services only. The power, range, and clarity of radio communications continued to improve through the 1930s and 1940s, thanks to advances in technology. In the early 1940s, radio systems finally were getting to a point where their operation would be practical in a commercial market.

Radio communication systems did play an important part in World War II. A company named Motorola was building backpack radios for the military, and these communications devices kept troops in contact on the battlefield. These devices, dubbed *walkie-talkies*, as well as handheld units called *handie-talkies*, offered two-way voice communications.

The next few decades following the war are when the most progress toward private radio communications was made. The FCC finally opened up spectrum for commercial radiotelephony use, and AT&T and Southwestern Bell introduced a private system in 1946. In this mobile telephony system, a phone call could be made to a car phone by means of the existing telephone network, and vice versa. All the caller had to do was ask for long distance and give the operator the mobile number.

The mobile telephone systems (MTSs) that AT&T operated in various cities brought new capabilities to private citizens, but they also quickly ran up against limitations. Due to the FCC's reluctance to open up more frequency channels for mobile telephony service, many of these systems quickly reached capacity. Much of the capacity problem stemmed from the method used to handle calls on the MTSs.

In a typical MTS, several towers around a city supported calls from the mobile units of customers. When a call was made, all towers in the system received the signal on the same frequency channel, and these separate receptions were then combined into a single, clear signal. In this manner, a person on a mobile phone could roam around the city, and one or more receivers always would be able to keep the call connected on a dedicated channel. When the person on the mobile unit hung up, then the channel was freed up on all receivers.

The fact that one mobile unit tied up a frequency channel across the entire city for the duration of the call is one reason the capacity of the MTS was strained. Because of this, most systems could only handle a few hundred users over large metropolitan areas. Just as the number of FM radio stations that can broadcast in a given area is limited today, so was the number of mobile callers then. Both systems operated at relatively high power and low frequency, leading to the similar capacity characteristics.

As customer waiting lists for mobile units soared, operators were desperate to come up with solutions to the problem of user capacity in their systems. A suggested method of getting around many of these barriers was the cellular concept.

A few companies, one of which was Bell Labs (the research arm of AT&T), began developing concepts of cellular radio in the late 1940s. Since the cellular concept called for a lower-power transmitter, the range of communications was reduced substantially to a "cell" that was only a few miles in radius. Additional transmitters then could be placed around this cell to create a group of cells. At this point, the system basically looks like a scaled-down MTS, simply with more receivers to cover a city.

However, new elements come into play to give a cellular system dramatic advantages—the most important being the concept of frequency reuse. Unlike MTS, the same frequency channel could be used in several cells throughout a city for different callers so long as the cells were not adjacent, where they would interfere with each other. The new system departed from the large-scale broadcast concept and looked toward making more efficient use of the frequency spectrum.

The new capabilities that had to be developed here involved the handoffs from one frequency channel to another. In the current MTS, users were passed to different transmitters on the same frequency. In cellular systems, adjacent transmitters operated on different frequency channels. Being able to hop onto different bands in different cells helped maximize efficient channel use. In this way, a single caller would not tie up a precious mobile line for an entire city, only a few square miles of it.

The cellular concept continued to take hold in the 1950s, when more refinement of the concept and different systems were suggested. As the 1960s approached, the technology necessary to accommodate frequency switching in mobile devices began to emerge. Indeed, one of the most significant discoveries of the century occurred around this time: the silicon transistor. First demonstrated in the late 1940s, the refinement and impending production of silicon transistors in the 1950s led to radios that were much more compact and useful.

From there, the rapid advances in transistor technology led to dramatic improvements in mobile communications systems. The new technology helped create radios that had far better electrical properties in a smaller package requiring less power. The new transistors quickly began to displace vacuum tube designs in almost all forms of electronic equipment. The new efficiencies discovered in silicon transistors finally made the mobile cellular concept a reality and helped put it on track to commercial viability.

Take note that "on track to commercial viability" meant that those early mobile cellular devices were still way out of the price range of most consumers. At this point, however, the rapid advances in integrated circuits were demonstrating how quickly the cost and complexity of electronics would come down.

THE DAWN OF COMMERCIAL CELLULAR

Mobile communications took a large leap into the real world with the development of the cellular radio concept. As mobile radio stalled up against limitations of capacity and spectrum use, the concept of localizing communications into smaller geographic regions blew the doors wide open on service capacity for radio systems. With cellular systems, radio channels could be reused over and over in large metropolitan areas, only limited by the density of cells an operator desires to deploy.

However, the technical obstacles to mobile communications were not the only barriers to its successful introduction. Many regulatory problems persisted. While the Bell System petitioned the FCC to open up wide frequency channels for a commercial radio system in 1958, it would be almost 20 years before a system would be implemented on a commercial basis. The debates over the function and control of mobile telephony systems stalled their implementation greatly because many smaller companies feared that the Bell monopoly would dominate wireless as well.

Eventually, the FCC announced that it would open up 2,300 channels worth of radio spectrum in 1974. This would be enough to kick-start the industry that so many private companies had been begging the regulatory body to open up. Several prominent companies such as GE, Motorola, and RCA were all eager to build equipment for systems.

The first large-scale cellular systems testing began in the United States in 1978. Many similar systems started in various countries around the globe, some even a few months sooner. The initial capacity and range of the system were small, and the equipment was expensive (thousands of dollars for a mobile phone). Nonetheless, it was successful. However, full commercial operation of the systems was still not allowed in the United States. Many other nations, such as Japan, forged ahead in this area without the regulatory bottleneck created in part by the FCC.

Commercial operation of cellular systems called Advanced Mobile Phone Systems (AMPS) began in the United States in 1983. The regional Bell company Ameritech started service in Chicago, Illinois, and several other companies soon followed around the nation.

Early cellular systems were bulky and difficult to operate. The quality of the connections and voice clarity were poor, far below those of burgeoning landline networks. The mobile units used for cellular communications were extremely expensive by today's standards, well above $1,000. And the costs for service were prohibitive, relegating their use mostly to professionals such as doctors and lawyers (or anyone else who could afford it). However, this didn't slow the demand for service—waiting lists soon developed for service providers that couldn't keep up with orders.

Service provider companies who got in on the ground floor of the cellular boom in the 1970s and 1980s would call this the "golden era," with relatively cheap spectrum available for the taking. Much like the days of the California gold rush, many wireless prospectors were hustling to apply for spectrum licenses to be granted. Many of the companies and individuals that eventually won spectrum licenses quickly turned around and sold them at a tidy profit.

As the 1980s came to a close, the cellular industry was at a crossroads. Capacity on the early AMPS in the United States was being strained in several markets. To make the situation more difficult, the possibility of new spectrum being made available to ease the capacity woes looked pessimistic at best. In the United States, many companies were looking at alternatives for a new generation of cellular service.

Several digital cellular systems were being investigated at the time. In Europe, regulatory bodies were moving ahead on plans to build a more inclusive cellular system, one that would allow roaming across all borders in the European nations. Their experience with earlier analog systems that were numerous and incompatible led them to favor a unified standard. The system being proposed also would include the latest digital technology, one that would support a host of added features such as a short messaging service.

The United States took a different approach, though. The FCC actually fostered the proliferation of multiple standards in the belief that it would further stimulate competition and force prices to consumers down. In a move consistent with its original charter, the FCC was navigating toward what it thought was in the best interests of the population at large. This path led to a different set of complexities in the U.S. wireless industry, where companies struggled to formulate a long-range plan in the face of uncertain technologies.

While Europe moved ahead with its unified Global System for Mobile Communications (GSM) cellular systems, the United States and some Asian nations went on to implement a variety of different systems. No one really thought much about being compatible with other nations at the time, except those in Europe, where their close proximity to neighbors made roaming across borders more important.

ACT II

The 1990s is when commercial cellular services really became practical for the average consumer. This decade saw the most rapid growth in services, while the price of these services dropped dramatically. It was becoming easier and easier for the everyday Joe and Jane to afford wireless services, and this fed the great wireless machine. More potential customers brought more competition and better economies of scale, both leading to cheaper products and services.

A dramatic shift started to take place in which mobile phones were no longer considered solely a tool for the doctor, lawyer, or affluent businessperson. Virtually anyone could afford a wireless phone, even if it only had the most basic service. Service providers also discovered several new pricing schemes that encouraged more consumers to take the plunge and buy a phone.

In this decade, the penetration rates for cellular subscribers soared. Many countries started the decade with only a few percent of their populations owning a cellular phone. At the close of 2000, several nations had more than 50 percent of their population connected wirelessly.

The start of the 1990s was a defining time in cellular systems in that it was the point at which most service providers started moving toward digital technologies. Current networks based on analog protocols such as AMPS in the United States and Nordic Mobile Telephone (NMT) or Total Access Communications System (TACS) in Europe were reaching their capacity. Many new digital schemes were proposed to help stuff more calls on the available frequencies. An additional positive was that the portable units based on digital technologies had far better battery life and could contain more features at a better price.

The adoption and subsequent development of digital networks took several years to accomplish. Even at the end of 2000, digital service coverage in many areas of the United States was poor. Many analog networks are still left to "fill in the holes" of digital services with at least voice support on the analog channel. Even with incomplete coverage, though, cellular service providers were signing up customers in droves as competition and better technology drove prices down to affordable levels for consumers.

Much to the surprise of many, the growth of cellular service in Europe and abroad was even more dramatic. While most people thought that a heavily regulated, unified system would not be able to grow as fast as one more geared toward free-market principles, just the opposite happened. The unified GSM networks were spreading throughout Europe, Asia, and dozens of other countries like wildfire. What was once considered inferior technology to American ingenuity has captivated the world and absolutely trounced almost all predictions of subscriber growth.

The divergent path that the United States chose to follow in the early 1990s is one of the reasons why people consider the United States to be behind other countries in terms of acceptance of wireless technologies. The variety of networks that exist in the United States today cannot interact except for the most basic voice services. While people in Europe can easily send messages to others' phones, people in the United States must have the same service provider—if the service provider even offers such a feature (most did not until 2000).

Here's another area where the United States took a different path from Asia or Europe. In the United States, service providers adopted pricing plans that have been termed *bucket plans*. This basically refers to the practice of giving a user a certain number of minutes for a monthly fee, say, 200 minutes a month for $39.99 a month. People could then make calls during the month that simply subtracted from their bucket of minutes. If the 200 minutes were not exceeded, no additional charges accrued.

In Europe, cellular service is predominantly pay as you go. While the monthly base fee may give the user some limited time to use, most everyone exceeds the basic fee and pays on a per-minute basis. Additionally, Europe has adopted a caller-pays system in which a person receiving a call on his or her cellular phone would not be charged for airtime. With most service providers in the United States, receiving a call is the same as making it—the airtime is subtracted from your bucket of minutes.

Many people in the industry still debate which system is better and which provides for more substantial growth. At this point in time, however, the statistics have provided an answer only as to which system encourages the most users to sign up. The European GSM standard and service practices have helped many nations reach penetration rates above 70 percent in some cases. The United States is just below 40 percent at the time of this writing, so there's still progress to be made.

WE'RE JUST GETTING STARTED

With all the growth and amazing progress made in the last few decades in wireless technology, it is hard to imagine that this is only the beginning. But it is. With two distinct generations of wireless communications behind us, the next phase opens up new possibilities with advanced data transmission capabilities. So begins the area of third-generation (3G) wireless networks.

Many research entities are predicting continued rapid growth for wireless services around the world (Figure 1.2). There is also a distinct possibility that many of them are underestimating the level of wireless growth. The vast majority of predictions about the number of cellular subscribers at the turn of the millennium have been low—some drastically low. Many forecasts in the 1980s said that there would be 100 million worldwide subscribers by 2005. This mark was passed way back in 1997. The United States alone passed this mark 5 years early.

FIGURE 1.2

Forecasted World Subscriber Totals

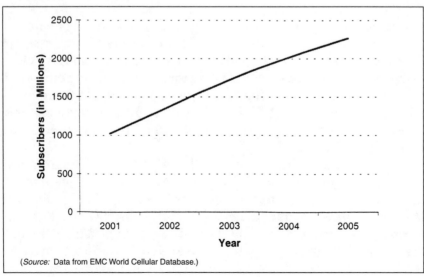

(*Source:* Data from EMC World Cellular Database.)

As if the proliferation of cellular phones for voice connectivity were not enough, the thought of also being able to transfer large quantities of data over the air has put the wireless industry into overdrive. The parallel boom of the Internet in the 1990s has set up the wireless industry for a much-anticipated encore. The combination of wireless capabilities with the resources available on the Internet has every entrepreneur chomping at the bit to develop something that hundreds of millions of cellular phone owners would pay to have.

The merging of the Internet and wireless communications has tremendous potential to change the lives and cultures of people around the globe. Never in history have two profound new media opened up ways to move information at the same time. Not only do we have a global network that stores vast amounts of information at various nodes, we also have the capability to access one of those nodes from virtually anywhere on the planet.

Truly, there are many possible applications out there that have yet to be discovered. While these new capabilities may not come about in the next few years, it is likely that we'll see some astounding new applications in the next decade. Few people had the foresight a decade ago to see how mobile data would empower people to communicate via short messages or e-mail. The same likely will hold for applications coveted 10 years from now.

SUMMARY

The events surrounding the discovery and development of wireless communications spin a fascinating tale of technology and shear determination to succeed. Many scientists and colorful characters of the recent past collectively are responsible for advancing our world to a point where instant communications are possible from virtually anywhere on earth. While many of these people have come and gone, the companies and technical wonders that sometimes bear their names live on.

Part of understanding where the wireless industry is going involves observing where it has been. Many developments that occurred with wireless telegraphy in the 1800s are being repeated in today's wireless market, albeit in a slightly different form. Keeping a perspective on telecommunications history can be a great advantage to an investor attempting to make sense of today's market. Ignoring trends of the past can lead to costly mistakes.

The important thing to draw from different events in history is an appreciation for the conditions at the time that either favored or hindered the development of technologies or the fortunes of companies. It would be a mistake to think that the failure of a technology or product in the past would lead to the same result today without considering external conditions that affect it. Looking at these elements with respect to the wireless market—the so-called driving forces—is where we'll turn our attention in the next chapter.

2

The Driving Forces
for Wireless

Your top wireless pick opened up this morning down 15 percent in a matter of minutes and continues to slide. What's worse is that you can find no good reason for the drop. The general market is up. The shares of some competing companies are stable. The only thing you can find is some obscure newsbyte from an analyst talking about a government body somewhere in South America announcing new spectrum allocation. This political bit couldn't have anything to do with my company, you think. Or could it?

We've all had episodes where the movement of stock seems based on no fundamental cause. Sometimes there are freak dips and spikes with stocks, and even the company itself will issue statements saying that it knows of no reason for the dramatic swings. More often than not, however, there is a good reason, and investors just don't make the connection. It is often related to an incomplete understanding of the industry and the prime factors that influence that particular market.

With the plunge in Nasdaq and dot-com ventures during early 2000, many people were wondering if wireless was a fad. Would it be essentially like Pets.com—a neat idea, but no business model?

Saying that wireless is a fad is like saying personal computers (PCs) were a fad during the early 1980s. Rather, wireless is real and is, in fact, in the early stages. Actually, there is already evidence of success, particularly overseas. In Europe and Asia, consumers are using wireless technology to make their lives easier, and businesses are using it to make their organizations run more productively. The United States is a little farther behind in its adoption of mobile technologies but should catch up soon.

In this chapter we'll look at the driving forces of the wireless industry and what guides its development. The overriding industry forces often are ignored; in fact, many analysts and industry followers suffer from tunnel vision and focus on technology adoption as the main driver for revenues (and ultimate success) of any given company. While technology certainly plays a role in the competitive wireless landscape, it is not the highest card in the deck.

If you look at the entire wireless market, it is driven largely from a consumer mindset. Foremost in the minds of consumers is brand, features, and quality/price. Most consumers could care less what technology is used to deliver a service.

A great example of this is NTT DoCoMo's i-Mode service in Japan. Widely regarded as one of the most successful wireless services, the technology that supports the service is arguably inferior and only supports packet data speeds of 9.6 kbps. While some people continue to argue that 100-kbps+ systems will take the market by storm, i-Mode keeps signing up users in droves while technically superior systems waffle in the slow lane.

Even if you think NTT DoCoMo erred by selecting a poor technology base, it obviously has done a number of things right. And all the things it has done right certainly have overcome any limitations in its supported technology. So let's consider some other areas that drive the industry.

BUY-IN FROM INDUSTRY LEADERS

Perhaps one of the most significant driving forces in the wireless industry is the buy-in from industry leaders.

MICROSOFT

For about 20 years, the mission of Microsoft was to have a "PC in every home and on every desktop." This made sense. The computer industry was undergoing a revolution in which PCs became dominant.

By the late 1990s, however, this seemed kind of quaint. Not everyone works at a desktop. Now, there are notebooks, personal digital assistants (PDAs), Web-enabled phones, and so on.

Bill Gates understood that technology was becoming connected, and Microsoft's mission statement was changed to "Empowering people through great software anytime, anywhere, and on any device." Yes, Microsoft made it the company mission to go wireless. And there is no doubt that this will have a tidal effect on technology for years to come.

As with anything at Microsoft, the company has taken its mission seriously. Now there is a new business unit called *Microsoft Mobility*. In 2001, Microsoft committed approximately $200 million to this division (one of the biggest incremental investments in the company's history).

Microsoft wants to create intelligent communications, which goes beyond just connecting devices. This involves three main areas:

- *Control.* Consumers and professionals need to have the power to get the information they need to make informed decisions.
- *Context.* Consumers and businesses should get the information they need when they want it. For example, if you are in an important meeting, you should not be interrupted by a nonpriority e-mail. However, if your daughter is trying to call, you might want your PDA to light up.
- *Synergy.* Wireless will become a seamless part of the many technologies of Microsoft, such as leveraging the 100 million users of Hotmail and the huge installed base of Microsoft Outlook.

ORACLE

The OracleMobile division has about 125 employees. The mission of the division is to build and host wireless Web sites. Of course, underlying the mobile technology are the database systems of Oracle. The database systems are critical to allow for transactions, security, and scalability. Moreover, Oracle handles many of the largest companies in the world.

With Oracle tools, programmers can easily build applications that allow for location, personalization, notification, and even voice. One customer is Jphone, a wireless company based in Japan. The company wanted to add location-based services for its devices.

Then again, Jphone had an incentive to innovate. You see, Jphone had to contend with the very popular NTT DoCoMo's i-Mode service that was sweeping Japan. In about a year, DoCoMo had 55 percent of the Japanese market.

Jphone wanted to create a system that allowed consumers and professionals to use its cell phones to locate convenient locations (say, a coffee shop or the nearest hotel). Creating the database was daunting. An Oracle8i database had to be populated with 17 million business references.

Moreover, the references needed to be geographically coded so as to be able to provide maps to the users. The database was a whopping 90 GB and required sophisticated searching technology to make it possible to provide real-time responses.

Within a few months, the service had 350,000 daily users. It cost Jphone about $6 million to develop the system, which was paid for in about 6 months.

SAP

This company is known as the Microsoft of Europe. Actually, five German engineers from IBM founded the company in 1972. The company grew quickly, becoming a dominant player in enterprise resource planning (ERP), which helps companies manage logistics, manufacturing, inventory, and finance. Clients include such heavies as Coca-Cola, DuPont, and even Microsoft.

The company has invested aggressively in developing wireless solutions. Categories include customer relationship management (CRM), business intelligence (access to data warehousing, reporting, and analysis), travel management, procurement (price comparisons and ordering), and supply chain management.

One of SAP's top customers is the Bosch Group, which has more than 190,000 employees in 140 countries. Bosch has always wanted to provide the best customer service but did not use state-of-the-art technologies. Rather, the company had a hodgepodge system that involved phones and faxes.

Then Bosch implanted SAP's Handheld Service. Basically, the company's service centers and field personnel were in real-time communication, making customer service much more automated. There was no more time-consuming report writing by the field technicians. Moreover, the system allowed for invoices to be printed out on the spot, the stock replacement parts to be updated immediately, and the necessary data to be transmitted to the company's Human Resources ERP system.

INTEL

This company has been leveraging its chip technology into the wireless space for many years. In fact, about two-thirds of all cell phones on the worldwide market have some type of Intel technology embedded. Furthermore, wireless devices increasingly will need more computation power, which will play to Intel's advantage. Its StrongARM processor has become important for PDAs and smart cell phones (so as to allow for handwriting and speech recognition). The company is also strong in flash memory technologies, which are extremely helpful for data applications (such as Web browsing and text messaging).

In pursuit of its wireless efforts, Intel has started the Intel Communications Fund, which has reached about $500 million. One of its investments is in Research In Motion (RIM), the developer of the BlackBerry device, which is a handheld e-mail device.

Jim Balsillie and Mike Lazaridis cofounded the company in 1984 in a small town called Waterloo, outside of Toronto. It was a good spot, however. Next door was Waterloo University, which has a top-notch program for computer science and engineering.

Lazaridis is the technical genius behind the BlackBerry technology (he graduated as an engineer from Waterloo), and Balsillie is the business brains (he graduated from Harvard Business School).

The company was visionary, developing products for wireless data applications in 1988. Balsillie and Lazaridis thought that e-mail would be the killer application and that the Web would be the underlying infrastructure. Interestingly enough, the company's RIM Inter@ctive Pager 950 is on display at the Smithsonian Institution in Washington, DC.

Simply put, companies have had a difficult time with mobile professionals getting access to e-mail. How do you make it secure?

How do you make it easy to get? What if the hotel phone system is incompatible? What about long-distance charges? Do you have to carry bulky equipment?

Intel met with RIM in 1997 in an attempt to pursue partnership opportunities. There were clear synergies, especially with Intel's chip technology. During that year, Intel made its investment, and BlackBerry now uses the Intel386 processor. This low-power chip made it possible for a BlackBerry device to last for 2 to 3 weeks on AA batteries.

In 2000, revenues for RIM increased 160 percent to $221.3 million. There were about 164,000 BlackBerry subscribers in 7,800 companies. Net income was $8.5 million. There was about $721.9 million in the bank.

SUN MICROSYSTEMS

The philosophy of Sun Microsystems is "the network is the computer." Since its founding in 1982, Sun has achieved about $18 billion in revenues in less than 20 years as the company emerged as a leading player in high-end hardware and software.

The company's philosophy fits very well with the wireless world, and it is no surprise that in October 2000, Sun announced its wireless initiative. It includes a new business unit, a Wireless Excellence Center (based in Stockholm, Sweden) and a $100 million venture fund. Moreover, Sun intends to leverage its Java programming language and its industrial-strength infrastructure products—which are likely to be instrumental for the third-generation (3G) buildout.

THE M&A FACTOR

In the race for wireless dominance, the giants—such as Microsoft, Oracle, IBM, and so on—not only will invest huge sums in research and development (R&D) but also will buy other companies. And if a buyout candidate offers critical technologies or customer bases, the premium can be significant for investors.

However, merger and acquisition (M&A) transactions can be tricky. If Wall Street does not like the deal, the stock price for the buyout target actually can fall. Moreover, it is not a good idea to buy a stock based on M&A rumors. While there may be a bump in the stock price, it will only be temporary.

Let's take a look at a wireless M&A transaction that was more than just a rumor. Extended Systems was founded in 1984 but was not located in Silicon Valley or any other high-tech hot spot. Rather, its headquarters was in Boise, Idaho. Initially, the company developed intelligent printer-sharing devices. However, the product line was phased out because of the emergence of local area networks (LANs).

In 1991, the company began development of products for mobile computing. Essentially, the products allowed for wireless connectivity to printers. The company also developed products for virtual private networks.

The company went public in March 1998. The underwriters were small (Volpe Brown Whelan & Company and Needham & Company). In all, the company raised a mere $9.6 million. The initial public offering (IPO) price was $8 a share, and for the most part, the stock traded at between $4.5 and $8 a share until about September 1999. It was at this time that the company announced that it was developing Bluetooth technologies (a short-range wireless technology we'll talk more about in Chapter 3). Wall Street went into a frenzy. By April 2000, the stock was selling at over $100 per share.

However, investors overreacted, and the stock price plunged. In fact, during March 2001, Palm saw an opportunity to buy the company at a bargain price. The offer was $264 million. Palm would not use cash to buy the company but instead used its stock. On the news, the price of a share of Extended Systems surged $3.50 to $23.13. Figure 2.1 shows the dramatic swings in the stock price.

Palm eagerly wanted to pursue the corporate market and saw Extended Systems as a way to do this. A customer survey from Palm showed that more than 40 percent of Palm's handheld units were paid for or reimbursed by companies and that 80 percent of Palm's handheld units were synched at work.

Extended Systems' Bluetooth technology would be instrumental for synching data. What's more, Extended Systems had a strong engineering staff, a worldwide sales force, and many enterprise customers, such as International Paper, British Airways, and DaimlerChrysler.

The acquisition also would be a blow to one of Palm's main competitors, RIM. All in all, it looked like a great deal for Extended Systems and Palm. However, the deal would soon fall to pieces.

By May 2001, Palm reported that its own financial situation was deteriorating rapidly. The company announced that its fourth-quarter estimates would be cut by a hefty 50 percent to between $140

FIGURE 2.1

Extended Systems Inc.

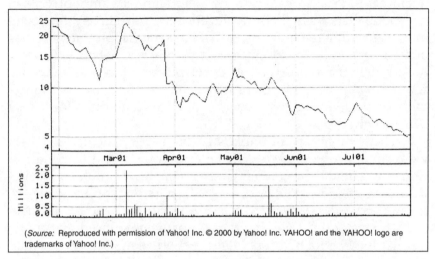

(*Source:* Reproduced with permission of Yahoo! Inc. © 2000 by Yahoo! Inc. YAHOO! and the YAHOO! logo are trademarks of Yahoo! Inc.)

million and $160 million. Losses also would widen substantially. A big problem was a delay in its new family of handheld computers, the m500. Palm also announced that it would institute price cuts and promotions for its product lines in order to work off existing inventory pileup.

In light of this, Palm and Extended Systems nixed their deal. The stock price of Extended Systems sank to about $8 per share. However, both companies said that they would continue to work together as partners.

FOREIGN M&A

M&A is not solely a domestic trend. Expect to see foreign buyers come into the U.S. marketplace. The deals likely will be extremely complex and require extensive regulatory approval (probably in both countries).

Let's take an example. John Stanton joined McCaw Cellular in 1982, where he went on to serve as chief operating officer and vice chairman. Then, in 1992, he founded Pacific Northwest Cellular, which merged with General Cellular to become Western Wireless. The company did its IPO in 1996.

During 1995, 1997, and 1999, Stanton purchased key Personal Communications Services (PCS) licenses. These assets were folded into a new division of Western Wireless called *VoiceStream*. VoiceStream transformed the licenses into a Global System for Mobile Communications (GSM) network (GSM has been adopted by 158 countries and accounts for 70 percent of the worldwide wireless market). In fact, VoiceStream was the only U.S. company with a nationwide GSM network. Moreover, the company had entered roaming agreements with 164 major wireless operators, allowing service in 171 countries.

However, having the licenses would not be enough to create a U.S. GSM powerhouse. Therefore, in 1999, the subsidiary was spun off (Stanton is the chief executive officer of both companies). As a separate company, VoiceStream could engage in an aggressive M&A campaign to realize its ambitions.

In July 1999, VoiceStream purchased Omnipoint for $4.6 billion, and then in October, it purchased Aerial Communications for $3 billion. Later in the year, as the deal was pending, Omnipoint purchased East/West Communications for $152 million.

In the summer of 2000, Stanton set his ambitions on Powertel. It certainly would be a friendly deal because Stanton and Alan Smith, president of Powertel, actually were very good friends. Both men helped create the GSM Alliance in 1995.

Even though Powertel had only 727,000 subscribers, the deal would amount to close to $6 billion. However, the company had spectrum licenses that covered about 25 million potential customers.

Meanwhile, the German telecom giant Deutsche Telekom contacted Stanton to discuss a buyout. In all, the deal would be valued at over $50 billion, amounting to a stunning $22,000 per customer. To put things in perspective, it would take 25 years to break even if VoiceStream received $75 per month from its 2.29 million customers.

Stanton still wanted Powertel, so he would purchase it too. However, VoiceStream would not be the buyer; rather, it would be Deutsche Telekom (this was done mostly for tax reasons). What's more, Deutsche Telekom agreed to invest about $5 billion to help VoiceStream bid for U.S. 3G licenses.

Investors panned the deal, though. The stock price of Deutsche Telekom fell 12.4 percent, and VoiceStream's shares fell 14.9 percent.

As the months went by, the stock price of Deutsche Telekom continued to deteriorate. The chief executive officer (CEO) of the company, Ron Sommer, was under incredible pressure to leave. However, he was able to keep the support of the board of directors and German politicians (since the German government owns about 58 percent of the company).

In addition, there was U.S. political opposition. Senator Ernest Hollings thought that the deal would give the German government essential control over VoiceStream. He feared that there would be an unfair advantage in terms of raising capital because the German government would not allow Deutsche Telekom to go bankrupt.

Despite this, the Federal Trade Commission (FTC) voted unanimously to allow the merger. The FTC thought that the merger would provide consumers with more choice and better prices.

Arbitrageurs were finding ways to make money trading off the uncertainty. Basically, in most takeover transactions, there will be a spread—which is the difference between the current stock price of the buyout target and the price at which the deal will be closed. However, not all deals happen—or the price ultimately may change, especially for megamergers. As a result, the spread can be significant. However, if the arbitrageur guesses right, profits can be substantial.

As for VoiceStream, at one point the spread had exceeded 30 percent. No doubt arbitrageurs had lots of questions: Would the CEO stay? Would the German government nix the deal? Would VoiceStream get cold feet? Would the U.S. government intervene and block the merger?

This is a high-risk game, and it is really not a good idea for individual investors to try it. You are going against well-heeled investors who can move much faster than you can—and with more money.

There is something else to be mindful of—flowback. It is very common that in a deal in which a foreign company buys a U.S. company, the U.S. investors will dump their stock. For example, a U.S. mutual fund may not even be allowed to own foreign stocks. The flowback can flood the market with stock and hurt the stock price, at least during the short term.

POLITICS AND MONEY GO HAND IN HAND

As seen in the preceding examples, politics plays a critical role in the wireless world. After all, anything that involves money is steeped in politics, and mobile communications is no exception.

Government regulatory bodies are the norm in the telecommunications industry, providing oversight and influencing the direction of the market. Furthermore, many of the nations of the world still have state-owned companies providing consumer services in the wireless market. Anytime you have money machines directly tied to government coffers, look out. Intense lobbying and political muscle are part of most major telecom decisions in most parts of the world.

A recent example of politics influencing wireless services is in China. Over the last decade, QUALCOMM has been desperately trying to sell the Chinese government on its Code Division Multiple Access (CDMA) technology. The company always has been rebuffed, and China deployed widespread GSM networks throughout the 1990s. In early 2001, the Chinese government agreed to deploy a CDMA network, much to the delight of QUALCOMM shareholders. However, Chinese officials have reversed decisions on numerous occasions only to re-reverse them again a short time later.

In addition, right on the heels of the U.S.-China riff over the midair collision of a U.S. spy plane and a Chinese fighter in early 2001, the network equipment purchases mysteriously were put on hold. While usually no explanations are given for the actions of the Chinese government, it is obvious that China is motivated to "play its cards right" when it comes to protecting its own interests and establishing permanent normal trade relations. As companies seek growth from global markets, such political dilemmas will be the norm and can make your investments a rough ride indeed.

Since wireless communications is pushing to become a global industry, there will be more cases like this in the future. Wireless is almost becoming a trade commodity like oil or crops. As more industrialized nations develop or adopt wireless technologies, the trade agreements negotiations have a new bargaining chip. A country that is strong in wireless technology manufacturing can offer it in return for assistance in other areas, such as agriculture.

This can work against nations, though, when they become too dependent on one or a few others for technology. For instance, if a new wireless technology is only supported or manufactured by one country, others may be less willing to adopt it for fear that it could be used against them in the future when they come to depend on it.

An example of this is wireless location services that are based on global positioning satellites (GPSs). Many U.S. companies use

GPS signals to accurately locate people, parcels in transit, or a host of other things. However, many service providers outside the United States are reluctant to adopt technologies that use GPS for one big reason: The U.S. Department of Defense controls operation of the satellites. Since in the beginning the system was used primarily for military purposes, it is not a great leap to believe that a change in relationship with the United States could cause the system to be turned off in a particular area, stranding users.

Even within the United States, a nation that prides itself on loosening the ties between government and enterprise, political influence reigns. Since the Federal Communications Commission (FCC) holds the power to deny or permit corporations to operate wireless networks (see the next section for more about this), companies have entire strategy teams preoccupied with tactics for maneuvering around the government.

Even in the early days of cellular in the United States, the entrepreneurs and young companies looking to exploit the new technologies completely bypassed the FCC in determining who to license spectrum to. They held their own auction and decided among themselves how to allocate the available licenses, saving themselves further delays from an already failed process within the government. The FCC likely will not allow this to happen again, though—because the financial stakes have risen tremendously, the government certainly will want to make the most money by keeping the process under its control.

In the end, a company that has strong ties to government regulators and people in other branches of the government will tend to have an easier time getting its products and services to market. Take a look at the boards of directors and advisory boards of some of the major telecommunications corporations in the United States. You will find many people who used to hold political positions in the U.S. government. Companies that are fortunate enough to gain insight from these individuals will have an edge in negotiating their way through the regulatory processes.

REGULATION

Any company that provides a wireless service or manufactures equipment must comply with numerous regulations. Since the mobile devices we carry radiate energy, governments obviously want to make sure they maintain safe levels. It is also important to make sure that various wireless devices operate at specific frequencies so that they do not interfere with each other. For this reason, governments often regulate the use of much of the frequency spectrum. This gives them the ability to charge high fees for companies to have the privilege of using certain frequency bands for commercial services.

As you delve into wireless investing, you will see the complexity of governmental regulation and how it can greatly affect your investment decision—good or bad. In the United States, the main governmental agencies involved include the following.

FEDERAL COMMUNICATIONS COMMISSION (FCC)

This agency was created under the Communications Act of 1934 and regulates interstate and international communications by radio, television, wire, satellite, and cable. A critical power of the FCC is that it holds auctions for spectrum that is given to the highest bidder. Yet the rules for being granted the spectrum are strict. Sometimes certain licenses are available only to small corporations with the intention of excluding the few heavyweights from taking all the licenses. Sometimes this backfires, though, because the small corporations have difficulty paying the government even on generous installment plans.

For example, a recent auction gave significant portions of spectrum in several markets to a company called NextWave after it outbid the competition. When the company couldn't come up with the money as promised according to the terms, the rights to the airwaves were taken back, and the bands were reauctioned with others in early 2001. The FCC raised over $16.85 billion for the U.S. government through this auction.

The problem was that NextWave was still contesting the loss of its licenses, which it continues to claim. A court decision in June 2001 reversed earlier outcomes and ruled that NextWave was in the right, leaving the whole auction process in disarray. What about the companies that won the licenses in the new auction? Do they have to give them back?

While this mess likely will be resolved soon, it demonstrates the strength of the FCC in guiding the market. While the government puts provisions in place to encourage speedy development of the wireless industry, it sometimes does the opposite. This example shows how attempts to kick-start the industry by putting licenses into the hands of more capable corporations actually dragged down an industry that is anxious to move ahead and catch up with other nations around the world.

The FCC is composed of five commissioners appointed by the President and confirmed by the Senate (each commissioner serves a 5-year term). Interestingly enough, more than three commissioners may not be of the same political party, nor may they have any financial interests in the communications industry.

However, the fact is that politics has a major impact on the FCC. With the election of President Bush in 2000, the agency is likely to take a shift toward more pro-industry emphasis in the telecom sector. This means that there is likely to be more megamergers.

FEDERAL TRADE COMMISSION (FTC)

Many believe that the FCC must approve telecom mergers. This is not the case. Rather, the FCC must look at issues regarding the transfer of spectrum to another entity. It is the FTC, as well as the Antitrust Division of the Department of Justice (DOJ), that ultimately approves a merger in the telecom world. There are a number of antitrust laws—Sherman Act, Clayton Act, and so on—that attempt to promote competition in the marketplace, which should mean lower prices and better quality of goods and services.

Like the FCC, the FTC has five commissioners nominated by the President and confirmed by the Senate (more than three cannot be from the same party). Again, with the Bush administration, it would not be surprising to see the FTC move toward a more lenient stand on allowing mergers in the wireless industry.

COMMITTEE ON FOREIGN INVESTMENT IN THE UNITED STATES (CFIUS)

President Gerald Ford created this committee in 1975. Essentially, the group has the authority to investigate the national security implications of direct foreign investment or acquisition. Members include the Secretary of Treasury (who is the chairperson), the Director of the Office of Science and Technology Policy, the Assistant to the President for National Security Affairs, the Assistant to the President for Economic Policy, the Attorney General, the Director of the Office of Management and Budget, the U.S. Trade Representative, the Chairman of the Council of Economic Advisors, and the Secretaries of State, Defense, and Commerce. After review by the CFIUS, the President has the ultimate power to block a merger. The process may not exceed 90 days. The proceedings for CFIUS review are not made public.

When Stanton negotiated the deal with Deutsche Telekom, he was required to undergo a CFIUS review. What were the national security concerns? Well, suppose the foreign country that owns the U.S. assets becomes an enemy. What if the service is shut down? Or what if a terrorist organization infiltrates the foreign country's own system and then affects the U.S. system?

Besides, the Federal Bureau of Investigation (FBI) wants to continue to be able to have wiretap capabilities so as to fight international terrorism and crime. As a result, the U.S. equipment must be maintained in the United States.

FOREIGN REGULATORY AGENCIES

Countries around the world have different rules about licensing the frequency spectrum within their borders, as well as for dealing with mergers and acquisitions. Of course, a key marketplace for wireless is Europe, which has been making great strides for unification under the European Union (EU), such as increasing the freedom of movement and reducing red tape. It is the Competition Division that regulates mergers and acquisitions activity in the EU.

In fact, the FTC and the EU have been working hard to harmonize regulations. This has been no easy feat. In the United States, the federal court system is an integral part of antitrust actions, which is not the case in Europe. Yet there have been moves to create a uniform filing form and uniform filing times and review periods that occur roughly at the same time.

STATE LAW

Do not forget that individual states in the United States can wield their powers. This has been the case especially with safety, as in the case of Patricia Pena. Patricia Pena's daughter died in 1999 as a result of a driver being distracted by a cell phone. As a result, Pena lobbied to restrict or ban cell phone use in cars. Since then, there have been nine ordinances passed regarding cell phone use. There is also movement in Congress to pass a national law.

A federal law is likely to have a significant impact on the wireless industry. After all, the telematics industry is based on the idea of using wireless technologies in the car.

STANDARDS ADOPTION

Note: In the discussion of standards, many technical terms and acronyms are used. More detailed discussion of these various terms is given in Chapter 3, and the terms are defined in the Glossary.

Most segments of the wireless market are heavily influenced by technical standards. These standards guide the way that equipment operates in order to ensure compatible systems. Essentially, technical standards can be seen as various "languages" that allow wireless devices to intercommunicate.

In order to understand a little about how standards adoption influences the wireless market, we'll take a brief look at how a standard comes about in the industry. Each stage of the process has some unique attributes and often is influenced by the other forces outlined in this chapter, especially politics.

A *standard* is a living document (one that is updated periodically) that outlines the technical specifications of any given wireless technology. The standard may specify such things as frequencies, power levels, or other parameters in addition to defining how to use the technology. This document is designed to ensure that all equipment that operates by its terms is completely compatible and meets all the stated goals.

The standards themselves often are developed by large committees (called *standards development organizations,* or SDOs) comprised of representatives from individual corporations that have a vested interest in the advancement of a particular wireless technology. Since these standards documents serve as design guidelines for the various wireless equipment, software, and operation modes, they are important to the success of a product in terms of reliability and compatibility.

The SDOs that exist in the wireless world are the groups that actually crank out the technical standards for wireless networks. Most large wireless companies have members of their technical staff participate in these groups in order to influence the decisions and obtain information about the industry. The standards that come from these groups can cover the air interface of wireless devices, the network interface, or other components of a wireless network. Below is a list of a few of the major SDOs operating in the world today:

- *Association of Radio Industries and Businesses (ARIB).* Japan's standards development body.
- *China Wireless Telecommunications Standards Group (CWTS).* China's main standards development body.
- *Telecommunications Industry Association (TIA).* A group accredited by the American National Standards Institute (ANSI) that develops North American wireless standards.
- *Telecommunications Technology Association (TTA).* Korea's standards development organization.
- *The Telecommunication Technology Committee (TTC).* Japan's national standards body that focuses on telecommunications.
- *Committee T1 (T1).* A U.S. standards body that focuses on network interfaces.
- *European Telecommunications Standards Institute (ETSI).* European body that worked to develop Universal Mobile Telecommunications System (UMTS).

As you may have noticed, many of these groups are organized around regions, continents, or countries. They organize to represent the interests of the governing bodies of the nations under their umbrella.

The next stage for a standard that has been completed at the SDO level is for it to be submitted to a wireless consortium or partnership. The wireless consortiums are groups that form not to develop standards but for the purpose of promoting or marketing various standards to international bodies. These consortiums usually are international and made up of or tied to a number of the SDOs. Some of these groups compile and disseminate statistics and other information that makes an argument for favoring the adoption of their standards over others. Some of the major wireless consortiums in existence today are

- *Universal Wireless Communications Consortium (UWCC).* A U.S. organization that includes about 100 carriers and equipment providers aimed at supporting solutions for Time Division Multiple Access (TDMA)–based wireless networks.

- *3G Partnership Project (3GPP).* Comprised of ARIB, CWTS, ETSI, T1, and TTA. Largely promotes the evolution of the open GSM standard.
- *3G Partnership Project 2 (3GPP2).* Made up of ARIB, TTC, CWTS, TTA, and TIA. Largely promotes the evolution of CDMA technology.
- *CDMA Development Group (CDG).* A group formed to advance the use of cdmaOne and cdma2000 throughout the world.
- *GSM Alliance.* A group formed to promote the GSM standard.

Most of the various consortiums and partnerships you see in wireless end up proposing standards and technology information to the International Telecommunications Union (ITU). The ITU is a charter organization of the United Nations and is widely recognized for setting the global standards for telecommunications. For instance, the group of standards that comprise the 3G radio interface for terrestrial wireless systems is called IMT-2000.

Looking at all these acronyms can just turn your eyes all fuzzy, so it helps to have a picture. For a graphic view of these various groups and how they all fit together, see Figure 2.2.

When looking at the various consortiums, it should be no surprise that companies tend to stick together in corporate cliques—sharing the same philosophies and visions for the wireless future. These collaborations tend to have profound effects on the market. When a few companies decide to band together and push into a new or existing segment of the market, competitors are forced to follow suit or risk losing some of their own share of a lucrative market.

An example is a powerful consortium that formed in 1994, the CDMA Development Group (CDG). This nonprofit group is supported by over 100 companies for the purpose of evangelizing CDMA technology and supporting its adoption. The activities of the CDG have included setting up teams to collaborate on standards, publishing white papers, and lobbying on behalf of member companies. The CDG has been instrumental in the adoption of IS-95 networks in several areas of the world, particularly South America, Asia, and the United States. One of its largest efforts in 2001–2002 is courting network operators that currently deploy GSM and TDMA networks in an effort to get them to change sides and join the CDMA team.

FIGURE 2.2

Wireless Standards Adoption Process

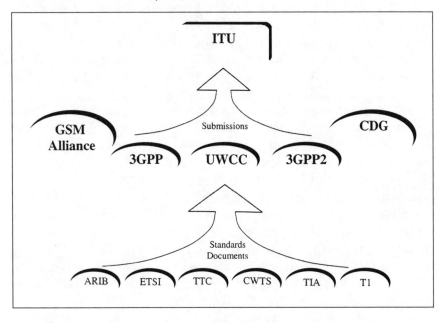

While it is hard to speculate about what success CDMA would have had without the CDG, it is safe to assume that it would have been significantly less. If all the companies that comprise the CDG had ventured forth on their own, their collective technologies would have had less of a chance of finding their way into commercial use.

It would be much easier to follow the wireless industry (and there would be far fewer acronyms) if all the various companies could agree on standards. Unfortunately, there has yet to be any case where all companies have agreed to adopt a single standard for equipment or services. Most wireless markets have at least a few competing standards supported by groups of companies. In the case of *Original Equipment Manufacturer* (OEM) companies or those which sell to service providers, supporting only select standards limits their available market.

For example, Nextel Communications offers service on a proprietary communications protocol called *iDEN*. This technology is similar to another called TDMA but is still in a class of its own. The phones that Nextel sells are all made by one manufacturer, Motorola, and are not compatible with other networks. As Nextel looks to upgrade its systems to 3G technology, it is in somewhat of a pickle.

With a nonstandard technology, there's little support for seamless upgrade options. And while Nextel is looking at the possibility of implementing cdma2000 technology that is supported by other manufacturers, it must deal with its Motorola contract that stipulates 6 months advanced notice if Nextel plans to use anything other than iDEN. Sole-supplier scenarios such as this can get sticky.

While other network operators may be in a better position than Nextel, the situation is not a whole lot better. Verizon Wireless and Sprint PCS use a technology called CDMA, which is incompatible with the network technology used by AT&T and Cingular Wireless. These competing technologies lead to many problems.

First, these competing technologies limit the number of suppliers that network operators can use to build their networks or supply handsets to customers. Sprint PCS, for instance, offers several phones from Samsung, a large CDMA handset provider. However, if you really like the features of the latest Nokia phones, you may be out of luck. Nokia has yet to be a significant supplier of CDMA handsets (although it is working to change this).

Another problem is that cellular users in the United States are limited in the collaborative features of their devices. For example, if both you and your friend use Verizon phones and service, you can send messages to each other and do other cool things like play games. If your friend has an AT&T phone and service, though, these functions do not work because of the incompatible networks.

In Europe and other nations that have agreed on a common technology called GSM, there are few problems with interacting with others wirelessly. This common standard adoption is one of the main reasons that GSM technology has become a huge success.

It also has allowed many European nations to quickly ramp up wireless penetration rates above 70 percent in some cases. Without all the added complexities brought about by multiple technologies, consumers adopt wireless services much more easily and in greater numbers.

The vast differences between the European and U.S. wireless markets due to standards adoption often is the subject of debate itself. Since the U.S. government's stance has long favored promoting competition in markets, the United States actually likes to see multiple standards competing in the wireless industry. The theory is that this ultimately will benefit consumers with lower prices and better features spurred on by competition.

In contrast, many European nations have made great strides toward unity, as evidenced by the formation of the European Union and a common currency, the Euro. The GSM standard for digital wireless devices also was a collaborative effort. Frequently it was weighed down by committee efforts, but in the end it came through and made it into commercial systems in the early 1990s. As stated earlier, GSM has far outpaced any other commercially embraced wireless technology.

When discussing which approach is better to evolving an industry, people usually favor one side or the other but not both. Not surprisingly, most Americans favor the pro-competition approach of multiple standards, whereas most Europeans favor the collaborative approach. This sentiment is mirrored in the corporate philosophies of wireless companies as well.

The problem for investors is that quite often the assessment of standards adoption wanders away from objective reasoning and leans more toward taking sides in a heated soccer match. Suddenly, nationalistic pride takes over, and individuals begin to emotionally cheer for a company from their nation to succeed in a market that doesn't play by those rules. It's a game of focusing only on the positives while trying to sweep the negative aspects under the rug.

While technical standards certainly are a driving force in wireless, the focus on adopted technology is quite often misplaced. Rather than understanding how a company's adopted technology helps it compete for market share, too many investors emotionally put money behind the technology they feel is technically superior. Their rationale is that if the technology is superior, everybody will flock to it while shunning the other, inferior technologies.

Unfortunately, this is a very short-sighted approach to investing because it overlooks many other forces that drive the industry. There have been many cases of high-technology markets where supposedly inferior technologies absolutely pummel the competition in the open market. Many people thought that Betamax was superior to VHS. The same was thought about MiniDiscs.

As stated earlier in this chapter, wireless is largely driven from a consumer mindset. The vast majority of consumers care little about the technology that is in their cellular phone or PDA. Their interest lies in the capabilities, quality of service, and price.

To some extent, technology plays a role in establishing these three things, but it is only part of the equation. Superior technology that gives a service provider cost advantages will not redeem a company that plans or executes its strategy poorly. Often, all a company needs is a "good enough" technology with a top-notch marketing and service team to beat the pants off the competition.

With most wireless service providers now migrating their networks to 3G technologies, there has been a tremendous amount of debate in the industry about which is the best path. While most of the world's wireless networks will migrate to a standard called *Wideband Code Division Multiple Access* (W-CDMA), other competing standards such as cdma2000 are being marketed as a better approach. Both standards have been approved by the ITU, with no preference given except to make them interoperable somehow.

As stated earlier, in the midst of these discussions, investors are watching the industry closely, attempting to get a read on just how pervasive certain standards will be. Most wireless companies have product portfolios that strongly favor one standard, so the acceptance of that standard is key to their revenue stream. Not surprisingly, each company pushes the technology standard that favors its business plan.

Too often the arguments and lobbying for standards adoption break down solely into a comparison of technical performance. Investors, journalists, and industry consultants are all engaged in a "my technology is better than yours" debate that too often takes center stage in the press. Additionally, many companies publish white papers and other materials to promote the financial advantages of implementing certain technologies.

The biggest flaw in almost all these discussions is the participants' attempts to lump the entire wireless industry in one pile. For instance, many investors are led to believe that the cdma2000 technology is a much cheaper way for network operators to deliver wireless data and voice services. A white paper published by QUALCOMM in 2001 breaks down the economics of various technologies and "proves" that its class of technology is magnitudes ahead of the competition when it comes to the costs associated with operating the system.

While in some cases this may be true, it will not be true in many other cases. Since various wireless networks around the world each have a unique makeup in terms of infrastructure, there is no single "boiler plate" spreadsheet that can be used to analyze the economics of migrating a network. Each network operator has specific needs, requirements, and goals for the future. Rarely will a network operator achieve the same results stated in white papers or marketing materials. Some will get better results in a few areas, but more often they'll achieve results far below what is predicted due to poor assumptions.

CONSUMER TASTES

It is natural to think that anthropologists will study remote cultures to try to shed light on modern culture. However, during a 10-week period in 2000, a group of anthropologists did 180 interviews in six countries to look at how people use cell phones (the countries included the United States, China, Japan, Sweden, France, and England). The study included visits at cafés, malls, train stations, and anywhere else people socialize with wireless devices.

One interesting finding was that people are starting to see wireless devices as fashion items. In China, for example, women wear their cell phones as jewelry.

Wireless fashion is no fluke. The force of consumer mentality is probably the most overlooked and least understood influence on the wireless market. It seems like the entire industry is still trying to figure out just what consumers want in a mobile device and what they would be willing to pay for. QUALCOMM shipped a hybrid cellular phone/PDA late in 1999, something that many thought consumers would flock to. It turned out to be a huge flop because it was too bulky and expensive. What many European companies are starting to realize is that wireless technology really creates a new lifestyle for people. The key to successful products and services lies in understanding the complexities of this mobile lifestyle in various cultures.

One company attempting to bring fashion to wireless is Palm. This company and Sanyo Fashion House (a major apparel manufacturer in Japan) introduced a spring line of raincoats. And yes, the inner pockets were perfectly fit for a Palm handheld unit (there is even a Palm logo on the pocket). But it is not cheap. The raincoats run between $185 and $695.

Palm even hired supermodel Claudia Schiffer for promotion. There is, for example, the Claudia-branded Palm V, which you can buy from ClaudiaSchiffer.com. The special device is metallic aqua and has fitness software.

If you stop to consider how you may have learned about cellular phones or services, you'll likely recall that you were exposed to them by a friend or colleague. While some people respond to ads or direct mail, many are driven to certain service providers when they see something really cool on a friend's phone.

Perhaps you've always thought that cellular phones were too cumbersome and bulky to be something you'd ever get. You couldn't imagine strapping a big black box to your hip. Then you see a friend's new sleek, fashionable communicator. It's so small that it fits in any pocket, and it even comes with a hands-free earpiece for easy use in your car. Only one service provider offers the phone, so it is probably in a good position to gain a new customer.

One example of consumer tastes driving wireless success in the United States involves AT&T. In the latter part of 2000, AT&T offered several new phones and service plans for the upcoming holiday season. The prediction by many in the industry was that consumers would gobble up new data-capable phones that could access the Internet.

To everyone's surprise (even AT&T's), the big hit was not the data-capable phones at all. It was the sleek Nokia 8260 model phones that were small, light, and fashionable. While the phones had messaging capabilities, they were much less featured than other makes and models. Even so, stores couldn't keep them on the shelves.

CONVERGENCE

TV, cable, movies, wireless—the dream of many media and telecom tycoons is to find ways to converge many media and, as a result, create huge competitive advantages. This was the thinking behind the megamerger of AOL and Time Warner, as well as the ambitions of Rupert Murdock of News Corp.

Even though convergence has not become a reality, it likely will gain momentum over the long term. And wireless will be a crucial part of the puzzle.

One person who has not waited is Jean-Marie Messier. In the mid-1990s, he became CEO of a sleepy French water company. However, this was too slow for Messier, so he launched an aggressive campaign to transform the company—now called *Vivendi*—into a media powerhouse. In his quest, he bought the French pay-TV company Canal+ (similar to HBO) as well as Havas (a software, books, and video game publisher) and Cegetel (the second largest cell phone company in France).

In the first part of 2001, Messier purchased Universal, which has a leading movie studio and music division; MP3.com, a top online music site; and Houghton Mifflin Company, the 169-year-old educational book publisher.

Central to Messier's vision is Vizzavi, a portal that allows cell phones to tap into the rich content of Vivendi. He thinks that people will want to have content provided anytime, anywhere, on any device. What's more, he thinks people are willing to pay for such services, perhaps on a subscription basis.

However, as with all convergence strategies, integration will be extremely difficult. Only time will tell if it will be a success.

SUMMARY

Understanding what drives the global wireless market is important for investors. While it is sometimes difficult to know which of the factors we've mentioned are the most important and which are the least, they all clearly play a role. In addition, there may be new forces coming into the market in the future as nations continue to deregulate and modernize their societies.

To recap, here are some of the important factors that drive the wireless industry:

- Buy-in from industry leaders
- Mergers and acquisitions
- Politics
- Regulation
- Standards adoption
- Consumer tastes
- Convergence

Clearly, wireless is no fluke. Companies such as Microsoft and Oracle are committed to wireless. These companies know that the world is going from the PC to portable devices. And for investors, the opportunities can be great. In the rest of the book we will look at the key industry segments and techniques for finding the companies that will benefit the most from these huge wireless trends.

3

Wireless Network Operators

That's it; you've had it. Your cellular phone has dropped yet another call to one of your most important clients. As soon as you get to a phone that actually works, you're going to drop your service after you give the provider a good razzing. Who in the world would buy stock in a company that has such a poor product and service? This company must be a bomb, you think, on the verge of bankruptcy. To your surprise, you find that the stock of your service provider is going gangbusters, actually a triple since the initial public offering (IPO)—even with a recent 35 percent drop!

So what gives? Can a company really have such subpar service and yet still prosper? Believe it or not, a company can—at least in this stage of the wireless market. Consumers, especially in the United States, seem to be willing to tolerate less than optimal quality of service for the benefits of mobility. Because wireless technology is still maturing, higher costs and sometimes poor service will be absorbed. However, network operators are seeing shrinking premiums for providing basic voice telephony services. At this stage, service quality is becoming more important to attract and keep customers. At the same time, technology is advancing rapidly, bringing new data and Internet access features to mobile devices. The network operators must continue to provide new services while searching for new revenue streams from growing customer bases.

Similar to other areas of telecommunications, wireless network operators play a pivotal role in the industry. In fact, the companies that operate the networks for services wield substantial power in the market because all the other segments are built to support or augment them. Without the service providers, there would be no wireless industry. Basically, they are the "center of the universe" for the wireless industry.

Since this segment of the wireless industry is so important, this chapter will focus on the wireless service providers and the important aspects of their business. These companies are the Sprints, AT&Ts, and Vodaphones of the world. Even if investors choose to pass by the opportunity to invest in wireless network operators, it is a good idea to understand their business anyway. Since they are the last stop on the food chain before the consumer, their position, strategy, and network technology factor into almost all wireless businesses.

For the most part, this chapter focuses on the mobile cellular industry. Most investors are familiar with the commercial telecommunications services that involve mobile handsets, and this is the area that has seen the most attention recently. The most popular items in this category are devices such as the prolific cellular telephone, personal digital assistants (PDAs), and pagers.

The major areas we will look at include

- Role in the industry
- Network technology
- Valuation metrics
- Key investment themes

While this sector of the wireless industry presents some of the best opportunities for investors, it is not the only game in town. There are dozens of other markets for wireless devices that serve more specific purposes. One example would be handheld bar code scanners that can be used in logistics to track inventories or to stage items in a manufacturing process. We'll come back to some of the other, less prominent (but still profitable) wireless sectors later in this book.

WIRELESS SERVICE PROVIDERS: THEIR ROLE IN THE INDUSTRY

Wireless service providers typically are huge telecommunications entities that have significant interests in several forms of communications and media. Since wireless capabilities have developed mainly as an extension to established wireline services, it should be no surprise that the likes of AT&T, Sprint, and WorldCom fall in this category. These companies already support huge telecommunications infrastructures and have the tremendous cash flow necessary to fund new products and services to the mass market.

There are currently only a handful of major wireless service providers in the United States. The six most popular that offer nationwide service include AT&T Wireless, Sprint PCS, Verizon Wireless, Cingular Wireless, Nextel Communications, and VoiceStream Wireless. The largest wireless service provider in the world is Vodafone, which has interests in several other service providers, including Verizon in the United States. Table 3.1 shows the approximate domestic subscriber base and reported revenues of each of these six service providers at the end of the first quarter of 2001.

TABLE 3.1

Major Service Provider Statistics for First Quarter of 2001 (1Q01)

Company	Domestic Subscribers	1Q01 Revenue (mil)
Verizon Wireless	27,100,000	$4,000
Cingular Wireless	20,535,000	3,341
AT&T Wireless	15,700,000	3,212
Sprint PCS	10,355,000	2,051
Nextel Communications	7,200,000	1,740
VoiceStream Wireless	4,400,000	732
(*Source:* Company filings.)		

Some of these companies, such as Verizon and Sprint PCS, were still part of larger parent companies as of early 2001. Sprint PCS has a tracking stock (NYSE: PCS) for its wireless business, and Verizon's stock (NYSE: VZ) represents the entire telecommunications business for Verizon Communications. However, Verizon does plan to spin off its wireless division in an IPO, and it wouldn't be surprising to see Cingular do the same.

Actually, the United States is one of the few countries to have so many network operators providing service in the same area. Several major markets in the United States have six or more operators competing for customers. Many countries in Europe, Asia, and elsewhere have only two or maybe three service providers for a given area. This is largely due to the U.S. insistence on fostering competition in the industry, whereas many other nations still have telecommunications industries that are under heavy government influence.

Even though wireless service providers sell end-user equipment such as cellular phones, most of them do not manufacture the equipment. They typically partner with equipment manufacturers and bundle the equipment with their service. It is also very common for the service provider to subsidize the cost of the equipment in return for a service contract, where the equipment basically will be paid for over the term of service. This is how you can walk into a Nextel store and walk out with a "free" phone. You simply end up paying for the phone and then some with your $39.99 monthly fee.

Wireless network operators appeal to consumers for the bulk of their revenue. Just like Internet service providers, they charge fees to consumers to use their services and connections. Not surprisingly, the price models are similar as well, with consumers typically paying a monthly access fee and then additional charges for special features or excessive use. The fact that carriers appeal to the masses for sales puts them in a complicated position. They must spend heavily in marketing their services, in building their service capacity, and in building a strong customer service department—all the while maintaining a high quality of service at affordable prices. It is a tough go for the service providers.

Because network operators are in the driver's seat of the industry, they often control the progress (or lack thereof) and direction of wireless services as a whole. Their investments in infrastructure and support services support literally thousands of smaller businesses. And their decisions in adopting technology can be either a boon or a bust to the balance sheets of some companies.

THE TECHNOLOGY

Unfortunately for the average investor, mobile communications involve some of the most complex, cutting-edge technology in use today. If you make toys, your technology platform is usually quite basic. A few lights and melody chips—maybe even a motor or two to give a toy a lifelike appearance. Wireless technology that goes into networks is magnitudes above this in complexity. Service providers need to have highly skilled staff in multiple disciplines to manage and service components of the network.

The good news, though, is that with respect to investing, there's really not all that much you need to know about wireless technology. Knowing the details of how things work is nice, but unless there's a strong correlation between technical specifications and revenues, it makes little sense to spend days trying to figure out just who has the upper edge in technology.

Having this information as a reference can be useful, though, because some limited technical terms often are used in press releases and news articles concerning wireless companies. Simply the sheer number of acronyms used in this industry is enough to boggle the mind (for which we include a Glossary at the back of the book).

When we talk about mobile networks that enable the wireless transfer of information while moving, there are three main areas:

- Satellite technology
- Land-based cellular technology
- Short-range technologies

Each of these segments applies to a different environment or locale. For instance, satellite technologies are used to establish networks with wide coverage areas—the entire globe, in fact. On the opposite end of the spectrum, short-range wireless networks are set up in what's called a *picocell environment*—an area of use that is only a few hundred feet in diameter.

Satellite technologies have a long history and are expanding in new ways. There was actually quite a bit of excitement about satellite wireless in the middle to late 1990s, when several ventures were underway to deliver global communications. However, in 1999, the spectacular failure and subsequent bankruptcy of Iridium, a $5 billion constellation of 66 low-earth-orbit (LEO) satellites, cast a dark cloud over this sector.

Another player, Globalstar, has been heading down the same path, unable to pay its debt and struggling to sign up even one-tenth the number of subscribers it had banked on. In 2001, Globalstar defaulted on some major debt obligations, and its stock capitulated.

Far from its peak of $47.75 in January 2000, Globalstar traded around $0.30 in April 2001. Hapless investors basically were left with only a significant tax write-off.

Today, most investors stay away from the area of satellite wireless. Many of them are still licking their wounds. Until a business model for the technology comes through with some decent success, there likely will be little market activity in this area. This is why we've left this in the niche market category (see Chapter 6) along with short-range technologies for now—cellular takes center stage.

Short-range wireless communications also have a long history, but the next decade will prove to be the most interesting for this category. Technologies with names such as Bluetooth, HomeRF, and IEEE 802.11 will start to make their way into networks around the world—but in an interesting way. Since none of these technologies will displace cellular networks, they will instead fill in certain markets and applications being offered in parallel with existing cellular services.

While all three of these areas sometimes have certain technical aspects in common, there are many areas that differ. Where we'll spend most of the time in this chapter is in the most prevalent technologies in the wireless sector—the cellular technologies. Cellular technologies have been developed in earnest for the last few decades, and their popularity has exploded. And from what we're told, it's only the beginning.

Since we can't possibly capture everything about cellular technology in this book, we'll focus on the area most publicized in the media—the air interface. The air interface protocols outlined here are the means by which mobile devices communicate through the air. You can look at the various protocols simply as languages that are incompatible, each having its own merits and demerits. The various technologies commonly are divided into *generations* roughly corresponding to the time frame in which they were deployed.

As we discuss various technologies, it is important to understand that there are basically two main types of information that wireless devices transmit. The most obvious one is human speech. However, while most people understand why voice communications are important to people, they may not see the importance of communicating data as well. Data communications can take many forms, but essentially they involve transmitting bits of information that could represent text, part of an image, or a file. As you'll see later, the job of sending and receiving data can be very different from transmitting voice.

The area of wireless technology that we're skipping over here is the fixed-network side, sometimes called the *backhaul* or *backbone*. While this area is vital to providing good wireless services, it is often removed from wireless discussions and instead included in discussion of telecommunications networks. Since it serves roughly the same purpose for landline connections, this area has a long legacy in providing voice services.

We would preface this entire chapter, though, with the statement that knowledge of wireless technology may not be a significant advantage for the investor. The technology buffs who have the inside scoop on how all this stuff works often make no better investment choices than those who are clueless in this area. Therefore, don't worry too much if this is all confusing or hard to remember. There are many other areas that are just as important, if not more so, when evaluating wireless companies for investment.

FIRST- AND SECOND-GENERATION (1G/2G) CELLULAR NETWORKS

The first generation of commercial wireless telephony generally has been understood to have begun in the late 1970s. While there certainly was a lot of wireless activity taking place before that time, the true potential of wireless services in the mass market began to come into focus in the late 1970s.

The first-generation (1G) networks being deployed in the United States consisted of an analog cell-based architecture called the *Advanced Mobile Phone System* (AMPS). Surprisingly, these networks are still used heavily today, although most service providers are replacing this infrastructure with more efficient digital systems. While the phones were heavy and the voice quality was below that of landline connections, the freedom of wire-free communications caught on fast. Through most of the 1980s, AMPS networks were deployed in earnest to increase coverage.

In the late 1980s, the AMPS networks began to show capacity strains, and newer digital technologies were being developed to succeed the original analog networks. A number of approaches were proposed around the world, and different nations took different paths into the next generation of cellular networks. Europe went through great pains to solicit collaboration from dozens of companies to develop and endorse the Global System for Mobile Communications

(GSM) standard, whereas the United States left the choice of technology open to private companies. Regulatory leaders in the United States hoped to supercharge the wireless industry by spurring competition between companies, thus driving end prices lower and leading to more widespread availability of services.

Demand also was starting to show for data services, something that the early AMPS networks handled poorly. The newer digital systems being suggested contained provisions to supply limited amounts of data more efficiently along with voice services.

Interestingly, the Internet was still nowhere near the mainstream culture yet, so today's wireless Web was not really on the minds of developers at this time. They simply foresaw the usefulness of eagerly adopted paging and messaging features integrated into cellular telephones. Only later did people start to realize increased value in a mobile terminal that not only could provide access to the omnipresent Internet but also could link people together with text messaging or chat capabilities.

In the United States, a number of new digital technologies came about in the early 1990s. The most popular ones were Time Division Multiple Access (TDMA) and Code Division Multiple Access (CDMA). Most of the Americas followed the U.S. lead, building out mostly TDMA and CDMA networks throughout the 1990s. Some service providers in the United States and other American countries adopted GSM as their air interface, but the number was far fewer.

Virtually all of western Europe adopted the GSM standard for the air interface of mobile devices. In addition, much of the Asia-Pacific region adopted it as well, with some in Japan and Korea being notable exceptions (opting mostly for a technology called Personal Digital Communications (PDC) and CDMA, respectively). Using this common protocol for services has helped enable roaming across borders in almost all European nations. Here's a look at some of the most common 1G and 2G technologies with a short description of each.

1G/2G AIR INTERFACE PROTOCOLS FOR VOICE

Advanced Mobile Phone Service (AMPS). This is one of the earliest protocols developed in the late 1970s and is often referred to simply as analog cellular. While it is old, it is still very popular and is the basis for many of the newer protocols.

Total Access Communications Systems (TACS). Based on AMPS, another popular analog system mostly in Europe and Asia. Many people in the United Kingdom still prefer this system.

Nordic Mobile Telephone (NMT). This was the first analog cellular system in use in Sweden and Norway. These systems now are still spread around many areas of Europe and Asia.

Time Division Multiple Access (TDMA). This protocol came around soon after the AMPS started to show some limitations. The main limitation that TDMA helped overcome was capacity—the ability to carry a certain number of calls or transmissions at any one time. It basically tripled the capacity of current cellular systems by using some digital techniques.

Code Division Multiple Access (CDMA). This protocol is fully digital in nature and offers many significant improvements over previous technologies in terms of capacity and voice clarity. Much of the early development of this technology was done in the military and brought into commercial use by QUALCOMM in the early 1990s.

Global System for Mobile Communications (GSM). This is a digital protocol deployed in the early 1990s that is similar to TDMA. Developed in concert with dozens of companies around the world, it is noted for being highly secure and reliable. It is by far the most popular protocol in Europe and the rest of the world (outside North America).

Integrated Digital Enhanced Network (iDEN). A proprietary standard developed by Motorola that is based on TDMA. It adds more features to the standard services such as direct two-way radio. Nextel is the main service provider that supports iDEN technology.

Personal Digital Communications (PDC). Established in 1991, this digital system is based on TDMA technology and operates in both the 800-MHz and 1.5-GHz bands. This protocol is operated predominantly in Japan.

Personal Handyphone System (PHS). A digital cordless phone system used primarily in Japan. The range of this system is very small. The system is incorporated with the traditional home phone system to offer better economy.

CIRCUITS VERSUS PACKETS

Particularly when we talk of wireless data communications, the concept of circuit networks as opposed to packet networks is very important. When you hear that a particular network is circuit-switched (or circuit-based), this means that a channel or physical line is dedicated to a communication between two points. This dedicated line is "tied up" until the communication is terminated on both ends. For example, a telephone call made from your home typically is serviced with circuit technologies.

One aspect of circuit technology is that there must be enough lines (or channels) to handle all the different communications taking place. You may remember trying to call friends or relatives after a major earthquake or other natural disaster only to get a message that all circuits were busy. Basically, the telephone service provider only has so many circuits to handle communications in any given area. And once they are dedicated, no one gets through until someone else hangs up.

Packet-based communications networks transmit data in discrete packages, sometimes across multiple circuits or paths. Whatever information is being sent is essentially broken up into chunks and sent along with some information that identifies the data and their destination. If you sent a friend a 10-page letter but sent each page in a separate envelope, you would be using packet technology (and wasting postage). Each envelope would have the destination (address), and if you numbered each page, your friend would have no problem compiling the letter in proper order to understand what you are saying. Packet technologies are a little more complicated than this because the data must all arrive at the proper point to be reassembled in a short period of time. Otherwise, you may miss some vital data (imagine if your friend didn't get page 6 that had all the juice on your coworker's love life).

One major advantage that packet-based technologies can provide over circuit-based networks is efficiency, especially when data are being transferred. Packet-based networks can take advantage of some basic characteristics of communication where circuit-based networks can't. Packet technologies can take advantage of the dead time in communications. When you browse the Internet, for instance, you can spend several minutes looking at information that was downloaded in a few seconds. Your service provider does not want to leave a circuit dedicated to you while you try to decide which digital camera has better features. At any instant, if a circuit is unused, sophisticated packet technology can borrow that circuit to service someone else's communication. In this manner, several different communications can be lined up on a single line or channel to fill in all the dead time. This allows a service provider to maximize the use of its network and serve more customers, thereby making more money.

There are also other characteristics of communications that can be exploited by packet technology. Most data communications are asymmetric in nature. This basically means that the amount of information traveling in one direction is not equal to the amount traveling in the other direction. When browsing the Internet, for instance, it is common to download about 5 to 10 times the amount of information that you upload. Uploaded information may be just mouse clicks, Web addresses, and some text strings, whereas downloaded information may be detailed graphics, animation, or music files. Packet technologies can be set up to handle asymmetric communications more efficiently, thus making the better use of available resources.

Many industry analysts believe that everything will one day be done through packet technologies, even voice communications (this is called *Voice over Internet Protocol*, or VoIP). The goal in the industry is to migrate telecommunications networks to an all-IP environment, where packet technology is used throughout the network. While this is technically possible and may very well turn out to be true, it is still a little farther out than most people think.

One company that is making progress in this area is Net2Phone, a provider of voice services through the Internet. While this company also has seen its stock suffer lately (from a closing high of $82.25 just after the IPO in September 1999 to $6.00 in June 2001), it continues to receive support in the market. Industry bellwether Cisco Systems continues to pour money into the company, supplying another $25 million along with Softbank in June 2001. This tends to indicate that despite current limitations, there is hope for the technology in the future.

Keep in mind, though, that there is a tremendous amount of circuit-based communications infrastructure in place around the world. All this equipment and technology are not going to be tossed out; rather, they will be optimized to keep up with consumer demands as much as possible. This already has been the case in the mobile cellular industry, where companies have been modifying older technologies to give them new, advanced capabilities. This practice commonly is referred to as *overlay*. The newer technology is overlaid onto existing infrastructure by making modifications or minimal changes to the equipment. This makes the introduction of advanced technologies more cost-effective, and it can preserve the function of the older technology as well, which still may be serving a large customer base.

Air interface technologies designed specifically to handle data were introduced into 2G systems and for the most part were not a huge change. They basically adapted the current hardware and wrote new software to send packets over the air to portable devices that had a compatible modem inside. For instance, AT&T and other service providers have built out a data network called *Cellular Digital Packet Data* (CDPD) to complement their voice networks. You can purchase a phone that supports the TDMA interface for voice and the CDPD interface for data from AT&T's PocketNet service. Here are some of the common air interface protocols for data in the second generation.

AIR INTERFACE PROTOCOLS EXCLUSIVELY FOR DATA

Cellular Digital Packet Data (CDPD). This protocol is currently in use by a number of carriers to complement voice services. It offers basic data-transfer abilities that can be used to send short messages, e-mails, or files. It overlays existing technologies to provide optimized handling of data on cellular networks.

Mobitex. Mobitex is a dedicated data-only network based on cellular technology that uses packet switching for maximum efficiency. The Mobitex protocol is an open international standard administered by the Mobitex Operators Association and supported by more than 20 operators around the world. With more than 30 networks on five continents, the Mobitex market is very large.

High-Speed Circuit-Switched Data (HSCSD). A circuit-switched data-transmission technology that supports speeds of up to 38.4 kbps.

This technology fits into TDMA and GSM systems, using voice channels to pass data.

THE NEXT-GENERATION (2.5G AND 3G) CELLULAR NETWORKS

As we just begin to move into the twenty-first century, most everyone in the wireless industry would agree that we are between the second and third generations of technology, which is often referred to as 2.5G. The third-generation (3G) technologies are starting to be implemented in 2002 but still have a few years before they become more widespread. How long the 2.5G era lasts is anybody's guess. Some people think that 2.5G technologies will be a big hit with consumers and therefore suspend the need even to offer a better, 3G solution for several years. Still others think that 2.5G technologies do not support fast enough data speeds to provide such applications as video streaming, so consumers will still press for more advances.

Another question that often comes up in discussions of wireless is what generation certain technologies fit in. The features of some technologies such as cdma2000 1xRTT put them in an area that many classify as 2.5G. Yet this technology is clearly advertised as 3G technology by some service providers on the basis of its 144-kbps peak data rate and other aspects. Investors really don't need to worry too much about the details of these arguments. Whether you call something 2.5G, 3G, or 394G doesn't really matter. It is more important to understand what capabilities the technology offers to consumers and where it fits into wireless networks.

The 2.5G technologies represent a sort of stepping-stone to get to the third generation. For the most part, they offer advanced data capabilities with higher transmission speeds and always-on connectivity. The *always-on* feature is basically just a term used to denote that the portable device can retrieve data quickly any time it is in range; there is no need to dial up a connection or wait more than a few seconds to pull up a data screen. Here are some of the common 2.5G technologies (note that most of them combine data and voice capabilities).

2.5G AIR INTERFACE PROTOCOLS

General Packet Radio System (GPRS). A packet-based technology that can be overlaid on TDMA and GSM architectures for data services.

With a standard IP layer built into this standard, it fits well with packet data applications.

Enhanced Data Rates for Global Evolution (EDGE). Similar to and based on GPRS, EDGE is seen as the next step toward 3G for TDMA and GSM networks. Using an enhanced modulation scheme, higher data rates are possible.

High Data Rate (HDR). Packet technology that is mostly applied to CDMA (IS-95)–based infrastructure to enable high-data-rate transmissions. This technology is part of a 3G evolution called 1xEV for CDMA networks.

Single Carrier Radio Transmission Technology (1xRTT). This is the first phase of a cdma2000 network, and some consider this a 3G technology. It offers theoretical data rates of up to 144 kbps.

i-Mode. Packet-based data service that is available in Japan. It has a relatively slow data rate of 9.6 kbps but is very popular.

IS-136B/HS. A technology that uses GPRS architecture for IS-136 (TDMA) networks. Data speeds range from 9.6 to 43.2 kbps.

If you know about the Wireless Application Protocol (WAP), you may be wondering why it is not included in this list or under any of the air interface protocol lists. Well, WAP is not an air interface technology. WAP is the technology needed on the handset and on a Web-based server to deliver Internet content over one of these air interface protocols (such as GSM).

If you're looking to invest in a wireless service provider, you'll usually find that each will announce support for a plan to implement one of these technologies in its network. Many have even already started the upgrades. Here's a general picture of how many of the major network operators around the world are upgrading their 2G networks before 3G based on their current network technology:

$$GSM \rightarrow GPRS \rightarrow EDGE$$
$$TDMA \rightarrow EDGE$$
$$CDMA \rightarrow 1xRTT/HDR$$

Again, this is not the path for all, since some will be implementing the other solutions mentioned. For GSM, many networks are already upgraded with commercial GPRS equipment, mostly in Europe and Asia. AT&T already has started to build EDGE into its network (yet it also will build a GSM network with GPRS capability in parallel). And some major CDMA operators such as Sprint and Verizon already have installed 1xRTT systems (which, again, many people classify as 3G systems).

While many of these systems were just being installed and tested in 2001, widespread commercial services are more likely to arrive in 2002–2003. At that point, consumers in the United States and around the world will start to get a flavor of some of the higher-speed services offered by many of these new technologies. It will be interesting to see just how many people drop the slower basic services in favor of these. This could be the best indicator of whether people will flock to the full-blown 3G services when they become available.

3G AIR INTERFACE PROTOCOLS

In the media, the standards for 3G services often are divided into two competing categories: wideband CDMA (W-CDMA) and cdma2000 (a version that uses a narrower band proposed by QUALCOMM). There actually are more versions than these two, but a vast majority of networks will end up with one of these flavors.

Of course, the original intention was to have only one standard. However, it shouldn't come as a surprise that the goal of a single, unified, worldwide standard would be plagued with problems and inconsistencies. In theory, it is a great concept: Develop an advanced wireless technology standard that will provide high-quality voice and data capabilities with seamless worldwide roaming capabilities. The implementation of this is a nightmare, though, and the battle for dominance continues to play out like a daytime soap opera.

One reason that the 3G dream of a unified standard has been so difficult to realize is that all the various participants come into the game carrying baggage from their existing infrastructure. The United States has a lot of CDMA and TDMA infrastructure. The European nations are predominantly GSM. Even though the frequency bands for 3G were specified and recommended back in 1992, the United States chose to implement part of that spectrum for existing wireless services. And this is only the beginning of the mess. When the focus shifts toward technical merits, the arguments quickly shift to which protocol is better, citing all sorts of technical figures.

However, another reason we have various proposed 3G technologies comes down to wrangling over intellectual property (IP). Various wireless companies developed and patented some parts of the technology necessary to carry out wireless communications. When these technologies end up within the protocol approved by standards bodies, they become what is called *essential IP*.

For instance, a large group of companies has essential IP in the GSM standard. Thus any company building equipment with GSM protocol technology must contribute a fee for using the patents. Organizations are even set up entirely with the purpose of governing the use and payment for IP among companies. Another example is that any company building CDMA (IS-95) equipment must pay fees to QUALCOMM because it owns a large base of IP in the 2G CDMA technology built into the IS-95 standard.

One of the main reasons that several flavors of 3G technology exist is based in the games played to avoid patented technology. Each company obviously wants to be well represented in the industry at the same time that it represses chances for its competition to thrive. In essence, all this comes down to giving your company an edge in the market to ultimately make more money.

What this translates into in the 3G arena is many companies trying to implement CDMA-based technologies without being under the finger of QUALCOMM. With more than a decade of CDMA experience, QUALCOMM has built a substantial IP base with hundreds of issued patents in this area. While most other wireless companies wanted to base their 3G technologies on CDMA, they didn't want QUALCOMM to dictate everything about the technology or have an unbalanced portion of IP in the approved standards.

What's interesting is that some companies around the world almost blame QUALCOMM for the multiple standards proposed for 3G networks. The sentiment is that if QUALCOMM had been more willing to share its piece of the CDMA pie with other companies, then maybe a single dominant standard would have evolved. However, QUALCOMM has insisted on IP royalty rates that many consider prohibitive, so other companies claim that they have no choice but to "design around" areas to which QUALCOMM lays claim.

As of this writing, though, QUALCOMM still claims that it has essential IP in all proposed 3G CDMA standards. It also insists on charging similar license fees while not participating in any of the groups that seek to settle and divide the numerous IP claims in various wireless network technologies. This leaves the door open for lots of litigation in the future. In fact, there may be some spectacular court cases coming that will rival such high-technology suits as those against Rambus or Avant.

Rambus also went after other companies, demanding royalties for its *Dynamic Random Access Memory* (DRAM) technology. After losing significant claims in a few court cases in May 2001, the stock of Rambus slid to a low of $9.00 in June 2001, far off the high of over $117.00 only 1 year earlier. The company even shocked investors with a report that costs for litigation soared to $7.3 million in the first quarter of 2001. These costs were far higher than any other expenses and took a big bite out of the $31.25 million in revenues.

Several major steps have been taken over the last decade to try to bring the various technologies and legacy systems together into a unified solution. The accomplishments have been dramatic, probably better than many expected, but there are still some major divisions being worked out. Probably the most profound progress was made through the Operators Harmonization Group (OHG), an international group formed in the late 1990s.

The OHG basically assembled to attempt to iron out the major differences between the competing CDMA systems promoted by two standards development organizations, the 3GPP and 3GPP2. The aim was to simplify the implementation of the IMT-2000 standard in handheld mobile units, which basically means aligning the air interfaces as best as possible. The two groups also recognized that while multifunctional phones would help in this endeavor, they would not be that saving "ace in the hole" because some modes are more difficult to couple with others. Basically, they saw that a single phone that talks all of these languages on all the bands was not feasible anywhere in the near future, so they had better trim down the protocol wish list. Significant progress was made, but much more can be done.

As we begin commercial deployment of some of these 3G systems in 2002, what we are left with today basically are these two major categories (W-CDMA and cdma2000) with various other flavors mixed in to address other less dramatic differences. Before we get too far and deep into the discussion here, let's define the two main categories of air interfaces for full-blown 3G services under IMT-2000.

POPULAR 3G AIR INTERFACE PROTOCOLS

Wideband CDMA (W-CDMA). This protocol is designed to integrate well with existing GSM networks. It is also coupled with the recommendations for frequency spectrum allocation because it requires a 5-MHz channel.

cdma2000 (IS-2000). This protocol is evolved from IS-95 (CDMA) networks. It includes the 1xRTT and 3xRTT versions and is more flexible with frequency spectrum allocation, operating in a 1.25-MHz channel.

While these two interfaces are the primary categories, the International Telecommunications Union (ITU) has defined a family of radio interfaces to cover all the bases. Figure 3.1, from the ITU, shows the five solutions and how they fit into the evolution of existing systems.

It is important to remember that all these protocols are relatively new and likely will continue to evolve. This is merely where

FIGURE 3.1

3G Networks As Specified by the ITU

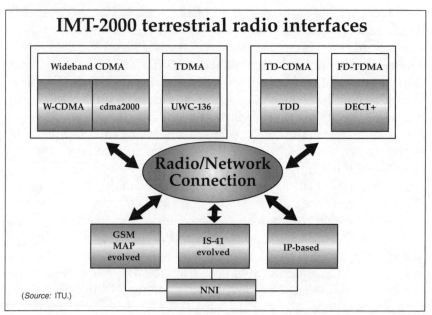

(*Source:* ITU.)

the wireless world is now, and there are still significant efforts being made to further improve the 3G landscape. Also, if the past is a good indicator, it is likely that changes in this area will never stop either.

WIRELESS NETWORK OPERATOR METRICS

With rapid growth in the Internet and the subsequent boom in the number of individual investors, stock analysis has changed tremendously. Advanced computing tools and free information over the Web have made it easy for just about anyone to "crunch the numbers" on their favorite stocks, looking for good buys or reasons to sell current holdings. Several new techniques have come about to help investors look at companies differently as well. Some favor core-value approaches, whereas others track growth or management effectiveness. Of course, they all attempt to predict how individual companies will perform in the future.

Companies competing in the wireless industry often are put through many different types of stock screens or compared in numerical analysis. Unfortunately, few of the quantitative methods used today account for all the intricacies involved in the wireless landscape, especially the service-provider segment. Not only are some qualities of the companies difficult to quantify, but there also is a large set of metrics that really don't make sense in many other industries besides wireless.

In this section we'll take a look at several of the metrics and other measurement tools that apply to different types of companies in the wireless industry. Some of these metrics have carried over from other segments of the telecommunications industry, but all of them collectively give a strong indication of the health of a company and its competitive position with respect to peers.

POTENTIAL CUSTOMERS (POPS)

The term *POP* carried over from another telecommunications business, the cable television segment. In that context, the term referred to the population of people that potentially had access to the cable service, those that were in the path of the coaxial cable. The number of POPs gave an indication of the extent of the network and essentially dictated the available market at any given time.

With respect to wireless companies, it means the same thing, only that the potential customers are simply those living in the areas where services are offered. Note, though, that in the wireless world this is an inexact measure because some of the population included in the POP figure actually may be out of the signal range of any towers. At best, it is a rough approximation of the network coverage and potential market.

The discussion of population coverage usually involves the two terms described below.

Licensed POPs. Licensed POPs include the population covered by spectrum licenses. If a service provider has a license to 10 MHz of spectrum in Atlanta, Georgia, then the population of this area is included in its figure for licensed POPs. With many service providers in the United States today, the licensed POPs are over 90 percent of the entire United States. Note that the network operator does not need to have an operational service in these areas, simply the permission to exploit the market. Sometimes this term for potential customers is simply lumped under a reference to allocated spectrum. The owning of rights to spectrum is basically wireless real estate on long-term lease from governments. For instance, a service provider may state that it has sufficient spectrum to provide service in 48 of the 50 top markets. This means that it owns spectrum rights to wirelessly connect customers in most of the populous regions.

Covered POPs. The covered POPs include the actual population that is covered by a network operator's service. In many cases, a service provider has only a partial network up and running in a given market. It is common for network operators to start service in the busiest areas of a market and continue to fill in the holes in coverage over time. It's more cost-effective to build capacity into dense urban areas where the usage is heavy and only extend the system area as users demand.

For instance, as of March 2001, AT&T Wireless reported 166 million covered POPs in its network. However, its licensed POPs were 216 million, which basically means that it is operating in approximately 77 percent of the area it has spectrum rights in. The other POPs that aren't covered yet are likely in less profitable areas or regions in which AT&T sees little demand for service.

TYPES OF NETWORK COVERAGE (EXPRESSED AS A PERCENTAGE OF POPULATION)

This metric does not always appear in company filings or statements, but a subset of it usually does. This subset is a breakdown of how much of the network is comprised of analog portions and how much is based on digital technology. Usually a network operator will state two things: how much of its network is digital (in percent) and how many of its subscribers use digital service (also in percent). Additionally, some service providers will indicate how much of their network is owned by them directly and how much of the network coverage is provided by partners.

These network coverage statistics are often overlooked, but there's a wealth of information contained in them. First, when looking at how much of any network is based on digital technology, the investor can get a good sense of how much future cash will be directed toward upgrading older analog equipment. For instance, Verizon Wireless has a disproportionate amount of its network still operating on analog, so Verizon typically invests more in infrastructure than other companies to upgrade this equipment. The company has been especially conscious of this recently and has made it a priority to modernize its network.

The reason that this is important is that the digital networks are much more efficient to operate. These technologies have much higher capacities and also offer more advanced capabilities to subscribers, such as caller ID and text messaging. This leads to higher revenue from digital subscribers who are taking advantage of the various services available on digital networks. Also, digital phones have longer battery lives and clearer signals. Overall, digital networks are a win-win for both customers and service providers.

The second metric that is important to note is the number of subscribers on digital service plans. Note that the percentage of digital subscribers can be vastly different from the percentage of digital network. For instance, Verizon Wireless reported in early 2001 that while its network was 80 percent digital, only about 60 percent of the subscribers were on digital plans. A year earlier, less than half of Verizon's subscribers were on digital services. Analog customers are almost likened to dead weight on a network operator who is looking for high growth. Sprint PCS has the upper hand in this category with its 100 percent digital network.

AVERAGE REVENUE PER USER (ARPU)

The ARPU probably is the most prominent metric for service providers because it generally measures the quality of customers the provider attracts. This number usually is stated in monthly terms, but some service providers state this number on a quarterly basis (3 months aggregate). A low ARPU relative to the competition shows that a company's services are more appealing to cheapskates. These customers may use the service less frequently or sign up for fewer features on the most basic plans. Companies sporting high ARPUs tend to attract the "power users," customers who make frequent use of the service and sign up for many of the extras.

In the pool of potential wireless service customers, business users tend to be the big spenders. A service provider that offers more features a business user would want tends to have much higher ARPUs. This is the case for Nextel Communications. Nextel consistently turns in ARPUs that are a solid 30 to 50 percent higher than the competition. One reason for this is that Nextel's products are specifically designed with features that appeal to business users, such as the Direct Connect feature. Another reason is Nextel's targeted advertising in the business space.

In the United States, ARPU tended to average around $45 for all wireless service providers in the year 2000. This is steadily decreasing as competition forces consumer prices lower and lower. Network operators such as AT&T and Sprint PCS typically deliver ARPUs around $60, whereas Verizon and other regional players are around $40.

One thing that significantly lowers ARPU is subscribers who are on prepaid calling plans. Such subscribers tend to use their phones sparingly or not at all, limiting the operator's income. You'll find many analysts divided over whether it is good to pursue prepaid customers. Some see it as a poor way to boost subscriber numbers while taking a hit on profitability. Others see some advantages because you can attract customers who normally wouldn't sign up for a service plan. The hope here is that once introduced to the advantages of a wireless device, people will convert their prepaid account into a more profitable service plan.

COSTS PER GROSS ADDITION (CPGA)

This metric is basically an indicator of how hard a service provider has to work to attract new subscribers. It includes all the sales and marketing expenses, as well as any equipment discounts or subsidies the service provider takes on in order to sign up a new user. A low CPGA relative to the competition indicates that the service provider is taking advantage of efficient marketing channels and is success-ful at branding its service. Higher CPGAs tend to indicate heavy spending in marketing services, offering phone subsidies, or holi-day seasons where promotion expense typically increases.

In 2001, the CPGA for most major service providers ranged in the area of $300 to $400. Additionally, you will almost always see the CPGA go up in the fourth quarter as network operators spend heavily during the holiday season to attract subscribers or encour-age giving cellular phones as gifts.

Some regional service providers can have lower CPGAs because their marketing is limited to smaller areas. Leap Wireless (Nasdaq: LWIN), for instance, delivers CPGAs in the low $200 range for its city-wide local cellular services. This doesn't necessarily mean that Leap has higher profit margins, though, because its ARPU tends to be much lower too—in the middle $30 range. Investors need to really look at the combination of all the metrics to see how well a company performs.

EARNINGS BEFORE INTEREST, TAXES, DEPRECIATION, AND AMORTIZATION (EBITDA)

EBITDA is a common metric used when evaluating any company, not just those in the wireless sector. This metric attempts to strip away noncore business costs to give investors a sense of how well the com-pany is delivering quality products or services to more and more customers. It is basically the revenue of a business minus the cost to produce the goods or services. Since interest, taxes, depreciation, and amortization costs can fluctuate from quarter to quarter without any direct connection to the financial health of a company, they are removed for easy comparison.

MINUTES OF USE (MOU)

While this metric is not often quoted in financial statements, it is sometimes mentioned in conference calls or analyst notes. This is the raw measure of time that the entire subscriber base used on a company's network. It is an indication of how well a given network operator encourages subscribers to use its services more frequently, thereby generating more revenue. The minutes of use obviously also will go up on a network that is expanding as well as a subscriber base that is increasing.

What is preferred is to have the MoU grow faster than the rate of subscriber growth. This indicates not only that a service provider is signing up more new customers but also that it is giving its existing customer base more reasons to use its service more often. This term is somewhat analogous to same-store comparable sales of a major retailer, except that the MoU reported often does not strip out the minutes used by new customer additions.

CHURN: NET TURNOVER OF ACCOUNTS

For some, customer churn is now displacing ARPU as the most closely watched metric for wireless service providers. While the initial focus of many companies was skewed toward profitable customers, losing these customers at a high rate caused priorities to shift a little. Customer churn is stated as a percentage of the total subscriber base and often is quoted as a monthly figure but sometimes shows up in annual terms. A typical total monthly churn rate for wireless service providers is 2.5 to 3.0 percent, which translates into about 30 to 35 percent of the customer base annually. Understanding churn and its causes can get very complicated.

There are various types of churn, and typically, churn is grouped into three categories: voluntary, uninitiated, and forced. *Voluntary churn* is probably the most important to watch and is composed of customers who dropped service due to dissatisfaction or in order to switch to a better/cheaper service with another provider. *Uninitiated churn* includes cases where customers leave a service because they've moved out of the coverage area, the operator has halted service in an area, or the subscriber dies. *Forced churn* is where the service provider initiates the termination of accounts due to the failure to pay bills or due to inactivity on the account.

QUALITY OF SERVICE (QoS)

This metric is somewhat less tangible than the rest and is tough to break down into a quantifiable number. Taken together, QoS refers to the ability of a service provider to enable clear, reliable connections and associated services on a consistent basis. It also includes the responsiveness of the company in terms of customer service for users. In general, this metric is understandably linked at least indirectly to customer churn.

There are some ways that companies can measure or at least get a sense of QoS, though. There are methods developed internally as well as provided by third parties that can track the number of dropped calls in a given area, for instance. There are also methods for measuring data throughput over the air interface or the performance of portable devices (battery life, for instance).

Where the QoS metric is used more often, though, is in the development or enhancement of the network. The service provider typically will target a specific level of capacity and QoS for any given area or region. Rural areas may be developed with a different QoS in mind than a thriving downtown area, for instance. Some systems, particularly CDMA networks, have their capacity tied directly to QoS as well. Depending on how the network is structured, the voice quality may suffer as the capacity of a CDMA cell is exceeded. For this reason and others, QoS and capacity can be tougher to measure objectively in CDMA systems.

KEY INVESTMENT THEMES

Several themes run through the network operator segment of the wireless industry. The various unique characteristics that set these companies apart from others are important for investors to consider in order to have realistic expectations of return. Here are some to consider.

STABILITY

As we discussed earlier, network operators carry a lot of inherent value due to their extensive network systems. When compared with other investments, then, these corporations tend to be more stable as a whole because the value of this equipment depreciates at a fairly predictable rate. The investment necessary to operate and maintain an expansive network also means that fast growth is very difficult to achieve and sustain. Typically, these companies take time to grow, especially at the more mature stage of the industry where we are today.

What this translates into is a slim chance that an investment in a wireless network operator will ever drop to zero or rocket 10-fold in a matter of months. If a network operator gets into trouble, it is usually bought out or liquidates its holdings, so shareholders get at least something back. Keep in mind, however, this does not mean that you can't lose a substantial amount of money. It only means that the investment risk and potential reward tend to be lower.

For instance, when the Nasdaq turned lower in late 2000, most telecommunications stocks followed. Between their peak in 2000 and mid-2001, wireless network operators took a heavy hit, losing an average of about 60 percent of their value. But this was relatively mild compared with many younger companies offering wireless applications or equipment. Many of them, such as GoAmerica (Nasdaq: GOAM—shown in Figure 3.2), Aether Systems (Nasdaq: AETH), and o2wireless Solutions (Nasdaq: OTWO), lost over 90 percent of their value from their respective peaks.

HIGH BARRIER TO ENTRY

As discussed in the preceding section, a large installed network makes service providers a more stable investment. This also makes it difficult for competition to pop up quickly in the market. Unlike other segments of the market, where a company can start with a few

FIGURE 3.2

GoAmerica, Inc.

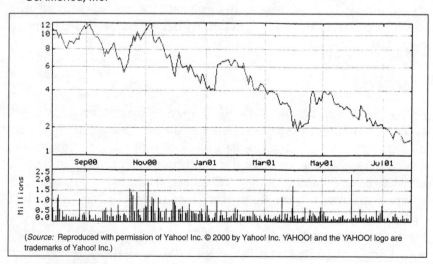

(*Source:* Reproduced with permission of Yahoo! Inc. © 2000 by Yahoo! Inc. YAHOO! and the YAHOO! logo are trademarks of Yahoo! Inc.)

million dollars, prospective network operators need billions even to start the race.

Wireless service providers have spent billions of dollars building the infrastructure necessary to carry out mobile communications. They must purchase or lease land rights to erect antenna towers that broadcast and receive mobile calls. They also must manage (or pay to lease) a complex landline network used to route the calls through traditional telephony channels. On top of all the equipment necessary for this, service providers also pay fees to license spectrum—basically they pay for thin air.

Licensing spectrum is analogous to paying for the rights to a television channel. The service provider is given a certain frequency band on which to operate the service and must adhere to certain requirements on where and with how much power it can operate. Auctions for regional spectrum in the United States in early 2001 netted over $16 billion for the U.S. government. Future auctions will likely net even more.

Because of the high stakes involved, the playing field in this segment should see few new players. There certainly will be more consolidation with smaller companies, but larger competitive threats can only come from other industry giants with lots of cash.

SUGAR DADDY

Another factor to keep in mind when investing in network operators is their relation (or lack thereof) to a parent company. Many wireless service providers are still part of larger telecommunications companies that provide other communications services such as cable television, high-speed Internet access, and long-distance phone service.

While many of the network operators are spinning off from their parents in the form of IPOs, some are still majority owned by past parents or other organizations. You may buy a stock thinking that you are getting a fast-growing wireless service provider only to find it weighed down by another division that isn't growing at all.

For instance, many investors bought Verizon Communications when the company was born in 2000 thinking that they were hitching a ride on the largest wireless network operator in the United States. Many did not know that they were buying all the long-distance, cable, and digital subscriber line (DSL) business too. Be sure to check out the company filings because they almost always separate out the wireless component of the business for analysis. In this way, investors can see if wireless is driving significant portions of the company's revenue or profit.

CASH IS KING

Wireless service providers are in a cash-flow business. The cash flow from operations is key to their ability to continue investing in expansion of their networks. A network operator that manages its cash flow poorly hampers its growth possibilities. Since growth comes at such a high cost, such companies must squeeze as much money as possible from their daily operations.

Their cash-flow scenario is also very important when is comes to managing debt. Most of the wireless network operators of the world are leveraged in debt, some of them to drastic degrees. Their ability to continue to borrow billions of dollars when they already owe so much hinges on their ability to demonstrate the capability of repaying the loans through extrapolation of their cash flow.

If service providers can't convince bankers or investors that the money will continue to pour in, they're stranded. A service provider with a strong cash flow and low debt is in a strong position, especially in a weak economy when things get tough.

NEW REVENUE STREAMS

Wireless service providers are always looking for new ways to make money. With the heavy competition in this segment, players are looking for something to differentiate them from the pack. The standard voice services supplied by network operators are generating less and less profit as the industry matures, forcing them to look elsewhere.

The biggest area that network operators are looking at for new revenue is in data technologies. As we discussed earlier in this chapter, new data capabilities offer one of the best opportunities for new consumer and business services. Network operators know that people are willing to pay a little more for these features, and they're working feverishly to capitalize on them.

Some other niche markets are finding their way into the mainstream with service providers as well. Location-based services, for instance, offer service providers the chance to give consumers unique capabilities based on where they are at any point in time. For example, a business manager may want to know where his or her field staff is at any time to respond efficiently to customers. The value added by these capabilities means that someone would be willing to pay for them.

CUSTOMER FOCUS

Network operators appeal to average people for the bulk of their income. In order to prosper, they must appeal to as many demographic groups as possible. This means that they must be attentive to a wide range of tastes and preferences among consumers and businesspeople. This also means that they must stay in touch with trends and consumer sentiment toward services.

While it is relatively easy for investors to assess a company's financial metrics, such metrics may not tell the whole story. A strong brand goes a long way in the network operator segment, and it's difficult to attach a dollar value to it. Yet even a basic evaluation of the less tangible aspects of a service provider's business, such as its customer focus and product mix, can be very important.

A big mistake that some investors make is to place too much importance on a network operator's back-end technology, spending little time to look at its customer focus. Such investors seem to believe that superior technology can make up for poor service and product placement. This is never the case. Network operators that have a relentless focus on building a strong brand by meeting the basic needs of their customers will win in the end.

SUMMARY

The entire wireless industry revolves around the network operators. Entire segments of the industry live or die depending on the direction that service providers take in bringing new capabilities to their customer base. For this reason, it is important for investors to understand as much as possible about the players in this segment—even if you invest in another area.

While this area of the industry is plagued with a significant amount of technical jargon, it is not critical for investors to have much depth of understanding here. Knowing the details of how all these devices work is not as important as understanding what technologies your investment choices have competency in. This ultimately dictates their available market and growth possibilities. Perspective on history and understanding technology trends can do more to serve as guidance for investment.

If you're looking at investing in a wireless network operator, keep in mind the following points:

- Many service providers are still part of telecom giants. Make sure that you understand the relationship of your prospective company with its parent.
- Do not expect phenomenal growth from a player in this segment. Tempered, long-term growth is more the norm.
- Avoid getting too deep into comparing technologies between service providers. Place more focus instead on product offerings and quality of services.
- Monitor the activity of several companies in this segment as it matures further. Consolidation of smaller players will continue until a few, dominant providers emerge. Often this comes down to one flagship corporation that leads the industry while a handful of others compete on a lower tier.

4

Wireless Equipment/ Component Suppliers

As a friend responds to a phone call during your lunch meeting, you notice that she carries the exact same phone as you. After she ends the call, you quickly pull your phone out to compare colors and screen icons. But you soon realize that her phone has many capabilities that yours does not—short messaging service (SMS), global roaming, and a cool Subscriber Identity Module (SIM) card. In addition, your phone mysteriously gives you a "No service" message. How did she make a call when you can't even get service with the same phone?

The fact that phones can look alike and yet have different features and capabilities highlights some interesting aspects of wireless equipment. Because there are a number of different network operators in the United States using various technologies to offer services, phones will have a whole range of different hardware and software components inside to provide custom features.

It is not uncommon for cellular phone manufacturers to make several models with different capabilities look the same. Since they are appealing to consumers at large, a stylish phone that is eagerly sought by customers helps give the company a strong brand identity. Therefore, many manufacturers attempt to make all their models look alike, whether they are sold with Code Division Multiple Access (CDMA) technology inside to work on Verizon's network or Global System for Mobile Communications (GSM) technology to work with VoiceStream's network.

The same holds true for manufacturers of other wireless equipment such as personal digital assistants (PDAs) or communicators. For instance, most consumers can recognize similar design and appearance aspects in all Palm handhelds—from the top of the line to the cheapest. Handspring PDAs have their own unique look as well.

Even for wireless component providers, the companies that make the "guts" of wireless equipment, it is important to support this type of scalability with a flexible product line. It is tough for a component manufacturer to compete, for instance, if all it makes is components for a single wireless technology. This limitation automatically locks the company out of several markets around the world and makes it less desirable as a partner due to its limited offerings.

In order to be successful in this segment of the wireless industry, players must plan their product lines carefully, with a strong vision of the mobile future. To capture the largest market possible, they must address several aspects of their product line, most notably:

- *Scale.* Companies must have products to address low-end models as well as more feature-rich high-end units.
- *Consumer appeal.* While component suppliers may be exempt from this, it is critical for companies making consumer products. Not only does the end-user equipment have to be technologically advanced, but it also has to look good. The style of equipment often has more to do with sales than the technology.
- *Global outlook.* Again, since wireless is a global market, players want to have products that are attractive for sale in Asia, Europe, or anywhere else in the world. With cultures and tastes being very different around the world, making products with global appeal can be tough.

Above all else, companies making wireless components and equipment are forced to compete on price. At this stage in the wireless market, excessive cost is not tolerated at any level. Even high-end equipment with large price tags has to keep realistic price targets to be successful. This is where manufacturing and operational efficiency can be a big boost in this segment of the market.

ROLE IN THE INDUSTRY

Companies that manufacture wireless components or equipment have a lot in common with other high-technology industries. Since they are basically providing the platforms and devices for services, they can be likened to computer companies that make desktop equipment, for instance. In fact, the client-server model for products in the computer industry can be applied loosely to the portable-handset/network environment in the wireless industry. For this reason, this area of the wireless market tends to be more straightforward than others.

Companies that dominate this space are said to provide the "nuts and bolts" of the industry. They have staff dedicated to developing advanced technologies to improve the performance of portable wireless devices and networks. These technologies can be in the form of physical hardware, software, or even intellectual property.

To better get a handle on this large segment of the wireless market, we will break down the companies and their products into three areas:

- Component level
- Portable equipment level
- Network level

Often companies play at more than one of these areas, but their business typically is concentrated heavily in one of them. Rarely does a company excel in more than one level.

Companies that offer component-level products basically are aiming to get their designs built into products at the other two levels. These are companies such as RF Micro Devices (Nasdaq: RFMD) and Texas Instruments (NYSE: TXN) that supply such items as integrated circuits, intellectual property, and Original Equipment Manufacturer (OEM) modules. Since wireless is such a high-growth market, suppliers in this area must have the capacity to produce their products by the millions. They also must be able to turn them around quickly.

Some of the components used in wireless equipment are commodity-type components, whereas others are more specialized. The components that fall in the commodity category generally are very low-margin, common parts that are easy to make. The specialized components tend to be more difficult to manufacture reliably and often command higher prices. Commodity components may be speakers, capacitors, and microphones, whereas specialized components may be special algorithms for filtering signals, digital signal processors (DSPs), or high-performance radio frequency amplifiers.

It is interesting to note that interwoven in this part of the industry is several other disciplines. For example, much of the production of wireless equipment is based on semiconductors and electronic circuits. Because of this, wireless is a significant driver for semiconductor manufacturers. In the last few decades, several semiconductor companies have shifted their business to strongly favor wireless communications products. Texas Instruments, for example, turned its focus toward DSPs in the 1980s, knowing that there would be tremendous demand for them in communications applications. The company's stock price was below $2.00 (split-adjusted) at the beginning of the 1990s and ended the decade at over $48.00. The company's growth during that time period is attributed largely to the growth in the wireless industry.

The portable wireless equipment segment is full of companies that manufacture a wide range of products. Most investors are familiar with cellular phone companies such as Nokia and maybe a few PDA manufacturers such as Palm because these products are used in the consumer market. However, most are surprised by the variety of wireless devices in the marketplace. The reason is that there is a huge market for portable wireless equipment in business applications, such as inventory management. Here are a few examples of less familiar portable wireless devices:

- *Wireless scanners.* These devices can be used to identify and track inventory in warehouses or in the field. Information is forwarded automatically to a central computer or server to improve efficiency. Symbol Technologies (NYSE: SBL) is a major manufacturer of wireless scanners.
- *Two-way pagers.* These devices have tiny keyboards so that short messages and e-mail can be sent and received remotely. Companies such as Research In Motion (Nasdaq: RIMM) and Motorola (NYSE: MOT) build two-way data communicators.
- *Global positioning system (GPS) receivers.* These devices use wireless connections to satellites to provide very detailed

location information. Garmin Ltd. (Nasdaq: GRMN) is one company building handheld GPS equipment.

The flexibility of portable wireless devices has led to an explosion of great ideas for where they can be used. Power companies are testing ways to read residential and business meters wirelessly. Huge warehouses employ wireless devices to track inventory.

Actually, new applications are being developed every day. Many of these applications are in what would be called *niche markets*, which means that the portable wireless equipment performs a small number of specific functions in a specific environment. Since the equipment is geared toward a specific application, it usually can be developed more quickly and made more cheaply. Don't be misled to believe that a niche market is necessarily a small market either; some of these niche markets make companies and investors very wealthy.

Network-level equipment often is sold by corporations that are heavily involved in many forms of communications. For instance, Lucent Technologies makes a variety of wireless base station equipment and network controllers, and the company also provides fiber-optic equipment and other products for wireline networks. In this category, it is also common to see manufacturers produce portable equipment as well as the networking products. Companies such as Motorola, Nokia, and Ericsson all make cellular infrastructure equipment as well as portable phones and communicators.

To get a better sense of important factors influencing each of these areas, let's look at each in a little more detail.

WIRELESS COMPONENT MANUFACTURERS

As stated previously, wireless component manufacturers make all the parts that go inside the wide range of equipment that consumers buy and network operators purchase to provide services. The names of these companies usually are not well known to investors, and sometimes these companies provide exotic components that investors have no clue as to their function. However, there are several major categories of wireless components in which a majority of companies participate:

- *Microprocessors.* A number of processor types are built into wireless equipment, the most prominent of them being
    - *Applications processors.* These processors are responsible for running the multimedia-type applications in a wire-

less device. For instance, this type of processor will handle video streaming, interactive games, or Internet browsing capabilities.

- *Baseband processors.* These processors handle the wireless operation of the device. They run software that captures and sends wireless signals and formats the information for use in the application stage.
- *DSPs.* DSPs play critical roles at both processing levels just described. They are particularly efficient at performing math routines that are very common in signal-filtering functions and encoding/decoding for some applications.
- *Radio frequency (RF) circuits.* RF components are the so-called front end of wireless equipment design. Since these circuits deal with transmitting and receiving the signals through the air, their efficient operation is critical to give a phone or other wireless device good reception.
- *Displays.* The displays used in wireless devices are becoming far more important than in the past due to the newer data capabilities used in wireless devices. With more media functions now possible on wireless devices, a nice color display is necessary. Liquid crystal displays (LCDs) and other display technologies are opening handheld devices to a whole new world of mobile applications.
- *Intellectual property (IP).* This covers several areas of wireless components. Patents are the most obvious and visible form of intellectual property, but a company that "sells" IP actually is licensing its expertise in a specific area of technology, not just the patents. With wireless devices becoming more and more complex, it is common for companies to buy out large portions of their designs from others.

To get a visual idea of how many of these parts fit into a mobile phone, a basic block diagram of the functions of a typical digital cellular phone is given in Figure 4.1. In this figure, the sections of the radio in larger boxes represent their relative importance to the overall function as well as the degree of complexity in development. For instance, the DSP and baseband processing sections tend to be very high-performance semiconductor chips that take sophisticated techniques to develop and integrate properly. They also tend to include more intellectual property. The smaller boxed functions such as mem-

FIGURE 4.1

Generalized Diagram of Digital Cellular Radio

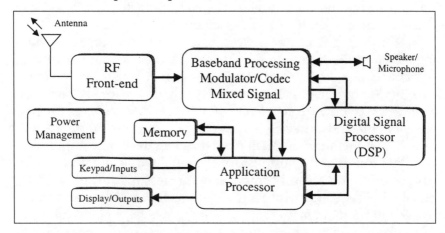

ory and keypad/inputs tend to be more straightforward and seen as commodity components.

Many of these same components (or variations of them) are used in the wireless network equipment. Wireless base stations also have RF circuits to handle the calls of customers. Often this equipment must handle multiple transmissions simultaneously from various customers, making high-performance circuitry a necessity rather than an option. Many companies that sell components will have product families that provide both network-side components and those for use in portable equipment.

A company that plays in the component space generally wants to become the number one supplier in one of these areas. Again, it is rare for one company to be particularly strong in more than one category. Rather, most focus all their efforts in one area but attempt to capture all areas of that one market. For instance, RF Micro Devices (Nasdaq: RFMD) strives to be the top supplier of RF components used in portable equipment as well as base stations.

APPLICATION/BASEBAND PROCESSORS

Just like the personal computer (PC) market where Intel and AMD battle furiously for market share of desktop microprocessors, the market for processors in wireless devices offers similar, if not greater, opportunities. As even the mighty Microsoft now recognizes, it is not all about desktops anymore. It's about having the ability to communicate and collaborate from anywhere. Most people agree that this means that portable devices that are connected wirelessly will overtake the market for PCs in a matter of a few years.

However, powering wireless devices is not as simple as shoving the latest Pentium into the device. The unique requirements of portable equipment, most notably low power consumption, make current desktop processors completely unsuitable for such an environment. Not only do processors in wireless devices have to operate very efficiently, they also must be optimized for running applications that are quite different from those on desktop computers.

In the relatively short history of digital wireless devices, there has been little need for the application processor. Most phones and other wireless equipment were simply cellular radios that transmitted information. In the last few years, however, a powerful application processor has become necessary because devices now are required to run more elaborate software to give users various multimedia functions.

Currently, many companies make and sell application processors and baseband processors separately. Since they are each dedicated to completely separate functions, this makes sense. Eventually, however, these two functions likely will migrate into the same semiconductor device. Almost all baseband processors made today incorporate some level of flexibility to tie them to an application processor.

If investors wanted to find the Intel of the wireless processor space, probably the closest company to that stage now is ARM Holdings plc (Nasdaq: ARMHY). ARM processor cores are widely hailed as best suited to run the baseband functions in most portable equipment. The company has been successful at licensing its intellectual property to many companies building wireless processors and claims to be designed into 75 percent of cell phones worldwide. Even Intel has licensed ARM's processor core to build its StrongARM processor family, which it acquired from Digital Equipment Corp.

DIGITAL SIGNAL PROCESSORS

Back in the early 1970s when cellular communications were starting to take off, DSPs had no presence in the market. The simple reason for this is that they were completely unnecessary in analog communications systems. What DSPs were needed for was digital communications. And without DSPs, digital communications would be almost impossible.

One reason that DSPs are so important is that they are needed to convert the human voice, which is inherently analog in nature, into a digital representation and back again. They are also very important in processing the signals that are transmitted and received between devices. On top of this, many newer multimedia applications, such as video compression, require DSPs to handle some of the processing workload.

DSPs are designed to do one thing very well, that is, math. What's interesting is that the mathematical functions required to process radio signals or application functions actually are relatively simple. The problem is that devices have to perform these simple functions billions of times per second to keep up. A standard processor is designed to be more flexible in the functions that it performs, so asking it to handle such a task would bog it down to a speed that would be useless.

One of the most common of these simple math functions is called multiply and accumulate, or MAC for short. This is simply multiplying two numbers and then adding the result to another number. Repeated MACs are absolutely necessary to enable digital communications, so DSP chips are optimized to handle MACs extremely efficiently.

One of the strongest players in the DSP market for wireless equipment is Texas Instruments (TI). With a strong focus on supplying DSPs to cellular phone manufacturers, TI was estimated to have its DSPs in 60 percent of all digital cellular phones in 2000. The business is growing rapidly too, even outside of wireless devices. In fact, TI was surprised to easily surpass its goal of $1 billion in wireless sales by the end of the decade (the company reached $1.3 billion in wireless component sales in 1998). Not only that, the company has been very successful at winning market share for DSPs used in wireless base stations, where the performance of each device is critical to support multiple users in any given area.

As with other components used in wireless devices, it is becoming more common to combine DSP cores with other functions in one semiconductor chip. Since the DSP functions are integral with the processing functions, manufacturers quite often combine them on the same silicon die. Look for more companies to offer processor-DSP combinations in the future in the form of a system on a chip (SoC) or in programmable parts.

RF COMPONENTS

Components used to actually transmit and receive signals through the air are unique in several ways. The semiconductor components often are not made of the common silicon materials used in most other integrated circuits. RF components are made from compounds such as gallium arsenide (GaAs) or silicon germanium (SiGe). These materials boost the efficiency of the components at the higher frequencies where they must operate.

RF components also must be very efficient in their operation. Since they handle the basic tasks of locking in on signals and transmitting voice or data to a receiver, they must be optimized to provide the best reception. The efficiency of these components has a direct effect on the end users' perception of their wireless service. With subpar RF components in a cellular phone, for instance, a customer may experience more dropped calls and poor coverage.

The various communications technologies used in cellular systems also literally will spell out performance criteria for radio devices to meet. For example, any GSM phone maker must make sure that its end product meets certain range and reception requirements. The RF circuits chosen for use in the phone and base station are the largest determining factor in meeting these requirements.

DISPLAYS

With the migration of consumer wireless devices away from telephones and into multimedia entertainment systems, the visual display in the handheld device becomes much more important. The popularity of PDAs and pocket PCs has helped spur cellular phone makers to incorporate similar visual interfaces into phones. The companies that supply the displays are in an envious position if they have a competitive product line.

One of several key factors in placing a large color display into a cellular phone is the amount of battery power it consumes. Since phones are already draining the battery to provide basic voice functions, adding a bright, color LCD makes it tough to still provide long talk and standby times. Therefore, one of the large technical hurdles in the area of displays is to make them consume as little power as possible while still giving a good visual experience.

Another pioneering advance in the area of displays is in the contrast. Since people are using their mobile devices more and more to view text and graphic information, companies are looking for ways to make the display more pleasant on users' eyes. For instance, a company called Three-Five Systems (NYSE: TFS) is a major supplier of cellular phone displays that is working on such a technology. Dubbed the PaperWhite LCD display, the background of the display looks white—or more like paper—than conventional LCD displays. This provides better contrast and gives the viewer the impression that he or she is actually reading off paper rather than a digital screen made up of pixels.

Along with vibrant color displays, many other new display technologies such as organic light-emitting diodes (LEDs) are being pursued that eliminate the need for backlighting a display. With a growing market for cellular phones, PDAs, and other mobile devices, there are lots of opportunities in this market.

INTELLECTUAL PROPERTY

As is the case with many other high-technology markets, IP plays a key role in this segment of the wireless industry. Since requirements for wireless devices push the limits of today's technology, protecting the inventions developed within a corporation is vital to keeping a competitive edge.

While some companies pursue the licensing of IP as a main source of revenue, many do not. Most companies seek patents on IP as a defensive tool, mainly to protect the products they sell from being copied cheaply. In both cases, though, the IP is key to the business.

Often IP takes the form of intelligent software. Companies often develop complex functions (algorithms) that handle specific tasks in wireless devices. They may then make these functions available to other companies to purchase so that they then can simply integrate them into their own designs. This saves the buyer considerable development time in creating the complex functions themselves.

IP also takes the form of patented ideas, ranging from system-level concepts to very detailed descriptions of hardware functions. Many communications companies patent various techniques they use to make wireless communications more efficient and/or cost-effective. If any standards-setting bodies (such as those explained in Chapter 3) vote to include these patented techniques into standards (making them essential), the inventing companies are then in a position to ask for royalties on the use of their design.

IP can become a double-edged sword, though. A trend in the last few decades has been for more companies to develop technologies only to the point of demonstrating their use and then quickly focusing on licensing them to others for manufacture. This is a fine line to walk because part of the value of any invention comes from continuous improvement in the process. Who better to improve a new idea than the original inventors themselves?

All too often a company is so focused on licensing a technology, that significant research and development (R&D) money is shifted to marketing, sales, and litigation teams to protect existing patents. Rather than steadily focusing on product improvement to give customers the features they desire, companies too focused on IP are absorbed with legal maneuvering and strategic methods to write patents and lay claim to inventions. In this process, the focus shifts toward competitiveness based on legal competencies rather than technical competencies.

Another important aspect of new inventions is that they often need optimization to make them more suitable for commercial markets. If a company develops a great new idea but does not go through the discipline of advancing it into a shippable product, what are the chances that someone else will get it right the first time?

For these reasons, it is a good idea for investors to be cautious of companies that sell themselves as pure IP players, especially in the wireless industry. These companies can be extremely attractive with unusually high profit margins, and investors may be lured to them based on a false sense of security in patent law. A company that applies its own inventions in successful products has more longevity than a company that simply provides the technology for a price. While there have been some successes in this category, it is definitely a high-risk area of investment.

As an example of the potential downside, one IP company that we mentioned before is Rambus Inc. While Rambus has proven to be an important player in the semiconductor memory market, the company took some hard hits in early 2001 when some litigation was ruled against it. While many investors bid the stock up less than a year before in expectation that every player would pay Rambus for its patents, many of the shareholders are now facing the prospect of the company losing the royalty stream at the hand of the courts.

Investors who were fortunate enough to buy into Rambus early in 1999 saw the stock soar fivefold within only a few months. However, many bought into the company or continued buying into the company in 2000 as the company continued to push farther for royalties in several technologies from every Dynamic Random Access Memory (DRAM) player in the market. While many investors saw the company's early success as the best indicator for future growth, it didn't actually work out that way. Those who bought the stock after it surged in June 2000 lost 80 percent or more of their capital in the next year. All the while many investors believed that the stock could go nowhere but up.

While Rambus does not compete in the wireless market, a very popular investment in the wireless space, QUALCOMM, is also thought of as more of an IP company than anything else. The company has a very strong patent base in CDMA (IS-95) technology and collects licensing fees from hundreds of companies that manufacture this type of equipment. Some investors tend to think that QUALCOMM is an exception to the rule with regard to IP and that it is almost a no-brainer in terms of long-term profits from its patents.

The problem with this view of QUALCOMM is that it doesn't recognize the factors that went into placing it in the position of authority it has today and what it takes to keep it there. Back in the mid-1990s when QUALCOMM was trying to sell its CDMA technology, it experienced a very cold reception in the market. Almost no one seemed interested in buying great ideas on paper if they still had to do the work of developing entire product lines. Also, because no one else supported various other segments of the wireless market with CDMA technology, few wanted to risk going it alone.

Thus QUALCOMM did what it had to do. It developed products on its own. It created a division to build infrastructure based on CDMA technology. It started a handset division to show how superior the phones operated. And it started a semiconductor group to actually design the circuits. All this effort eventually was enough to win over the support of several players in the industry, and QUALCOMM's stock soared in hopes that more would follow.

Going forward in 2001, though, QUALCOMM has been busy divesting itself of many of these divisions. The company no longer manufactures phones—this division was sold to Kyocera. The infrastructure division was handed over to Ericsson after a long period of litigation between the two over patent rights. And the company came close to spinning off the semiconductor technologies division late in 2001 but withdrew the plan to do so. The new QUALCOMM is one that no longer has its revenue balanced between the various divisions. A vast majority of the profit comes from patent licenses and royalties.

This change in strategy is meant to propel the company to higher heights. With lots of high-margin revenue flowing from IP licensing and royalty fees, the company looks to be one lean and mean competitor. However, like the case of Rambus, investors would be wise to question the growth sustainability of this model. Many of the businesses that QUALCOMM has divested from are part of its core competency and are integral parts of its technology (IP) development.

This is not to say that QUALCOMM will suffer the same fate as Rambus. However, there are similarities in the business model, and investors need to understand the risks here. The high-growth business that made investors so much money in the late 1990s (those that sold anyway) has changed substantially. As a general rule, the premium placed on IP fades away as technologies mature. We've already seen evidence that QUALCOMM is lowering licensing fees to gain share in certain markets such as China.

For the stock to continue to go up, QUALCOMM will have to find new areas of growth and penetrate new markets. It is just not as simple as sitting back and collecting fees. Royalty streams can be great forms of sustaining income for corporations, but they fade with time and need to be replaced constantly with new revenue streams to keep a company growing.

PORTABLE EQUIPMENT

This segment of the wireless industry hosts the companies that are most well known to consumers and investors. Companies such as Sony, Nokia, and Palm are almost household names. In fact, Nokia was ranked as the fifth most valuable brand in 2000 in Interbrand's Annual Survey, putting it in a class with Microsoft and Coca-Cola. Since consumers carry and see these items every day, they tend to be the first choice of investments for many individuals. Because of their high level of exposure, these companies are in a unique category with specific attributes.

Companies that build portable equipment for the consumer market typically build one or more of the following:

- *Cellular telephones.* Basic handsets that provide voice services over wireless connections. Dozens of companies such as Nokia, Ericsson, Motorola, Siemens, and others make all types of cellular phones.

- *Pagers.* These come in several flavors: one-way, two-way, simple numeric, or alphanumeric. Motorola is a major manufacturer of pagers with its Flex product lines.

- *Wireless communicators.* These are a level up from pagers and support more advanced features such as e-mail, guaranteed delivery, and organization functions. Research In Motion makes a line of popular devices called BlackBerry, although most of these are too pricey for consumers.

- *Smartphones.* This is a class of cellular phones that contain some enhanced features such as Internet browsing capabilities or some multimedia functions. Some phones will play MP3 files, for instance.

- *Personal digital assistants (PDAs).* This category encompasses tools that have limited information management functions and simple applications. They often have the ability to be expanded with modules to give them various functions as well. Many models are also capable of wireless data transmission. Palm and Handspring are major manufacturers of PDAs.

- *Pocket PCs.* Often confused with PDAs, these devices may look the same but have much more advanced capabilities. With high-resolution color screens, lots of memory, and fast processors, these portable devices can run applications similar to a desktop PC. Compaq's iPAC models of pocket PCs are very popular.

- *Hybrid phones.* This emerging class of devices is a cross between a PDA and a cellular phone. Often it looks like a bulky phone until you flip open a cover to display the PDA screen. Kyocera has a popular hybrid that combines a cellular phone with a Palm-type PDA.

- *CB radios.* Although not as popular as they used to be in the 1970s and 1980s, citizen band radios are still popular for short-range voice communications. Motorola makes a line of pocket-sized radios called Talkabout.

- *Wireless PC cards.* Small cards that fit into expansion slots of laptop computers and enable them to send and receive data over a variety of wireless networks. Sierra Wireless makes a variety of cards that fit into laptops for use on networks operated by Sprint PCS, AT&T, Metricom, and others.

If you're looking at investing in a company in this area, probably the most important step to take before any other evaluation is to look at what market(s) the company focuses on. While many of them focus heavily on consumers, some also target the business space. While many companies also balance between the two, some are dedicated exclusively to one or the other. This is important to see early on because it factors into how you evaluate a company's strength down the line.

CONSUMER SEGMENT

For companies playing in the consumer segment, their business has much more to do with brand appeal than others. While an OEM component manufacturer may be able to correct for part quality problems in short order, a flawed product can have long-lasting consequences for consumer equipment companies. If you have a bad experience with one company, it is likely you'll make all future purchases from a competitor.

The element of consumer brand is important for investors to factor into these types of investments. A company in this area can have good management, efficient manufacturing, and a host of other great qualities, but without a strong brand, the company always will be fighting an uphill battle. Keep in mind, too, that some companies can have strong brands in certain countries but be totally unknown in others.

In the early 1990s, one company took a commanding lead in the cellular phone market. With over half the market in 1996, Motorola appeared to have a lock on the market for years to come. Unfortunately, its lead slipped away quickly, mostly to one competitor, Nokia. Many investors were surprised that a company with its roots in paper and rubber boot manufacturing would take over a technology powerhouse like Motorola.

Obviously, there had to be more than one thing wrong at Motorola to lose the lead so fast. However, the quick reversal of leadership in the cellular handset market also had a lot to do with what Nokia did right. Here are just a few elements that effected the change:

- *Focus on technology, not features.* Motorola continued to build technically advanced handsets, while Nokia built simpler models that people found more appealing. In the end, Nokia put more focus on how the phones looked on the outside, whereas Motorola concentrated more on what was inside.

- *Lack of focus on growing market, GSM.* Nokia got a huge boost by having the foresight to put most of its efforts into GSM technology, which is now by far the most popular digital cellular technology in the world. Motorola's lack of sincere presence in GSM products (or digital cellular as a whole) gave it little opportunity for above-average growth.

- *Ease of use not on par.* By and large, consumers did not like the interface elements of Motorola phones. The ergonomics of the devices were a level below Nokia's models, which were found by consumers to be much easier to use. Motorola's handsets were geared more toward functionality that came with the cost of complexity, whereas Nokia stayed with the more simplistic approach of supplying the basics.

After losing the crown of number one global cellular phone supplier, Motorola still struggles to turn its handset business into a true competitor. Still reeling from their April 2001 admission of its first quarterly operating loss in 16 years, Motorola is pinning its turnaround hopes on next-generation equipment. To this end, Motorola has been eager to place the first General Packet Radio System (GPRS) cellular phones into the market, hoping this will give it an edge in the coming years. With many laps yet to go in this race, it will be interesting to see where it goes from here.

Manufacturers providing portable equipment to consumers are also subject to other forces, such as consumer spending cycles and fashion trends. Managing the product line also becomes critical to success. A recent illustration of a company's failure to do this effectively involved Palm in early 2001.

Following the Christmas season in 2000, Palm had a whole new lineup of its popular PDAs coming out of development. In tight competition with Handspring, Palm promoted its soon-to-be-released products a little too early in the first quarter of 2001. When product shipments were held up due to manufacturing problems, sales dropped off dramatically as inventory piled up. The timing of the delay was particularly bad because vendors and resellers did not have the opportunity to reorder in Palm's fiscal fourth quarter. Palm was forced to cut prices aggressively and offer additional incentives just to move inventory, and the company ended up taking a big hit on earnings.

The net result on Palm's stock was not pretty during this period. When news of the revenue shortfalls hit the market, the stock got whacked for a 48 percent loss in a single day. Competitors such as Handspring and Research In Motion did not fare much better in the following months. Along with the souring economy, many of the PDA manufacturers saw their stocks tumble by 75 percent or more by mid-2001. While better timing may not have spared Palm's stock completely, bad timing certainly did not help. Some analysts estimate that this little goof cost the company several hundred million dollars.

The relationship between equipment manufacturers and service providers is also important for investors to understand. Making products such as cellular phones is not as simple as designing a cellular phone and putting it in stores. Equipment makers must work with service providers to build products they think their customer base wants and needs. Even though they are separate companies, they are largely dependent on each other to succeed.

For example, take a look at AT&T's service coupled with phones from suppliers such as Nokia and Ericsson. In order for AT&T to launch its new data and messaging services in 2000, it had to work with these manufacturers to produce equipment compatible with its network infrastructure. Nokia produced a line of phones that supported messaging functions similar to the Short Messaging Service (SMS) used pervasively around the world on GSM networks. Ericsson, meanwhile, produced handsets that had data modems built in to work on AT&T's Cellular Digital Packet Data (CDPD) network in order to provide its PocketNet service. Both companies had to work closely with the service provider to make the launch a success.

This scenario demonstrates the importance of business relationships in the wireless industry. Equipment manufacturers and service providers must have good working relationships to compete in such a challenging market. In somewhat of a codependent relationship, they do whatever they can to support their partners so that they may see the benefits returned. In July 2001, when AT&T Wireless (NYSE: AWE) finally was separated from its parent, AT&T (NYSE: T), many of its partners, such as Motorola and Ericsson, took out large ads in financial papers to congratulate the company and wish it future success. While public accolades may not have a direct impact on revenues or profits, they can build success in other, indirect ways.

As most knowledgeable investors know, these types of collaborations between companies don't just happen overnight. It takes a long time to build these relationships, and they can be damaged quickly. One example of a partnership strained early on occurred when Nokia discovered a software glitch in its CDMA handsets supplied to Verizon Wireless in early 2001.

A relative newcomer to CDMA technology, Nokia was happy to have negotiated an agreement with Verizon to supply a new model 5185i phone beginning in 2000. Nokia's first attempt to supply CDMA phones to Sprint PCS a few years before didn't go well because consumers complained about poor quality, but the company claimed to have improved the products. Still, a problem surfaced when the company was testing the phones to see if they were compatible with Verizon's future network upgrades to cdma2000. With the discovery that calls were dropped on the new network Verizon quickly put an end to promoting Nokia phones and relied instead on other manufacturers. Two slips is all it took to undo years of hard work and cast a dark shadow on Nokia's hopes to grow its CDMA phone business. Both episodes not only marked failures of the products but also damaged the relationship with both service providers, making future collaboration unlikely.

Investors looking for opportunities in this area would be wise to look into these types of relationships and make note of them. Quarterly and/or yearly Securities and Exchange Commission (SEC) filings often indicate who a manufacturer sells to or has partnered with to provide wireless services with its equipment. Frequently, companies will cite their relationships in terms of ongoing risk because termination of their collaborations for whatever reason will hurt sales. With a substantial amount of division in the U.S. wireless market, it pays for investors to know who's on whose team. These relationships also can give hints of where future possibilities in partnering or mergers and acquisitions (M&A) can occur.

BUSINESS SEGMENT

Equipment manufacturers selling products into the business segment are subject to a different range of influences. Not as dependent on a strong consumer brand to succeed, they work at developing a strong product line and a good reputation in the industry they serve. Supplier relationships become very important at this level, and competition is fierce. Since wireless devices can bring high levels of efficiency to the operation of a business, customers become dependent on their reliable performance and therefore desire a complete package of products and ongoing service from a supplier.

For instance, Symbol Technologies has built up a sizable customer base by providing millions of rugged handheld scanners for use in numerous enterprise applications. Not only does the company make point-of-sale bar code scanners for a company's retail operations, but it also makes portable wireless equipment for managing inventory more efficiently. Symbol Technologies' products and services help any company that wants to track and store any sort of information transfer. Some of its most popular offerings include its wireless local area network (LAN) systems that allow workers to move about with portable PCs or other custom handheld devices while still being connected to the office's wired network.

As Symbol Technologies started to sell many of these new systems in the mid-1990s, business took off. In the 4 years between 1996 and 2000, Symbol Technologies was growing revenue at a compound rate of about 17 percent. Its net income was doing even better, growing at a 23 percent rate. If an investor had bought $10,000 worth of Symbol Technologies stock in early 1996, the stock would have been worth over $60,000 by the end of 1999. While a vast majority of investors have not even heard of Symbol Technologies or other business-focused companies, such companies certainly were making somebody a tidy profit. While passing on investing in the Ciscos, JDSUs, and Nokias of the world to find a quality unknown company may not be popular at parties, sometimes it can be more rewarding financially, especially when the media hype around popular stocks wears off.

Since business applications for wireless devices tend to be very specific in nature, most portable wireless equipment is customized for various clients. In such cases, the customer obviously must be interested in a large quantity of equipment, because significant effort is necessary to develop custom products. These supply agreements typically take the form of long-term OEM contracts, where the equipment manufacturer delivers specified products and ongoing support services. This type of business model tends to be very similar to other business-to-business industries, such as jet aircraft sales to airlines. The announcement of significant contract signings is a strong driver of the stock.

While the consumer segment of the market for wireless equipment is driven largely by the phenomenal consumer uptake of wireless technology, the business segment is more subdued. This lower level of growth, however, typically is made up for in profit margins and stability in contracts. Owing to the different nature of the market, stocks that derive substantial revenue from the business segment tend to be more stable over time. The consumer-oriented businesses tend to be more exposed to swings in the market resulting from consumer trends, macroeconomic factors, and holiday buying cycles.

WIRELESS INFRASTRUCTURE EQUIPMENT

Equipment used in building cellular wireless networks has many common attributes with standard wireline communications infrastructure. The only major difference is the last few legs of the communications link, where the signal is passed over the air to the mobile customer. Beyond this, most functions for routing the signal to the correct destination are built on the existing, wired telephone network.

Figure 4.2 shows a typical breakdown of mobile communications infrastructure. The towers on the far right coupled with the base transceiver stations (BTSs) are responsible for sending and receiving the wireless signals to and from mobile customers. The base station controller (BSC) coordinates the operation and functions of the individual base stations. A mobile switching center is then used to connect the mobile traffic (whether voice or data) to the standard telephone network.

This figure also illustrates how the model will change slightly in the next generation of infrastructure. Rather than having the Mobile Switching Center (MSC) route traffic onto circuit-based networks,

FIGURE 4.2

Typical Wireless Infrastructure Configuration

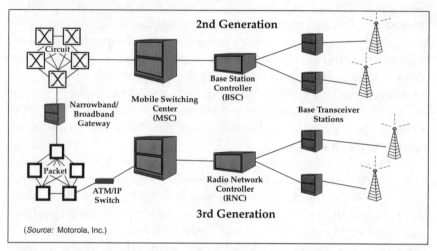

(*Source:* Motorola, Inc.)

Asynchronous Transfer Mode (ATM) switches will route Internet Protocol (IP) traffic onto packet networks. The demand for data in next-generation networks demands this IP functionality in newer networks. The long-term goal is to have an all-IP network someday, but this is a long way out. First, we have to be able to send voice and video reliably over packet networks.

Most of the discussion about wireless infrastructure equipment centers on the base stations, controllers, and switching centers. Sometimes referred to as the *radio access network* (RAN), the network of multiple base stations can be set up quite differently for different technologies. For instance, operation at different frequencies may require individual base stations to be much closer together. However, most cellular systems follow this general architecture.

It is actually somewhat common to see companies making both network infrastructure and portable equipment. Top companies such as Nokia, Motorola, and Ericsson all have large divisions working in both areas. This actually makes sense, too, because the technology that goes into handset design is similar to that which goes into the base stations. From there, it's not much of a stretch to get into manufacturing some of the other network elements, such as switches and controllers.

Supplying both cellular infrastructure and handsets can be beneficial to companies as well because they can take care of multiple requirements for their customers. If a company such as Motorola has had a good relationship in providing handsets to customers, it is easier for it to sell the customer on its new line of wireless network equipment the next time its contract is up for evaluation.

At the turn of the millennium, the leading provider of cellular infrastructure equipment in the world was Sweden's Ericsson. The vast majority of its revenue comes from building equipment into all kinds of wireless networks. While its lead in this market is now coming under attack from Nokia, Nortel, Motorola, and others, Ericsson still maintains good working relationships with dozens of network operators. Even though the company has struggled to succeed with portable units, its radio network business has been a star performer to date.

Wireless infrastructure providers stand to make a lot of money as network operators look to build out their next-generation networks over the next several years. Since many of the service providers around the world need substantial upgrades to their existing systems, companies such as Nortel, Lucent, Motorola, and others are working feverishly at securing contracts.

One factor that could influence the growth possibilities of infrastructure providers significantly is the cost of spectrum licenses. When network operators began bidding for third-generation (3G) spectrum, market sentiment toward wireless opportunities was at its peak. The hyperbole and fervor surrounding the possibilities of 3G caused many operators to bid astronomical amounts for spectrum in countries such as the United Kingdom and Germany, sending many of them deeply into debt.

With many of the major service providers struggling to maintain cash due to a heavy debt load, some are speculating that the purchase of infrastructure equipment may be delayed significantly. In somewhat of a ripple effect, infrastructure providers are having trouble selling their products because few have the cash necessary to buy them. This has led to the somewhat risky practice of what's called *vendor financing*, where the equipment provider actually facilitates a loan to the network operator so that it may purchase the provider's equipment.

What this means is that equipment providers are now shouldering more risk by becoming creditors to cash-poor operators. Many infrastructure providers have taken the stance that they really have no choice and view it as more of an investment than a risky loan. The outcome of these financial arrangements, however, could spell trouble for some equipment companies that may be cash-poor them-selves. Some operators such as Turkey's Telsim already have defaulted to companies such as Motorola and Nokia for hundreds of millions of dollars.

WIRELESS EQUIPMENT MANUFACTURER METRICS

Like the wireless service providers, there are a number of metrics that analysts and investors use to discern the quality of an investment in a wireless equipment manufacturer. Since their businesses share similar aspects with other industries, the metrics used here tend to be common across other sectors of the stock market rather than unique to this space. Nevertheless, it is worthwhile to go though some of the more important metrics to consider when evaluating an investment here.

Here are some important things to consider when trying to gauge the strength of a wireless equipment manufacturer.

ADDRESSABLE MARKET

The addressable market represents the total available market to a company's products. Since wireless networks have numerous incompatible technologies, the application of certain products on some networks is impossible. The product line and assortment of technologies supported then define the addressable market for the manufacturer. For instance, a maker of portable CDMA equipment cannot consider much of Europe as its addressable market because most all networks operate on the incompatible GSM technology.

For instance, shown in Figure 4.3 is a breakdown of addressable markets by technology in terms of the number of subscribers for each. The Personal Digital Communications (PDC) market opportunity is limited because its growth over the time period is very low. Each of the other technologies shows sizable growth, but GSM shows to be the largest opportunity by far in terms of sheer numbers. If an equipment manufacturer has no products compatible with GSM technology, it is missing most of the market.

Since most companies in this segment exhibit core competencies in only one or few technologies, almost all have some limitations in their addressable markets. This must be accounted for before looking at growth possibilities. For instance, investors must not make

FIGURE 4.3

Cellular Subscribers by Technology

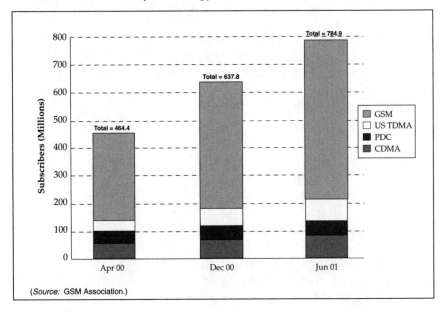

(*Source:* GSM Association.)

the mistake of looking at statistics for cellular phone growth in the future and estimate market share for any company without first considering how the market will be divided based on technology. Keep in mind also that this makes growth estimation difficult because you are making an estimate on top of an estimate.

INTELLECTUAL PROPERTY

Attempting to gauge a company's strength in intellectual property (IP) simply by counting the number of patents issued or pending is a poor way to evaluate this aspect of the company. Most patents filed in the United States end up being irrelevant in the economy because they contain little value that consumers or other companies would be willing to pay for. Yet it is far too tedious for investors to look through a company's patent portfolio and gauge which ones are significant and which are just ancillary to doing business.

A better approach is to look at a company's plan and process for extracting value from its IP. Has the company successfully defended its inventions in the past? Does it even have a legal team to address the issues with IP? Does the company have a strong history of converting its past patents into successful products?

Understanding a company's approach to leveraging its IP and how it fits into its business plan is far more important than simply the sheer numbers of patents. Most quality companies have plans to organize their IP and use it actively to further their businesses. This can take several forms, such as licensing the technology, trading it for IP in other areas, or aggressively defending against competitor advances in the market.

PROFIT MARGINS

As with all investments, a company's ability to make a profit is key. While many investors tolerated soaring revenue coupled with continuous losses in the late 1990s dot-com era, most have come to the reality that the "new economy" is a farce. Companies still must have a solid business plan that has strong potential for a decent profit.

With the soaring popularity of mobile wireless devices, many equipment providers have been sacrificing profitability for growth in market share. While this tactic may be lauded during good times, it can be particularly painful in down markets when buying cuts back dramatically. Late in 2000, many cellular phone manufacturers such as Motorola and Ericsson were hit hard by the economic downturn. Growing inventories made their poor profit margins even worse, leading to substantial losses in both their phone divisions.

Hopefully, the trend of companies and analysts giving undue attention to market share at the expense of profitability will change as the market matures further. Historically, a company's market share has been touted above all else. Investors should keep in mind that even a company claiming a 95 percent market share that is unprofitable is not worth an investment. Keep an eye on the profit margins of each division within a company and compare them with those of competitors in peer segments. Some divisions may have very low profit, but at least one or more should be generating decent income.

INVENTORY MANAGEMENT

When looking at an investment, be sure to check the operations of the company. By being diligent in going through a company's balance sheet, investors can get a good idea as to the company's effectiveness with respect to inventory management.

As the Palm example we discussed earlier in this chapter shows, poor inventory management can be devastating. When Palm raised $874 million through its initial public offering (IPO) in March 2000, no one even considered that the company would be in a cash crunch a little more than a year later. Effectively managing component purchases while timing product releases properly is a tough job, one that is handled best by experienced management.

PRODUCT LINE MIX

Wireless equipment providers are asked more and more to provide solutions for a company, not just a single product. Often a service provider wants a partner who can support several areas of its business, such as both infrastructure and network services.

An equipment provider is also much stronger if it provides products across multiple technologies. Having a broad technology base opens up opportunities with more customers and helps balance the revenue for a company because some technologies may fall out of favor or go obsolete.

It is also good to pay attention to what markets (regions or countries) a company's products are aimed at. Many equipment manufacturers have products that sell well in a few countries but may be poor or nonexistent sellers in others. If a company wants to increase revenue from other markets, it needs to tailor its products to that region. Rarely does one phone or portable device sell well in more than a few countries. For instance, Japanese and Asian consumers may prefer metallic-colored, clamshell-style phones with big displays, whereas Latin Americans may prefer flat colors on a phone with smooth contours. These differences in consumer tastes are one reason why Nokia has done so well with its removable phone faceplates— customers have the ability to customize the phones to their liking.

SUMMARY

Wireless equipment manufacturers are the key partners for network operators. The relationships between the two must be strong in order for the overall product and service to be successful. Even companies that sell components or devices to the business segment need to have a team attitude to succeed.

Along these lines, investors should understand where an equipment provider fits with respect to its peers and competition. It is not enough just to know that the company whose stock you own makes equipment for CDMA networks. Who are they partnered with? Are they particularly strong in Korea or possibly weak in the U.S. market? Corporate relationships take a long time to build in this area, so don't expect a company to win over customers instantly—even if it has superior products.

Many of the players in the wireless equipment sector are well-known names that almost every investor knows about. Yet there are hundreds of unknowns that compete in this area—stocks that most people haven't even heard of. Since wireless is booming and has many years of growth ahead, there is no shortage of companies trying to get a piece of the wireless pie. This leaves investors with plenty of opportunities to invest in an equipment or component manufacturer.

If you are considering investing in a wireless equipment or component supplier, keep the following in mind:

- *Understand the core technical competencies of the company.* You don't have to know how all the technology works, but you should understand what markets are open to the company and where its strengths lie.
- *Take some time to look at the relationships the company has with peers and service providers.* Looking into the background of senior management can give some clues as to who they may be working with too (unless they left their previous job on bad terms, of course). The fact that a company has large facilities located in other countries also can indicate good working relationships in those regions.
- *Be careful when investing in companies that rely on IP for a vast majority of their revenue—these are risky investments.* Companies that have strong track records in converting inventions into commercial products tend to be more stable in the long run. There's more money to be made in the end product than just the idea.
- *Look beyond the popular names in the consumer segment to find a few companies that are boring yet highly profitable.* Com-

panies providing wireless equipment and services to businesses have a bright future, especially in the United States.

■ *Understand that companies making equipment by the millions have to manage inventory (and all operations) very carefully.* Swings in the economy tend to affect these companies significantly too because customer purchases will vary dramatically depending on the overall economic outlook.

5

Wireless Enterprise Solutions

Jane is a top salesperson for a thriving high-tech company. She is constantly away from the office meeting clients. Most of the time she is in the United States, but sometimes she deals with some accounts in Europe.

However, she knows that her productivity could be higher if she did not have to deal with red tape. She must record the contracts on a variety of paper forms and fax them back to corporate headquarters. Errors are inevitable. Sometimes the fax is not clear, nor is the handwriting.

Furthermore, Jane gets updates on inventory on a weekly basis. In other words, for an order that must be filled quickly, she does not necessarily know if there is enough on hand.

With effective technology solutions, she could reduce mistakes, lower transaction costs, have more time to spend with customers, and have real-time information.

Jane is not an exception. There are many inefficiencies in corporate America. Technologies such as wireless will become critical in making business run much smoother.

Such technologies applied for business use are known as *enterprise solutions*. This is a fancy term, but you will hear it a lot. There will be some companies that make substantial profits from this segment of the industry. In fact, some of the biggest high-tech companies—such as Oracle and PeopleSoft—made their fortunes by focusing solely on the enterprise marketplace. Over the last 20 years, the corporate world has become centered on the desktop personal computer (PC) as a tool for improving corporate operations. Achieving full benefits of this desktop tool meant networking the PCs and providing applications that allowed people to collaborate through them. As stated earlier, though, the average corporate employee is moving farther and farther away from the desktop and more toward a myriad of wireless tools.

This recent move toward wireless tools means that the wireless enterprise segment is still in the early, formative stages, basically where the PC industry stood 20 years ago. This leaves many high-growth opportunities waiting to be discovered in this area. There are literally hundreds of young companies currently competing for a piece of this market.

Due to the underdeveloped nature of the enterprise segment, investors see it as having the best chance of producing at least a few mammoth companies and stratospheric stock returns. This allure to find the eventual Microsoft of wireless enterprise already has led to a rush into the few public companies addressing this area in 1999–2000, such as Aether Systems. With an early jump in the market, Aether Systems started selling wireless products and services to Fortune 500 companies and financial institutions. Using a growing stock price as leverage to buy other companies, Aether was able to expand its product base and customer list substantially. The company's market capitalization soared, and it looked like it was only the beginning.

However, the market compression that began in 2000 short-circuited what would have been a period of heavy investment in this market, with lots of companies going public to raise funds for growth. With the souring economy, many enterprises put off decisions to implement wireless solutions in their businesses, thereby putting a huge damper on the market at the time.

Poor market conditions didn't kill the wireless enterprise segment, however; it only put more pressure on companies to perform. Many went into belt-tightening mode, conserving cash in order to make it to the next round of funding or to a time when they could make an initial public offering (IPO). There still remains a vast field of private companies pushing ahead in this area.

In the coming years, many of these companies will file IPOs, merge with others, or go out of business. A select few will go on to grow their revenues substantially and possibly be bought out by the giants already working in enterprise software. The goal in this area of investment is to find those select few companies and hold them as the market matures.

While it would be great just to provide the names of the companies that eventually will dominate the wireless enterprise space, clairvoyance is not one of our strong suits. What we can do, though, is break down this market, look at the corporate needs that drive it, and examine what various companies are doing to fulfill those needs. This discussion should give investors a strong background to evaluate the hundreds of companies that will rise to address the many facets of this market.

There is a major force driving corporate America toward wireless. First some background: Since the advent of the industrial age during the mid-1800s, the concept of the corporation was as a separate entity. A company had a defined set of suppliers and customers. And there also were the vicious competitors. However, there was very little integration between these players.

Since the mid-1990s, however, with the emergence of the Internet and globalization, leading companies do not consider themselves separate. Instead, they have recognized that the rules of commerce have changed radically. Rather, to succeed, companies need to collaborate—even with competitors. Simply put, no company can do everything. Building walls ultimately will lead to disaster.

Interestingly enough, a big reason that many e-tailing companies failed is that they did not partner. They thought that the virtual world was superior to the bricks-and-mortar world. This was the case for eToys. And for the first few years, the company was the leading online retailer. However, even though the company wanted to remain virtual, it still had to build huge distribution centers. During the Christmas season of 1999, the company learned that sending products to customers is extremely complex.

Amazon.com had another approach. The company teamed up with the major bricks-and-mortar retailer, Toys"R"Us. It was a powerful combination. Amazon.com leveraged its technology, and Toys"R"Us leveraged its distribution. By the end of 2000, the joint venture was a great success, and eToys eventually had to be liquidated for scrap.

THE COLLABORATIVE ECONOMY

It seems kind of odd, but one of the companies that has been extremely effective in integrating enterprise technology is United Parcel Service (UPS). UPS believes that we are involved in the *collaborative economy*. One of the company's mottos is "Collaborate or suffocate." In fact, UPS is becoming a model of the New Age corporation.

On the face of it, UPS looks like a typical bricks-and-mortar company. There are more than 150,000 delivery vehicles and 500 airplanes. Service areas span more than 200 countries and territories (every address in the United States is covered). The company carries goods that represent about 6 percent of the U.S. gross domestic product.

In reality, however, the company is more like Microsoft, that is, a high-tech powerhouse. On average, UPS spends about $1 billion per year on technology research and development (R&D).

UPS has no choice. The company's customers demand timing and predictability for shipments. They are imperative.

One of the most critical investments started in the mid-1990s with the development of the so-called Package-Level Detail (PLD). Essentially, every UPS package would become a "smart" package. The PLD would hold the necessary information to identify the package. UPS then integrated this information throughout its organization, including inventory, purchasing, accounts receivable, and management reports.

The underlying glue for this complicated system is connectivity through wireless communications. In fact, UPS has its own cellular system. Wireless pervades the company's operations.

The benefits are enormous:

- *Visibility.* Customers are connected in real time to their shipping information. The result is a positive customer experience.
- *Brand value.* UPS becomes a trusted brand in terms of delivering on its promises. As a result, there is much more customer loyalty.
- *Cost savings.* UPS estimates that its technology system saves the company about $5 million per day in terms of customer support costs. Whereas in 1996 about 17 percent of customer requests were automated, now the level is about 90 percent.

While UPS is at the forefront of enterprise wireless solutions, others certainly will follow—which will be an enormous opportunity for enterprise solutions developers.

As we continue, we'll look at the major trends affecting the enterprise wireless market and ways to zero in on companies that likely will succeed.

THE TRENDS IN THE ENTERPRISE

There is no question that wireless will become an integral part of many companies. As stated earlier, it is essential for collaboration. Here are some of the other driving forces:

- *Mobile worker.* More and more, workers are not in their offices at their desks. Rather, they may be working at home or traveling. To meet this need, a substantial investment is required in enterprise wireless technologies. A study from International Data Corporation forecasts that by 2004, about 50 percent of the U.S. workforce will spend 20 percent of its time away from the office. Moreover, a study for Cahners-In-Stat estimates that the number of professional wireless data users will increased from 800,000 in 1999 to 9 million in 2003.

- *Cost factor.* The cofounder of Intel, Gordon Moore, gave a speech in 1965 in which he discussed *Moore's law.* He had been graphing memory chip performance over the years and had realized that every 18 to 24 months a new chip would have about twice as much capacity. This law has held up. In fact, as the power of the chip increases, the costs to make the chip fall. You are getting more bang for the same buck. This is the special nature of high tech. And the same holds true for the wireless industry. Devices are getting more powerful, smaller, and cheaper. Thus, for a corporation, it is more attractive to implement wireless technologies than to hang onto outdated technology. It also helps that airtime fees have been declining as well. Ten years ago, a cell phone bill easily could cost $1,000 or more per month. Now you can get a flat rate for less than $200 per month.

- *Next-generation networks.* Enterprise applications will require the ability to transmit data communications effectively. Legacy networks, though, were built primarily for voice communications. However, with the substantial investments in middle-generation (2.5G) and third-generation (3G) technology, the infrastructure will allow for better enterprise solutions.

- *Wide application.* Wireless technologies have potential impact on many areas of the enterprise. The following subsections discuss some of the main areas that will benefit.

SALES FORCE

As stated at the beginning of this chapter in the example with Jane, a company's sales force can be a major beneficiary of wireless technologies. Having the right data at the right time can mean the difference between closing a sale or not. Moreover, having up-to-the-minute data can be an effective way to build existing relationships with customers.

Some important features for sales automation include

- Integration with customer databases and customer relationship management (CRM) systems
- Real-time access to customer order status and product availability
- Expense reporting
- Customer tracking

INVENTORY MANAGEMENT

Many companies have sophisticated inventory systems, but typically they are tied to fixed locations. For example, a warehouse may have a bar code machine. With wireless devices, inventory changes can be recorded on an anytime, anywhere basis.

Having better inventory systems will mean fewer costs of holding inventory and better order fulfillment and tracking. In the process, there also should be greater customer satisfaction.

Technology features for inventory management include

- Bar code systems
- Real-time tracking
- Mobile forms fill-in

FIELD SERVICE

When UPS delivers a package to you, you must sign off on the electronic clipboard of a field service representative. Many companies do not provide such sophistication. You are likely, instead, to sign your name on a piece of paper on a clipboard.

Features include

- Customer information
- Information tied into the inventory system (or any other pertinent system)
- Calendars (for scheduling)
- Electronic fill-in forms
- Expense tracking

PERSONAL INFORMATION MANAGEMENT (PIM)

This is a basic feature of almost all enterprise solutions and is integral to most other solutions. PIM capabilities have been sold to enterprise customers for some time now. At first, it was in the form of Franklin planners. In the mid-1990s, it shifted to digital media platforms such as Newtons and Palm Pilots.

Today, many PIM features are even supported on cellular telephones. Just about any portable device has many PIM features included, such as

- Scheduling calendars
- To-do lists and/or electronic notepads
- Contact lists
- Electronic business card indexes
- Expense tracking
- Meeting/event reminders

M-COMMERCE

For enterprises that want to give their customers the ability to purchase items from wherever they are, wireless solution providers can supply the necessary infrastructure. Many companies offer secure portal extensions to a company's internal network to allow people to shop from available inventory.

Many people today balk at mobile commerce (m-commerce) because they don't see much merit in buying goods over a medium where the product can't be seen or touched. While this may be true, more compelling m-commerce solutions lie with the wireless device simply handling the purchase while a customer actually is viewing the item to be bought. This scenario is a reality today in many ways. Grocery stores have gone completely wireless, where a mobile device tracks and bills a customer for each item placed in his or her basket. No more standing in line; just walk out with your goods and get the bill later.

To equip an enterprise with m-commerce capabilities, wireless solution providers can help in a number of ways:

- Create the access portal
- Build the "wireless storefront"
- Implement security features
- Establish a billing system
- Support multiple portable device types

ENTERPRISE RESOURCE MANAGEMENT

Most enterprises have critical applications that run on some level of the network within their business. An e-commerce site such as eBay or Amazon.com, for example, cannot tolerate any network downtime. In addition, financial companies depend heavily on market data delivered in real time. A network hiccup or crash of a server can mean a loss of millions to these businesses for every hour the problem goes unresolved.

In critical applications such as these, some enterprises have added wireless monitoring capabilities to their critical network elements. Now the information technology (IT) staff can be alerted immediately to any problems or unusual activity in the network. If they are not on site, they have wireless tools that allow them to access important information about the problem so that they can take immediate action to resolve it. Some companies even have sophisticated abilities to direct changes in the resident network, such as routing traffic onto a backup server or system until the problem can be addressed.

Here are some of the features that resource management solutions can include:

- Immediate alerts to system faults
- Remote access to server log databases
- Control capabilities

FINDING THE RIGHT COMPANIES

For the most part, successful software companies are high-margin businesses that scale nicely. And this likely will be the case with the emerging market for enterprise wireless software solutions.

Why are the margins high? Let's take a look. Suppose that XYZ Wireless wants to develop a new application. This means investment in an R&D project. Say the project takes 6 months and costs $5 million.

Next, the software will need to be distributed. For the most part, this is very cheap. Duplicating software on a CD-ROM may cost $2 a copy, or if the software is distributed over the Internet, the cost could be much less, say, 25 cents per copy.

If the price of the software is $5,000 per copy, it will only take 1,000 copies to break even. The cost of distribution for the Internet would be only $250 and $2,000 for CD-ROMs.

To calculate a company's gross profit margin, first subtract the cost of goods sold from sales, and then divide that number by sales. Multiply the answer by 100 to get the result stated as a percentage. The formula is

$$\text{Profit margin} = \frac{\text{sales} - \text{cost of goods sold}}{\text{sales}} \times 100$$

In this example, if the company sells its software via the Internet, the gross profit is $5 million minus $250, which is almost 100 percent.

Of course, there are other expenses, such as for the sales force and marketing, that may comprise 20 to 30 percent of sales. With the profits, the software company can then spend more money on R&D to expand its product line.

To see how profitable a software company can be, look at the example of Siebel Systems. Tom Siebel cofounded the company in 1993 to develop software that would help companies better manage their customers [called *customer relationship management* (CRM) *software*]. Before this, he was a vice president at Oracle and even talked to Oracle about pursuing the industry. Oracle thought the industry would remain a niche.

Some niche! By the end of 2000, Siebel Systems had increased its revenues 118 percent to $1.76 billion. The margins on the software licensing revenues were a stunning 98 percent (the services part of the business had margins of 37 percent). Operating profits were $388 million.

The company went public in 1996, and a $10,000 investment in Siebel Systems at that time would be worth $74,000 today (Figure 5.1).

There's something else important about the software industry: Software companies that dominate their industries tend to soak up much of the profits. This has been quite consistent for the software industry since the early 1980s.

Let's look again at Siebel Systems. In the first several years of the CRM industry, there were hundreds of competitors. However, Siebel Systems was the company showing the most momentum in market share. By 2001, the company had about 20 percent of the marketplace.

Below Siebel Systems were five companies that had about 20 percent of the market share. On average, Siebel Systems was five times bigger than these five competitors. The remaining 60 percent was held by much smaller companies (about 60 in all).

FIGURE 5.1

Siebel Systems

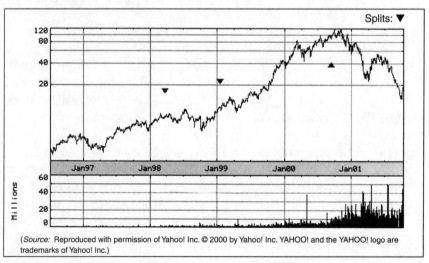

(*Source:* Reproduced with permission of Yahoo! Inc. © 2000 by Yahoo! Inc. YAHOO! and the YAHOO! logo are trademarks of Yahoo! Inc.)

In fact, the 20-20-60 market share structure indicates that the industry is still in a high-growth phase. What does a market look like when it is mature? This is shown by the traditional database market. Here, the top player is Oracle, with 40 percent of the market. The next five companies hold 40 percent of the market, and 20 percent is distributed among niche companies.

Why is there such a substantial growth in market share? There are a number of reasons. First of all, the leader has a high stock value, as well as reputation, and has a much easier time purchasing competitors (which can help boost market share and add new product lines). Next, companies must spend large amounts of money to introduce new technologies. They would rather stick with those companies with which they are familiar. Third, the leader gets much more press coverage and has more brand loyalty than the competitors. Whenever a company is thinking of buying a new product, the leader likely will be the first company to come to mind.

To see the stark difference in valuation, in the middle of 2001, Siebel Systems had a market capitalization of $19 billion. Of the next top five competitors, none had a value above $1 billion.

This is not to say that focusing solely on the market share leaders is foolproof. Sometimes the market leaders can fail (as we'll see in the case of WordPerfect). Rather, it may make more sense to focus on a few of the top market share leaders. If one of these prevails, the upside can be substantial.

Moreover, in the emerging wireless technologies, the marketplace is not at the phase at which Siebel Systems finds itself. Rather, it is in the early stages. There are no clear market leaders yet. Just as with CRM, it takes at least 3 to 4 years for clarity to become apparent.

In the rest of the chapter we will discuss some of the key factors to look for when trying to find the next market leaders for wireless enterprise developers.

GETTING THE BENEFITS, PUTTING OFF THE HASSLE

While a new wireless enterprise solution may provide great benefits for a company, what if it is difficult to install or to maintain? What if it does not work in all environments?

Companies are willing to make investments in IT solutions as long as they can push the hard stuff to the technology provider. And enterprise wireless solutions involve complex technologies. A developer must deal with different networks, protocols, operating systems, and devices. For a company's in-house IT department to develop these technologies certainly would be a stretch. So why not outsource it?

What's more, companies need to get to market quickly. Thus it makes sense to rely on technologies that work.

However, the traditional software model relies on licensing technology to a customer—taking a one-time fee. When there are upgrades, the software company will get additional fees. However, there is often a year or two until the next upgrade.

What's more, a customer must deal with integration and maintenance of the software solution. The costs, in fact, can be much more expensive than the licensing fees because the customer must hire more IT people and consultants. This is known as the *total cost of ownership* (TCO).

Currently, before a company purchases new technology, it will take a hard look at TCO. If an enterprise developer's technology requires heavy software solutions on the customer side, expect resistance. It will certainly be a tough sale.

However, there is a better software model: The *application server provider* (ASP) *model* is also popular. Essentially, this means that the enterprise developer will manage all the technology and allow the customer to get the benefits. With wireless technology, this is much easier—since the customer is connected to the central servers of the enterprise developer.

With the ASP model, the upgrades occur continuously. If a change is made, the software company programs its servers. Instantaneously, all customers have access to the upgrade. There is no need for another installation. Moreover, an ASP company can charge on, say, a periodic basis, such as every month. This helps provide stability to the revenues stream.

An example of this type of application service is a messaging product called MX from the company MobileSys. This product is comprised of a dedicated messaging network that is managed by MobileSys. The network securely connects any number of applications from a customer's intranet to a variety of wireless devices.

Since the company bypasses the public Internet and transfers messages securely to the wireless service provider, it can guarantee message delivery within minutes. Not all companies need guaranteed message delivery from corporate applications such as e-mail and network monitoring, but it is critical to some. Since the customer does not have to host or support any elements of the solutions, its job is much simpler.

ADOPTION

Who is currently using enterprise products? Are they well-known customers? What types of customers are they? How long have they been customers?

In many cases the customers will be concentrated in a specific industry. This can be a double-edged sword. Is the technology flexible enough to be transitioned to other industries. Or do other industries even want the technology? If so, the enterprise developer has strong growth opportunities.

Different industries place very different demands on wireless applications. Financial institutions, for instance, demand high levels of security and redundancy. Applications developed with high levels of encryption also may serve other areas well, such as consumer m-commerce. Other markets, however, such as field service management, may be more concerned about geographic coverage than security.

MULTIPLE REVENUE STREAMS

While a company should not be spread out in too many directions, it is nonetheless a good sign if there are multiple revenue streams. Enterprise solution providers often provide various levels of their products, just like most software makers. Customers can purchase a full-featured package of software and services or choose to implement only a few basic tools, such as simple messaging. This helps the providers develop a product line that has something for everybody and provides several sales channels to drive revenue. If one or a few of the market segments turn sour, the others can make up for it.

GLOBAL OPPORTUNITIES

If enterprise solutions work in the United States, they probably will work in other countries as well. This can be a great boost to a company's growth rate as long as there is a management team to make it happen. Look to see if the company has named key vice presidents for global operations.

It's also a boost if a company has foreign backing. A foreign company that has a financial interest in a wireless enterprise solutions provider can provide vital connections to customers and partners in other countries. This support can help the company jump quickly into global markets when it is ready to expand.

MERGERS AND ACQUISITIONS (M&A)

Acquisitions can be an effective way to strengthen a company's technology portfolio. Why build it when you can buy it?

However, keep in mind that the history of M&A—especially in the technology sector—is replete with disasters. Integrating complex technology product lines, as well as different company cultures, can lead to many problems.

Since this sector of the wireless market is still in the early stages, there undoubtedly will be a high level of consolidation. There are far too many small players in the market wooing corporate clients. Many of these small companies will need to merge with partners and even competitors to remain viable.

In times of consolidation, it is essential for investors to evaluate the deals that companies in the sector are making. Does a buyout or merger look more like a move of necessity (or desperation), or is it supported by a strong vision for the combined company? Are the two companies involved both weak players with little or no revenue, or is it the case of a strong player acquiring a vital technology to fill out its product line?

Be especially wary of mergers that occur in response to competitors' mergers. If a company moves to buy or consolidate with a company because every other competitor already has, then it is likely left with the bottom of the barrel in terms of a partner.

CUSTOMIZATION

Not all companies want to outsource their solutions. They may have a strong technical staff that can add value to enterprise solutions. Also, a company may have special needs that a one-size-fits-all solution does not handle properly.

Thus it is important to have enterprise solutions that can be customized. This requires the solution provider to maintain a staff that is well acquainted with customers' needs. Staff members must be able to foresee how the customer would want to expand its product to make it flexible.

In this area, it is nice to see some senior management with backgrounds in the industries they now serve. What better way to understand the needs of your customers than to have been one yourself at one time?

IT SPENDING

Although the 1990s were a boom time for IT spending, there was a slowdown in early 2000. There are many reasons for this. The economy was slowing, and companies already had invested huge sums in new technologies. When IT spending falls, there is likely to be a significant impact on enterprise software developers. Although wireless enterprise solutions typically are not expensive items, they are nonetheless discretionary.

GIANTS

The enterprise market leaders—such as Microsoft, Oracle, and IBM—certainly pose threats to upstart enterprises solution providers. These market leaders have the resources, talent, and distribution to make their products dominate. And as we've seen in Chapter 2, these companies already have begun initiatives to focus significant energies in the wireless space.

Obviously, this can mean trouble for small companies going up against the giants. However, companies that already have partnerships or funding from larger companies are sitting in a good position. The relationships between the players often were established early on, so it pays to check into these.

RESEARCH & DEVELOPMENT (R&D)

The software industry is replete with examples of how companies have failed to maintain their technology lead. A classic example is WordPerfect. The company was the leading developer of word-processing software for the PC. In 1994, the networking software giant Novell purchased WordPerfect for $1.4 billion. However, WordPerfect thought that transition from DOS to Windows would be slow. This was a huge mistake as Microsoft quickly ate the market share of

WordPerfect. Within 18 months, WordPerfect was sold to Corel for about $100 million.

One way to analyze a company's technology is to see how much is spent on R&D. True, this is a very rough indicator. After all, a company may be spending money on the wrong things (such as what WordPerfect did). Thus it is important to look at a company's press releases to see the direction in which the technology is headed.

However, as a general rule, look for companies that spend 8 to 12 percent of sales on R&D. This is not a perfect rule, but it is a good guide. Less than 8 percent dedicated to R&D may be too little to remain competitive in the future. More than 12 percent may starve current operations and marketing from much-needed funding, which will constrict cash flow.

DAYS SALES OUTSTANDING (DSO)

This is a critical statistic for software companies. How does it compare with the rest of the industry? For example, Siebel Systems compares favorably, with its DSO at about 75.

The DSO shows how fast a company is converting its sales into cash. By looking at a company's balance sheet, you can calculate the DSO by using the following formula:

$$DSO = \frac{current\ A\ /\ R}{sales\ for\ the\ period} \times days\ in\ period$$

For quarterly earnings reports, sales are given over a 90-day period, but this equation can be used for any reporting period (quarterly or yearly).

The DSO will change frequently. Also, if a company begins to enter foreign markets, the DSO will tend to increase temporally. However, if there is a large jump in the DSO—say by 20 to 30 percent during the quarter—there should be concerns. The software company may be having trouble selling its software.

UBIQUITY

One of the keys to Oracle's success has been that its database hooks into just about any type of technology environment. As a result, a company is not faced with getting rid of legacy systems in order to bring in new Oracle systems.

The same principle is vital for enterprise solutions developers. For the most part, large organizations will have a variety of wireless devices—cell phones, Palms, Handsprings, and so on. If an enterprise solution cannot integrate these devices seamlessly, it probably will languish. Remember: The mantra for wireless is anytime, anywhere, and on *any device*.

Another aspect that makes this even more difficult is the number of wireless service providers, especially in the United States. The technology servicing the devices is often incompatible, compounding the problem. For instance, a solutions provider may have to supply messaging solutions to a customer who has devices operating on Sprint PCS's or Cingular's wireless network—which are incompatible with each other.

NETWORK LIMITATIONS

Let's face it, the wireless infrastructure has many problems. There may be areas where there is no coverage, for example. So how do you conduct business if the only device you can use is wireless? Basically, the technology should be developed to deal both online and offline.

One company, Everypath, builds its products with this in mind. The company considers itself not simply a wireless company but an information and collaboration company as well. It provides solutions for accessing and passing information through a variety of means—wireless, PCs, or even the standard telephone.

TOO INNOVATIVE

Ironically enough, a product can be too good. This is the case when the product is ahead of its time. Thus the product eventually will be a big part of corporate enterprises—but no time soon. Unfortunately, the results can be disastrous for the company that introduced the product. The huge investment in R&D to develop the product will cripple the company as competitors introduce products—that have incremental changes—and take more and more market share away.

Of course, it is not easy to determine when this happens. However, if the product is revolutionary—a huge jump from the last generation—there is a good chance that the company may be walking the plank.

A classic case in point occurred when Informix, a leading database company, purchased Illustra in February 1996 for $400 million. With the acquisition, Informix would be able to develop a revolutionary new database system that would handle such complex data types as digital images and video. The new product became known as a *universal server*.

In December 1996, Informix launched its universal server product. The chief executive officer (CEO) of Informix announced that the product had a year lead against the competition. He said that the software represented a fundamental change in the database industry and would have a substantial impact on the company's revenues for 1997. The stock price at the time was about $26 per share.

Unfortunately, customers did not have an immediate need for the product. Moreover, the technology was available only for a few platforms. Meanwhile, Oracle began a price war, and Microsoft introduced new products that were competitive with Informix's offerings.

By April 1997, Informix announced that it would severely miss its numbers. In May, the company released its financial report, and the company had a loss of $140.1 million. The DSO went from 84 to 130. The stock collapsed to $7 a share.

SECURITY

Even though collaboration will be important, there is still a need for security. Perhaps customer information needs to remain private, or a company is negotiating a big deal or a merger. If a wireless device cannot keep such communications confidential, then it will have serious problems in the marketplace.

Currently, wireless security is somewhat lax. In early 2001, researchers from the University of California at Berkeley found security holes in the so-called Wired Equivalent Privacy (WEP) algorithm of the Institute of Electrical and Electronic Engineers (IEEE) 802.11b standard. Basically, WEP is supposed to protect wireless communications. In fact, some hackers were able to break into corporate networks remotely, say, from a laptop in a car across the street from the company.

Another example occurred in Japan. Hackers located a security hole in NTT DoCoMo. Whenever a call was made, it would be redirected to 110, which is the equivalent to 911 in the United States. The 110 service had to be shut down. What if someone had an emergency and needed help?

When looking at an enterprise application, therefore, make sure that there are many security features. Here are some things to look at:

- *Encryption.* This is a special way to encode data to make them extremely difficult to decode.
- *Authentication.* This validates the identity of the user, which can be done using such things as passwords, smart cards, and biometrics (say, a thumb print or an eye scan).
- *Access.* A company should be able to control the level of access for a device. For example, an engineer may have his or her access limited to a certain project, whereas the CEO will have complete access.

Actually, the high-tech security industry is likely to get a nice boost from wireless companies that need security infrastructure. The three main groups to benefit include

- *Antivirus companies.* These companies, such as Trend Micro (Nasdaq: TMIC) and Symantec (Nasdaq: SYMC), build software tools to combat and prevent virus intrusions.
- *Digital identification companies.* A digital ID uses sophisticated technologies to authenticate the user you are communicating with. A top company in the field is VeriSign (Nasdaq: VRSN), a company that did not collapse during the high-tech bear market of 2001.
- *Network protection companies.* These companies develop technologies to protect servers from attack (known as *firewall systems*). Companies include Check Point Software (Nasdaq: CHKP) and Internet Security Systems (Nasdaq: ISSX).

SIGNS OF A BREAKOUT

The wireless enterprise marketplace is still in its infancy. Many of these companies will have small revenue bases (if any revenues). Therefore, applying traditional value metrics makes no sense. Yet there certainly will be much money made from this sector—as well as the other emerging market areas (as discussed in the next chapter).

This is why many of the factors mentioned in the preceding section are quite subjective. In the end, you are making a gut decision on what direction a market is headed. Of course, this is highly speculative. Then again, because of the high risk, you have the potential for gaining high returns.

Actually, venture capitalists make their money by making these types of decisions. In other words, when looking at enterprise developers and other emerging market players, basically you need to assume the role of a venture capitalist. In Chapter 11 there is a section entitled, "Thinking Like a Venture Capitalist." When investing in early-stage wireless companies, look at this section. It will give you a framework for picking the future big winners.

Keep in mind that early-stage companies can take quite a bit of time to hit critical mass. As we will see in Chapter 7, it took almost a decade for QUALCOMM to become a winner.

So what signs should you look for to see if an early-stage company is ready for a break out? In the rest of this chapter we will take a look at two key elements: momentum and insider buying.

MOMENTUM

In the late 1990s, many day traders made lots of money by *momentum investing*. That is, they would buy stocks because the stocks were going up quickly. Of course, momentum investors got burned when the Nasdaq went into a bear market. As a result, momentum investing got a black eye.

Basically, when an early-stage company is breaking out, it usually will not be short term. Success tends to breed more success. As the company signs a big deal, other potential customers will take notice and will start to buy the company's products. This means that there will be an acceleration in revenues and profit growth. Quarter after quarter there will be surprises for Wall Street. And the stock will continue to zoom.

Yet investors will think that the trend will end or that the stock price is too high. Perhaps the stock has already doubled or tripled. It certainly can't go any higher, right? If a company is truly in the breakout mode, the stock can go much higher. On the other hand, the reverse is true. When earnings start to decelerate, it takes a long time to reverse the trend.

Let's take an example. Lightbridge (Nasdaq: LTBG) was founded in 1989. The company's first product was called *Credit Decision System*, an expert system that automates the approval process for people buying cell phones. The company then leveraged this technology into other products for customer service for the telecom industry.

Looking at the business model, the company had products that were in high demand. Cellular companies have big problems with churn rates. Lightbridge helps reduce this. What's more, Lightbridge has a business model that is based on recurring revenue streams. A major show of strength was the customer list, which included such "biggies" as GTE and AT&T Wireless.

In the third quarter of 1998, Lightbridge's stock price ranged from $4 to $7 per share. The company's earnings report, though, indicated that the company was showing strong growth. Sales reached $15.6 million, which was a 65 percent increase from the same period a year previously. The company turned a profit of $700,000, although this was down from $900,000 a year previously. However, the company stated that it had set in motion cost controls so as to boost margins.

Another positive was that the company was expanding into Europe and Asia. In addition, the company struck a major deal with TeleCorp (an affiliate with AT&T Wireless). The third largest cellular phone company in Mexico reported that after using Lightbridge products, the amount of fraud in its system was reduced by 50 percent. New customers included Symbio Systems, KG Telecom, and Centennial Wireless.

The first report was no fluke. During the first quarter of 1999, revenues reached $19.3 million, which was up 45.5 percent from the same period a year before. Cost controls were taking effect as net income reached $1.5 million, up from a loss of $15.4 million a year previously. The CEO said, "The investments we made in 1997 and 1998 in data center capacity and performance improvements prepared us for the Company's record-breaking transaction volume."

Even at this time, you could have bought the stock for $5 to $6 per share. The momentum of success continued for Lightbridge. By the end of 1999, the company had generated $89.7 million in revenues, which was a 41.6 percent increase from the year before. And net income was $10.1 million, which was up from a loss of $6.9 million. The stock reached almost $35 per share by the end of the year (Figure 5.2).

F I G U R E   5.2

Lightbridge, Inc.

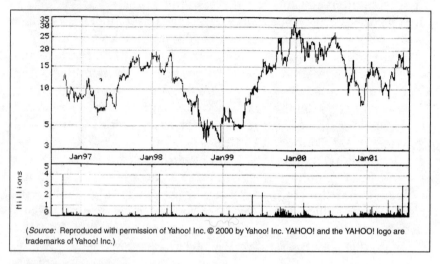

(*Source:* Reproduced with permission of Yahoo! Inc. © 2000 by Yahoo! Inc. YAHOO! and the YAHOO! logo are trademarks of Yahoo! Inc.)

INSIDER BUYING

The phrase *insider trading* brings visions of Ivan Boesky and Gordon Gekko. It is illegal for people to invest based on nonpublic information. You may pay heavy fines and even can go to jail.

However, there is a legal form of insider trading, that is, the transactions from officers, directors, and major shareholders (known as *insiders*). By virtue of their positions, insiders are privy to nonpublic information. In other words, they know if a big deal is about to be signed or a new technology has tremendous promise. And they also know when a big deal falls through or the business starts to deteriorate.

During the 1930s, the federal government wanted to place restrictions on insider sales. One idea was to prevent insiders from trading stocks. However, this seemed a bit too extreme. After all, it is good for management and directors to be owners of a company's stock.

A compromise was struck: Insiders would be required to disclose their buy and sell transactions. This rule, in fact, can be a good indicator for individual investors. However, you need to be patient. Insiders tend to invest early. It could take 6 months to a year to see an uptrend. The main reason is federal regulation: If an insider makes a profit within 6 months, it must be given back to the company. Basically, this encourages insiders to invest for the long term.

However, the wait is a good thing. This gives investors time to do the required research on the company.

So where do you get the information? With the Internet, it is easy to access free information about insider sales. Two great sites are *www.insiderscores.com* and *www.insidertrader.com*.

Insider buying is much more predictive than insider selling. When an insider sells stock, he or she may not necessarily be negative about the prospects of the company. For example, the insider may be forced to sell stock, such as for a divorce or to pay a tax bill. The insider may want to diversify his or her portfolio. Or the insider might want to enjoy the wealth and buy a new boat or house.

As for insider buying, the insider must fork over hard-earned dollars. This definitely shows a certain amount of faith in the company. Keep in mind that the executive probably already has substantial stock in the company (such as through an employee stock option plan). Yet the insider would rather buy more shares.

Now there are parameters to look for when analyzing insider buying. Obviously, an insider who buys 100 shares would not be very convincing. Here's a look at the key factors.

TYPES OF BUYERS

Focus on senior management, such as the CEO, chief financial officer, chief operating officer, vice presidents, and board members. These are the people who have the best access to nonpublic information. Lower-level employees or major investors do not have much access to the internals of the company.

HOW MANY BUYERS?

There is a concept called *clustered buying*. This is when three or more insiders buy stock—at the same time (say, within a few months of each other).

Even though insiders are privy to nonpublic information, this does not mean that an insider will be correct in how Wall Street reacts. Actually, investors may not consider the news to be worthy, and the stock may not move. However, when several insiders begin buying, this provides much confidence in the stock price climbing.

HOW MANY SHARES?

As stated earlier, small lots of shares are not very significant. You want the insiders to purchase substantial amounts. There are several ways to look at this:

- *Percentage of the buying compared with the number of shares outstanding.* If this is 10 percent or more, then it is bullish.
- *Percentage of the buying compared with the number of shares already owned by the insider.* If this is 50 percent or more, then it is bullish.
- *Percentage of the buying compared with the salary of the insider.* If this is 25 percent or more, then it is bullish.

INDUSTRY INSIDER BUYING

Look at other insider selling at wireless companies. Is there a trend of increased heavy buying across the board? If so, this indicates that the marketplace is experiencing a growth spurt.

EXAMPLE

When the telecom market plunged in late 2000, so did the shares of InterVoice-Brite (Nasdaq: INTV). This developer of telecom equipment saw its stock plunge from $38 to $6 (Figure 5.3).

One of the problems with the company was the integration of a recent merger (between InterVoice and Brite). In the short run, profits suffered. Yet the stock was still selling at about 10 times earnings and less than 1 times sales.

Five insiders continued to be bullish on the stock, putting about $5.5 million into the company's stock. There were no insider sales. By the summer of 2001, the stock had doubled to $12.

SUMMARY

The wireless enterprise market is still young and promises substantial growth in the future. Businesses that are seeking market advan-

FIGURE 5.3

InterVoice-Brite, Inc.

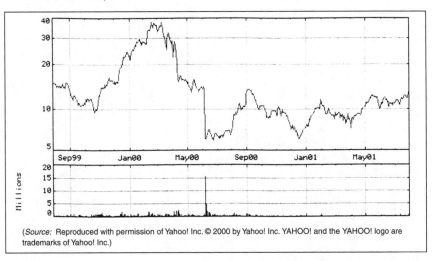

(*Source:* Reproduced with permission of Yahoo! Inc. © 2000 by Yahoo! Inc. YAHOO! and the YAHOO! logo are trademarks of Yahoo! Inc.)

tages are routinely turning to wireless solutions to improve operations. In many cases, wireless tools and services are critical to the success of the company.

The emerging nature of this market makes it a particularly risky one for investors. There are hundreds of players competing in this segment, with many of them offering similar products and services. Consolidation in this area will continue for years as the weaker players are weeded out.

Tremendous opportunities lie in this area for investors as well. The challenge to investing successfully in an enterprise solutions provider comes in being able to see the early signs of success. It is not as simple as crunching the numbers and monitoring objective metrics. Growth in these companies has a lot to do with relationships and leadership.

Once you find the right companies in this market, it takes patience to reap the rewards. While surges in stock prices can produce handsome gains for those lucky enough to time it right and sell at the top, there's greater opportunity for profit in holding a long-term winner.

6

Emerging Technologies and Markets

A great uncle left you a small but significant inheritance on his death. You remember that he would always tell you to invest in the future and take risks. Being young and decades away from retirement, you decide to take the money and invest it in an emerging segment of the wireless industry. With most of your personal funds secured in stable growth areas, you decide to risk a portion on a really forward-thinking company—one that envisions the mobile world years from now. But most of your early research finds most companies looking to third generation (3G) and beyond insanely valued—even for high-growth stock. You figure that the cat's out of the bag on wireless and begin looking elsewhere.

Not so fast. There's a tremendous amount of potential in wireless, and it is largely untapped. It's only a matter of where to look.

When digital wireless technologies were being developed in the early 1990s around the world, no one really knew for sure where the best profit opportunities lay. All they knew was that demand for cellular phones was surging, thanks to new technology that made portable devices smaller and lighter. Providing for simple data features was thought by some to be simply a rudimentary add-on feature to augment all the other, more desirable functions of a mobile phone. Little did anyone know that Short Messaging Services (SMSs) would be such a raging success. Today, some service providers find a sizable chunk of their revenue—10 to 15 percent—coming from this simple add-on feature.

The same will hold true in the future. It is impossible for anyone to look much farther than 5 years into the future and tell you for sure what the wireless world will be like. People often are surprised by which services or types of devices consumers flock to, even the companies producing the products and services. For instance, there was widespread belief that Research In Motion (Nasdaq: RIM) was doomed with its costly, redundant BlackBerry device. Why would someone pay several hundred dollars for something they essentially could have in a cheap pager or smart cellular phone? Obviously, thousands of people see some good reasons, and in 2001, RIM was looking to expand overseas.

Many companies are pushing radical ideas in the wireless space. While some have succeeded, some will struggle to complete their vision and ultimately die out. Metricom set out with its novel Micro Cellular Data Network in the mid-1990s only to find that it couldn't sign up enough subscribers to keep the business alive and support expansion plans. Iridium and Globalstar also had trouble making their emerging technology [low-earth-orbiting (LEO) satellite systems] support overly optimistic business plans. While there may be more failures than successes in this category, the companies that prevail can provide great returns for thick-skinned investors.

With numerous past examples of a lack of vision—and more often a completely wrong vision—investors all have an opportunity to evaluate for themselves the chances of various companies becoming the next to accomplish what no one expected. There are far too many wireless applications that anyone has yet to imagine, so don't stop short and deduce that everything worth following is already overbought. Remember from Chapter 1 that most of the history of wireless communications was in the form of broadcast media. It has only been about 20 years since the idea of personal, mobile communications has taken hold in society. This leaves decades of further possibilities.

For an investor to increase his or her chances of finding a winner in the emerging category, he or she must forego the desire to invest in a well-known entity. A company that has an exciting vision for the wireless future that is shared by many on Wall Street is likely already overvalued and overanalyzed. Companies that receive a disproportionate amount of the spotlight tend to be distracted from the primary goal of making their products or services work and end up victims of their own market success.

As with picking stocks in general, there are some basic recommendations that investors should follow when looking at companies developing emerging technologies:

- *Leadership.* The officers of the company should have demonstrated competency in the industry. For instance, if the chief executive officer (CEO) of a hot start-up in this area left the cattle business to start the company, watch out. Look for people who may have left respected companies. Sometimes teams of people leave a large corporation because they have a great idea that a shortsighted management didn't embrace.

- *Industry support.* You'll undoubtedly find a number of companies in this area that claim remarkable things. Strangely, all the mainstream companies in the industry seem to ignore the company even though the product or service would be of great benefit to them. If industry heavyweights won't back up an emerging company's claims, this probably means that the claims are just that and nothing else. Look for a company that has funding from industry bellwethers or working relationships with respectable peers. This helps legitimize their claims.

- *Past success.* This goes along with the leadership quality. A company that has bounced around from other lines of business is a high-risk venture. If the company couldn't get its first business (or product) right, this reduces the odds that the second will do any better.

- *Smart backing.* Check into the people or ventures that are supporting the company. Do they have a good track record? Are they well-known names? Sometimes people who have lots of money but little knowledge of what they are getting into are the ones who fund a company.

- *Regulatory/consortium connections.* Standards bodies, consortiums, and political agencies hold significant power in the wireless industry. Companies developing emerging technology or applications should have some presence or experience in these areas because they will have to deal with them at some point, usually when near shipment of a feasible product.

Like all other guidelines about investing in wireless, these rules are by no means hard and fast. However, most of the success stories in the industry tend to have these qualities. At the very least, a company who does not fare well in these areas will have an extremely difficult time forging its place in the marketplace.

In order to look at many of the high-growth possibilities in this developing portion of the wireless market, we'll divide them into two major categories: emerging technologies and new consumer applications. The emerging technologies tend to have more to do with advanced hardware and systems, whereas the applications typically are based on software.

The consumer wireless applications market will be discussed later in this chapter. We'll first take a look at a few of the emerging wireless technologies fighting for a piece of the mobile future. Some of these technologies are simply new processes that seek to solve long-studied problems, such as limited battery life in portables or incompatible systems. Others are completely new ideas for providing mobile services to people in different environments. Emerging technologies in this category can be driven by a number of things, including

- *Cost reduction.* This involves substantially cutting down the investment necessary to enable wireless communications. The motive can be to make the infrastructure more efficient or to realize cost savings in producing mobile devices.
- *Improved features.* This involves eliminating headaches that consumers deal with in current mobile devices, such as short battery life, incompatible networks, or even a poor visual experience.
- *New capabilities.* This involves introducing new functions into mobile devices. Some current concepts include making your cellular phone into a virtual wallet with point-of-sale functions, using wireless technology to itemize and pay for grocery items automatically as you leave a store, or using cellular signals in novel ways to map real-time traffic patterns or get census information.

EMERGING TECHNOLOGIES

Emerging technologies constitute one of the more exciting areas of wireless simply because it involves the most forward-thinking solutions. Many of these technologies are still in the early stages of development with no commercial exposure but a lot of promise. Some are just now coming into the commercial market, where some of their benefits are now being realized. In the rest of this chapter we'll delve into a few of the areas that are showing promise in the industry. Keep in mind that in the coming years, even more emerging markets will appear.

We'll start by taking a look at a few of the emerging technologies in the wireless market. Then we'll explore the area of consumer applications in wireless devices—a market for services that is emerging with the advent of the wireless Internet.

SOFTWARE-DEFINED RADIO

A software-defined radio (SDR) is a wireless transmission device— either a portable unit or a base station—that has its primary radio functions defined in software. Makes sense, right? Well, cellular phones today already have many of their functions programmed into software, so when does a unit become *defined* by software as opposed to just including software?

Today, most discussions of SDR technology refer to the idea of using software code rather than fixed circuitry to perform the transmit and receive functions of the radio. This is significant because the radios have to transmit and receive information according to a certain protocol—such as Global System for Mobile Communication (GSM) or Code Division Multiple Access (CDMA). If this function is fixed in silicon chips as it is today, then it cannot be changed easily. However, if it is executed in software, it can be changed much more easily, even on the fly.

Back when we discussed wireless equipment manufacturers in Chapter 4, we looked at the basic architecture of a cellular radio and looked at some of the major functions. This included the processing section (both baseband and application), the digital signal processor (DSP), the radio frequency (RF) front end, and other areas. What SDR technology seeks to do is to make all major functions fluid—so that the core wireless function of the phone can be easily changeable. This includes the baseband processing, DSP, and some portions of the RF front end. This would be analogous to having a personal computer (PC) that could switch to any operating system—DOS, Windows, Linux, and so on—at the push of a button.

The major advantages that SDR technology will bring are in three main areas: protocol compatibility, ease of upgrade, and spectrum efficiency. With respect to protocol compatibility, many people see SDR as the savior of the wireless protocol snafu. In the envisioned scenario, an SDR handset will be able to adjust its transmission parameters to match whatever base station is in the area. Another scenario has cellular base stations around the world fitted with SDR technology. In this case, the base unit can identify users dynamically as they pass through the cell and adapt its parameters to best serve them.

SDR technology has the potential to solve many ongoing problems in the wireless industry. Since it basically aims to align the various air interface protocols to make them interoperable, this technology has the promise of eliminating a lot of the headaches for consumers in dealing with incompatible services and equipment. Some service providers have even been calling publicly for SDR technologies to be implemented in equipment. In June 2001, Verizon Wireless' CEO Dennis Strigl called on the great minds of the industry to develop technologies to bring the two major 3G air interface protocols, wideband CDMA (W-CDMA) and cdma2000, together in a single network solution. His comments were thought to reflect a common feeling in the industry, where service providers are frustrated with having to deal with multiple incompatible technologies.

The second major advantage that SDR technology brings is the ease of upgrade to radios—both mobile and base station modules. Newer features and services can be added to existing hardware simply by installing new software. Another positive feature of the software upgrade is that it can be done over the air interface. Rather than taking your phone into the service dealer where technicians plug it into a PC or program it through keys, users will be able to just call in for an upgrade.

Some cellular handsets that entered the market in mid-2001 have so-called over-the-air configurability. However, the downloading capability of these handsets is in the area of applications—not the core radio functions. For instance, users can download different games or utility programs to work with data. Quite a bit of work still needs to be done to be able to change a phone's operating properties with information downloaded over the air.

The third major advantage, and one most coveted by the Federal Communications Commission (FCC), has to do with the spectrum efficiency of the technology. What the FCC is hoping for is the capability of radios to be "smarter" in the ways they use frequency spectrum. SDR base stations could optimize the use of the licensed band to squeeze more users and bandwidth in the available space. Smart radios could adapt to make use of underutilized frequency bands. Making the wireless network more efficient means that network operators won't keep pounding on FCC doors asking for more licenses.

To this end, the FCC has been placing some attention on the regulation of SDR devices. In the past, the regulatory requirements for wireless radios in the United States had detailed parameters for operation of the devices according to a specific protocol or mode. These parameters were necessary to keep all devices operating in an organized fashion. For instance, the FCC didn't want to allow anyone to make a wireless radio that could be converted easily by a consumer to use on emergency or military frequencies. If an SDR unit could change its mode easily after it was shipped from the manufacturer, it would void any regulatory approval by the FCC and make it illegal. To tackle this issue, the FCC has been meeting with some of the major players in the industry to fashion new rules that allow for proper regulation of devices that can change operational modes. So far the process has gone well, and both the FCC and the industry are making progress toward the goal of commercial SDR devices.

In addition to companies working on SDR technology for the military and government, several companies are working in the area of SDR technology for consumer applications. Most of the activity in this area is currently in semiconductor components—development of the actual processor cores that can handle a variety of communications protocols. As of 2001, commercially available software-defined processors are still a few years out, so the device manufacturers have yet to get into the game.

Many semiconductor manufacturers are working on building hardware that is capable of an SDR solution in a handset. Chipmakers Xilinx (Nasdaq: XLNX) and Altera (Nasdaq: ALTR) both offer programmable chips that can be reconfigured for new functions. Start-up companies such as Morphics, Chameleon Systems, and QuickSilver

Technology are all working on new processor architectures that are designed specifically to change functions on the fly. All these companies are still fighting against current limitations in the technology, such as power consumption and cost. They are also competing against the status quo—low-cost Application Specific Integrated Circuit (ASIC) solutions.

The ASIC solutions used in wireless units today still have some advantages over SDR. While they have their functions fixed, they are cheap when purchased in quantity and are getting small enough to fit multiple functions in a cellular phone, for instance. It's possible that as advances in ASICs continue, multiple radios simply will be built into one portable device. Then a simple layer of software would just select which function to run and shut down the other circuits. This would achieve the same goal as SDR but be limited to what is fixed in the phone without the provision for over-the-air downloads. Indeed, cellular phones already exist today that operate in analog modes such as Advanced Mobile Phone Systems (AMPS) and digital modes such as Time Division Multiple Access (TDMA).

A forum has already been established to provide an industry resource to companies working with SDR as well. The SDR Forum has been meeting regularly since 1996 and has many of the industry heavyweights on its membership roster. This nonprofit body seeks to develop and promote standards for SDR technologies and work with international bodies at aligning current technologies. If you were looking for an SDR company in which to invest, the membership roster of this organization would be a great place to start. The organization lists over 100 members, and many are public or later-stage private companies.

MICRO-FUEL CELL TECHNOLOGY

Even though fuel cell technology has been around for decades, it has yet to prove economically feasible in consumer applications. This is starting to change, though, as fuel cells are starting to creep into everyday power applications, bringing with them some cost benefits.

Fuel cell technologies have been explored for a number of applications outside the area of wireless technology. In fact, the benefits that fuel cells will provide such other areas as the automotive industry should far outweigh their significance in the wireless market today if certain hurdles can be overcome. Yet the possibilities in this area still offer a tremendous benefit to consumers and the environment, especially when you consider how many millions of toxic cellular phone batteries are purchased and disposed of every year.

There are a few public companies that are pursuing micro-fuel cells for items such as laptops, cellular phones, and personal digital assistants (PDAs). Since our society is becoming ever more dependent on portable power, it is not likely that we'll be shunning batteries in the future. Fuel cells fit the bill perfectly for economical, environmentally safe power. They just need a little time to get there.

Some of the major advantages that drive fuel cell development for portable devices include

- Increased capacity
- Long usable life
- Environmental friendliness

The increased capacity that fuel cells offer depends on the type of fuel cell. The efficiency of different methods varies depending largely on the type of fuel fed to the cell. For most applications in portable devices, fuel cells generally promise an improvement of 5 to 10 times what today's batteries deliver. This basically means that your cellular phone will stay on standby for more than a month or give you a talk time of 24+ hours.

The usable life of fuel cells also goes way beyond the capabilities of today's batteries. Even the best batteries, such as lithium ion (Li-ion) and nickel metal hydride (NiMH) batteries, degrade significantly after about 300 to 500 charging cycles. This puts their usable life somewhere around 1 to 2 years depending on how much you use them. Fuel cells can go far beyond this because nothing wears out in the cell.

Fuel cells are also praised for their limited effects on the environment. Because the by-product of most fuel cell operation is water vapor, there's not a whole lot of damage fuel cells can do. Even disposable zinc-air fuel cells are nontoxic, although they do contribute to landfills to a tiny degree.

While fuel cells offer a lot of potential in the market for portable electronic devices, there are a few significant barriers that need to be overcome before a commercial product is feasible. One major limitation is in storage of the fuel. For instance, hydrogen fuel cells must have complicated and expensive systems coupled with them to either store the hydrogen in its purest form or refine it from another fuel.

Since the efficiency of a fuel cell usually is tied directly to the purity of the fuel, the method for storing and recharging the fuel is critical.

Direct methanol fuel cells seek to overcome the problems of storing hydrogen by using cheap and safe methanol as the fuel. However, these systems have their own problems and may not match the efficiency of hydrogen-based fuel cells. These complications, along with other issues, lead most workers in the industry to believe that fuel cells won't appear commercially until sometime around 2005.

There are only a handful of companies working in micro-fuel cell technology currently, and some of these are trading publicly. Manhattan Scientifics and Mechanical Technology both have high-profile research projects underway, with some of the most prominent minds in fuel cell technology working on their teams. Motorola also has a division working with the Los Alamos National Laboratory on a methanol fuel cell for portable devices. Another company called Electric Fuels Corporation already sells commercial zinc-air batteries for cellular phones and PDAs that basically are a fuel cell (only they are not rechargeable).

SMART ANTENNA SYSTEMS

Smart antenna systems are actually a group of technologies designed to improve the performance of cellular base stations. By optimizing several aspects of how a tower transmits and receives signals to individual users, the technology can increase the capacity and range within a particular cell profoundly. Smart antennas can be added to cellular and Personal Communication Service (PCS) base stations that employ any air interface technology from GSM to CDMA or even 3G systems such as W-CDMA.

What smart antennas essentially do is actively manage how the different radio transmissions are done in the base station. By focusing the signals toward users rather than broadcasting them in all directions, the tower can reuse the same frequencies to boost capacity. A tower therefore could track one user to the north and use the same frequency channel to service another user in the south. The advanced processing that takes place in these systems also improves the signal quality, providing better clarity and fewer dropped calls.

Once their function is understood, the usefulness of smart antennas is fairly obvious. With more and more people signing up for mobile services, the capacity of current networks is under strain.

Service providers such as Verizon and AT&T spend hundreds of millions of dollars annually to upgrade capacity and service quality in major markets such as Los Angeles and Florida. Merely improving the performance of existing base stations can save companies the cost and time of building new towers in already dense areas.

Several prominent companies are developing smart antenna technology in the United States and abroad. While some major service providers and equipment vendors have experimented with their own technology, the most progress has been seen from companies such as ArrayComm and Metawave. ArrayComm is led by cellular phone pioneer Martin Cooper and probably is the most vocal proponent for the spectrum-efficient technology. Companies such as AirNet Communications have partnered with ArrayComm to incorporate smart antenna technology into its proprietary software-defined base stations. Metawave has customers around the world using its products to increase capacity in CDMA and GSM systems.

While smart antenna systems are available commercially today, the technology is advancing rapidly, so new ideas are coming about all the time. With a constant need to improve capacity, many related technologies are also coming about that seek the same goals—serve more subscribers with better quality. One example of this is superconducting filter technologies. This technology uses high-temperature superconducting (HTS) materials (in a cryogenic cooler) to filter signals more efficiently, therefore allowing a system to add more users while improving the quality of signal reception.

The superconducting filter market alone is a big reason why many investors are looking at emerging markets in the wireless space. The major public companies working in this segment have already had their share of the spotlight in early 2000. As shown in Figure 6.1, the stock of Superconductor Technologies (Nasdaq: SCON) soared over 20-fold in the first quarter of 2000. By May 2001, however, the stock had settled back down close to its September 1999 level.

Much of this gain was fueled by excessive speculation when people saw HTS technology coming into the mainstream. This transition from emerging to mainstream often leads to dramatic surges in the stock of emerging companies. However, the shares usually settle back to a more realistic level over time, as seen here. Whether there will be a second act for this segment is still being debated.

With rapid growth rates in wireless subscribers and shortages of spectrum in some countries, smart antenna technologies are already

FIGURE 6.1

Superconductor Technologies, Inc.

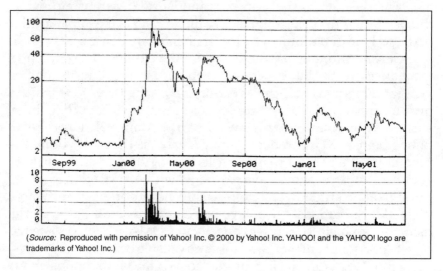

(*Source:* Reproduced with permission of Yahoo! Inc. © 2000 by Yahoo! Inc. YAHOO! and the YAHOO! logo are trademarks of Yahoo! Inc.)

providing much needed relief to some service providers. Keep in mind, though, that a slowdown in subscriber growth or ease of spectrum strains will decrease the need for these types of solutions. Smart antenna solutions must remain cost-effective; otherwise, they will become an expensive extra rather than a necessity in a wireless system.

HIGH-ALTITUDE PLATFORM SYSTEMS

High-altitude platform systems (HAPS) are either aircraft or large balloons that usually are piloted in the upper atmosphere (50,000 to 70,000 feet up) for extended periods of time. The crafts may be manned or directed automatically by computer control. These vehicles are loaded with a payload full of radio gear to provide wireless services over certain regions on the ground. You can think of it as a big cellular base station floating in the sky or as an extremely low-earth-orbiting satellite.

Where HAPS really show their promise is in the cost necessary to deploy wireless infrastructure. When you consider that a radio platform at an altitude of roughly 50,000 feet can cover an area of over 5,000 square miles, the idea of HAPS really starts to make sense. It would take hundreds of cellular towers or costly satellites to provide similar coverage. A service provider essentially can give up the massive up-front costs of building a terrestrial network in exchange for the recurring costs of operating planes or balloons.

HAPS are broken down into mainly two categories: fixed-wing aircraft and balloons (also called *aerostats*). The fixed-wing aircraft systems keep the radio payload aloft for only several hours at a time and must schedule new flights routinely to replace planes that are running low on fuel. Balloons, on the other hand, can remain aloft a lot longer, some for years. Each system has its own benefits and drawbacks.

Some systems even use a combination of fixed-wing aircraft and balloons to provide reliable service to an area. Customers would not be very happy about a blackout in their service, so redundancy is very important with HAPS. There always must be a backup in place in case something happens to the primary system.

At first thought, it seems like it would be extremely expensive to operate a HAPS. If you have a balloon system, you have the high cost of multiple platforms for redundancy. Fixed-wing aircraft systems must cost a bundle in fuel and salaries for the pilots. However, when you compare these costs with alternatives such as satellites and terrestrial systems, proponents of HAPS claim that they're actually lower. Here's a breakdown of the main advantages that HAPS bring:

- Reduced infrastructure cost
- Faster means of providing service in new areas
- Ease of service upgrades
- Better reception

Most companies that are pursuing HAPS tell network operators that their systems cut the cost of wireless services by 25 percent or more. HAPS also tend to have much lower upfront costs to get a network going because the equipment costs much less. Instead, the cost is spread more into the ongoing operation—paying for fuel, pilots, and crews to keep the system going. The upfront cost advantage is especially important to smaller service providers who don't have billions sitting in the bank earmarked for infrastructure expansion.

The HAPS also have a major advantage in the time it takes to get a network operational. While traditional terrestrial systems have slow buildout due to the need for hundreds of tower sites, HAPS can be launched in a fraction of the time. Even the time necessary to get a satellite aloft for service is more than most service providers can bear. Proponents of HAPS think that the time-to-market advantage they hold is extremely attractive to network operators rushing to expand their coverage. It is foreseeable that operators could even put a HAPS in place temporarily while they are getting a terrestrial system installed or satellites into orbit.

Another advantage of HAPS is that the radio hardware can be changed easily to meet the service needs of consumers. While not realistic, the president of a mobile service provider could place a call to the HAPS operator and within a few hours change the entire operation from, say, mobile service with GSM to CDMA. It would take months and billions of dollars to do this with a terrestrial system. Hardware upgrades and new service features are as simple as changing the payload of the next flight.

The upgradability benefit is important for service providers when it comes time to upgrade service. For instance, when 3G-type phones start hitting the market with such advanced features as full-motion video, the operator could easily add the new service options to his or her next scheduled flight. If the network operator is signing up too many customers, the operator can quickly add more capacity to the system by adding more platforms or just more radios to the existing payload.

The last advantage listed is generalized as better reception. While HAPS will not give customers better reception in all cases, they will provide better coverage overall due to the location of the radio platforms. This is mostly an advantage over terrestrial cellular systems because users must be within range of a tower. Hills, valleys, and even large buildings can make coverage difficult for tower systems. Since HAPS are always overhead, the effects of terrain and other disrupting objects are negated. As long as they are not deep in a building or underground in a bunker, users should be able to connect to the system.

There are only a few companies currently pursuing deployment of HAPS. Washington, DC–based Sky Station wants to deploy lighter-than-air balloons at 70,000 feet that remain operational for 5 to 10 years. A private company, Angel Technologies, is looking to start a broadband data service in dense metropolitan areas through high-altitude aircraft flown in 8-hour shifts. One of the few public companies in this segment, Platforms Wireless, has a lower-altitude system that provides mobile services over an area comprising roughly 140 square miles.

MORE TO COME

Besides these areas, many other emerging technologies are coming into use in the wireless industry. For instance, a few courageous companies, such as Telespree Communications, want to sell disposable cellular phones that can be purchased at any grocery store or gas station. Once the time on the phone is used up, it is simply tossed in the garbage. Many people liken this type of product to disposable cameras, which oddly soared in popularity even though the concept initially seemed very strange to people.

Another private company, Commil, based in Israel, wants to make Bluetooth networks operate according to cellular principles. Bluetooth access points currently do not let users leave a small area, but Commil's solutions would allow a person to roam over a larger area while maintaining a session on a portable device.

If you keep an open mind and look beyond the popular wireless stocks, you're bound to find many more interesting stories. Keep in mind that many past attempts to apply some new ideas in the mainstream market have failed, so a great idea doesn't necessarily make a great investment. Make sure that there is a legitimate need in the market for advanced products. As we've stated before, superior technologies don't just sell themselves—they have to create value.

WIRELESS CONSUMER APPLICATIONS

Giving wireless devices the ability to connect to the Internet has led to an explosion of players in the wireless applications segment. Even though this segment is still in its infancy, companies are scrambling to be the first to offer a variety of services that may be useful to mobile users. While the currently available applications and services are somewhat limited, many companies expect the future of wireless Internet applications to be very lucrative.

Most of the companies that build wireless applications fall under the software and services category because they are developing and selling products that enable wireless hardware to do different things.

New wireless applications also are being discovered every day, so new companies keep popping up in this segment. For this reason, this segment tends to have a lot of small, young companies. There also tends to be more privately owned or pre-initial public offering (IPO) companies in this segment.

The products sold in this market can be broken down into various levels of software and services that go into hardware with wireless capabilities. Similar to how we use PCs, wireless devices soon will see many more capabilities added to them in the coming years simply by installing software. While the cellular phone you have today may be capable of only limited computing functions such as calendars and address books, future devices will be configurable to run software that maps routes, gathers specific information from the Internet, or plays any number of interactive games.

To enable this expandable functionality, a wireless phone or other device will have a few levels of software built in. It will have a piece of software that acts as the operating system, much like Windows or DOS has done on the PC. There also may be middleware applications that enable specific hardware functions on the device or work as a translator for applications written in various languages. Then on top of this there will be the user applications, the actual programs that do the stuff you want.

As a basic example of these levels, let's look at a Palm PDA. Many PDAs operate with the Palm OS as their operating system software. This piece of code works with the hardware in the PDA to perform low-level functions. On top of the Palm OS, a user can install thousands of different applications. If you want to download a mapping application, let's say, you need to make sure that the application is written for the version of Palm OS you're using.

We already discussed a large portion of the wireless applications space in Chapter 5. The consumer applications segment is also growing at a rapid rate and actually has a few less impediments to growth. First, companies that build applications for consumers do not have to deal with multiple network configurations and legacy issues that businesses have. The software written for wireless devices has to interface with the relatively few service provider networks and, of course, the Internet.

Since the wireless applications developers are targeting a consumer space that already uses mobile wireless devices, their available market is well defined. Many of the companies in this category are partnering with service providers to offer subscription-based services, content, or software to wireless subscribers on their networks. For instance, a network operator could provide you with cellular service as well as the phone and preprogrammed access channels to specific sources of information (content) on the Web. The service provider may make agreements with several content or applications companies to include in their service.

One company making headway in this area is go2 Systems. Go2 Systems offers mobile users location services through its wireless devices. The company has partnered with several major service providers in the United States, such as AT&T Wireless and Sprint PCS, to offer its directory services to all subscribers with Internet-enabled phones. The company's wireless applications center on the capability to find any number of retail outlets, restaurants, or landmarks. The company is essentially a mobile Yellow Pages with turn-by-turn direction capabilities. A subscriber simply enters a query for, say, the nearest Starbucks, and the go2 Systems software will send the subscriber the location relative to his or her position along with directions to get there.

If you're an investor who can tolerate high risk, this is probably one of the best categories for you. Many of the investment choices in this segment are young startups that have great ideas and a lot of technical talent. Since this segment of the wireless market is so young and still changing, it is hard to pinpoint exactly which products really will be embraced and which will flounder—hence the risk.

This market, especially the wireless Internet portion, is very similar to the wired Internet applications market in the mid-1990s. The Internet was so new and could be used for so many cool things that companies sprang up all over trying to capture a piece of what was thought to be a huge pie. As the market has developed, though, many companies have fallen off the radar screen or have been left behind, usually because their products didn't add real value. While it is nice to be able to check sports scores from your cellular phone, the real money to be made will be in applications that add high value or capture strong cultural trends.

Another prominent player in this space is Openwave Systems, the world's largest provider of mobile Internet software solutions. In fact, this company has a giant lead in this new market. Essentially, the company licenses various applications technologies to wireless and wireline carriers, as well as portals and broadband providers. For these customers, it is a quick and inexpensive way to generate revenue from their subscriber bases.

Openwave has a broad suite of software solutions, which is called the *Openwave Services OS*. The suite includes a mobile browser (which is embedded in more than 70 percent of the world's Internet-enabled phones), personalization services, e-mail, media content delivery, unified messaging, and so on.

The breadth of the services has been strong enough for Openwave to clinch deals with many top telecom companies, such as AT&T Wireless, Verizon Wireless, Sprint PCS, and Nextel.

Interestingly enough, even though 2001 was a particularly tough year for telecom, Openwave was able to produce impressive results. As of the end of June 2001, the company had a 218 percent increase in annual revenues to $465 million. The company also was cash flow–positive. The total number of active mobile subscribers surged from 4.2 million to over 21.6 million by the end of June.

In fact, the success of Openwave has much to do with the importance of alliances and mergers and acquisitions. You see, Openwave is the result of a merger between Phone.com and Software.com. Both companies had several years of talks with each other, discussing the trends in the wireless and wireline industries, strategic plans, and possible alliance ideas. In late 1999, the CEO of Phone.com, Alain Rossman, talked with the CEO of Software.com, John MacFarlane, about the possibility of a merger. MacFarlane, however, wanted to remain independent.

Then, in April 2000, Phone.com agreed to purchase Onebox.com, a top developer of unified messaging technologies. In the due-diligence process, Phone.com realized that Software.com was a major supplier of software to Onebox.com. Seeing this as another reason for a merger, Rossman again approached MacFarlane. Instead, however, MacFarlane wanted to pursue a strategic alliance. As these talks progressed, MacFarlane was becoming more receptive to the idea of a merger. However, if there was to be a deal, it would have to be a "merger of equals." In other words, in the merger, the shareholders of each company would own roughly 50 percent of the new merged entity.

Both parties studied the benefits of the merger:

- There was cross-selling of products from Phone.com and Software.com.

- There was little overlap between the two companies' technologies.
- The new company would have a solid management team. In fact, during the merger agreement, a board member of Phone.com, Donald Listwin, decided to quit a high-profile job at Cisco to become the CEO of Openwave. This was certainly a positive signal; he obviously saw tremendous opportunities with the new company.

By early August, both companies announced that they would merge. Today, the combined company, operating as Openwave Systems, so far hasn't missed a beat. With a strong track record to date, it should continue to be a major player in the future.

FOLLOWING THE EARLY ADOPTERS

When looking into the future of wireless applications and their acceptance in the consumer space, most people look to Japan. The nation tends to be one of the earliest adopters of new technologies and services, and one company there is forging ahead in the wireless Internet. NTT DoCoMo supports one of the most successful consumer wireless services in the world, called *i-Mode*. Within 2 years of the service launch, the company already had 20 million customers signed up. It continues to be a big hit, and many companies around the world are scrambling to duplicate its success.

What makes the i-Mode service popular is the Internet-based applications offered to customers. NTT DoCoMo set up a system for attracting and generously paying application developers to write Internet content that could be accessed from i-Mode phones. As a result, even though i-Mode requires application developers to write in a nonstandard language called *Compact HyperText Markup Language* (cHTML), applications soared in number. Part of this was due to the ease of writing in cHTML but a large incentive was the ability to make a good profit.

Since the initial success of i-Mode, NTT DoCoMo has launched its next level of service called *i-Appli.* These new phones took consumer applications to a new level, where the individual customer could install applications directly onto the phone. By placing a Java operating system on the phones, the company provides customers with the ability to download any number of applications written in the Java language. The software would then be resident in their phone and stay there until it was replaced with a new application.

Adding new capabilities such as this to wireless devices has continued to fuel the explosion in wireless applications. For investors looking at a company that builds end-user applications, it is important to determine whether the company has a good sense of what consumers really want and need.

SUMMARY

Emerging technologies are never boring, and those in the wireless space are no exception. Several product and service concepts receive accolades from some and chuckles from others. For the most part, many of these far-out concepts are years away from commercial viability. Once these emerging technologies reach commercial operation, they either become integrated into the mainstream market, migrate into a niche market, or simply die out in the face of competing methods.

It's a good idea for investors to keep in touch with significant events that happen in many of these emerging technologies. Even if many of the companies working in these areas are still private and offer no chance for investment today, they may offer an IPO in the near future. Some even have the real possibility of taking a leadership role in the industry someday. After all, the Ciscos and Intels of the world had to start somewhere too.

With respect to the consumer applications portion of the wireless market, investors will find that companies come and go very fast. It is not uncommon for a few students to get together and turn out a successful wireless application in a matter of weeks, spawning a new company. Indeed, many of the application developer programs run by device manufacturers encourage anyone with an idea to offer it up to mobile subscribers.

In time, though, large players such as Openwave Systems will form in the various segments of the applications market to dominate it. This offers investors an opportunity to get into a great stock early on. Watching the trends in early-adopter countries can give hints to how the consumer applications market will develop around the world, so it's a good idea to keep in tune with global trends.

For many investors, young companies in emerging markets can become very emotional investments. Too often investors are so excited about the prospects of a company's idea that they lose sight of rationality and transfer the same exuberance to evaluation of the stock. In this case, it is very common to see investors ride a stock into bankruptcy, still singing the praises of the technology all the way to zero. To minimize the excessive risk in this area, investors should avoid "falling in love" with a stock. Great technology has never saved a bad business.

At the very least, don't risk any sizable portion of your assets in this area. The chances for a positive return on any one investment are much less than in other areas of the wireless industry. What usually happens in this segment is that a few companies go on to provide tremendous returns on investment while the vast majority go bust. For this reason, it may be good to spread your investment between more than one company working in an emerging market. No matter how you approach it, keep in mind that when investing in emerging markets, you could lose a significant amount of your initial capital.

7

IPO Fever

An upstart wireless company plans to do an initial public offering (IPO). The company has a lot of potential, and it looks like the IPO will be hot. The company doesn't have much revenue, though. But, hey, aren't young companies supposed to be kind of raw, anyway? So you call your broker to get shares. She says that it might be difficult, if not impossible. Should you buy the stock after its IPO, or forget about it?

Imagine if you got shares in the IPO of Microsoft or Dell or Oracle. If you held on—even for 5 years—you would have made a bundle.

Perhaps one of the all-time IPO success stories for wireless companies is QUALCOMM. The company went public in December 1991 at $1.54 per share (adjusted for three splits). Unlike Dell or Microsoft, however, the QUALCOMM IPO was not a runaway success; rather, it merely plodded around.

The visionary founder of the company, Dr. Irwin Jacobs, had developed a new cellular standard called *Code Division Multiple Access* (CDMA). However, many other standards were competing with his. How would he stand out? He was convinced that his solution was the best and ultimately would prevail. He would take any opportunity to make his views known on the subject. Simply put, he would not give up until CDMA became massive.

It was not until March 25, 1999 that the stock went into hyperdrive. This is when QUALCOMM ended its dispute with Ericsson over patents concerning the CDMA technology, and investors started to take notice of the possibilities.

In 1999, QUALCOMM reached $3.9 billion in sales and $307 million in profits. The number of subscribers for CDMA doubled to 41 million. The stock price surged beyond $350 per share.

A $10,000 investment at the time of the IPO would have been worth about $260,000 by the time QUALCOMM hit its high. The company's founder, Irwin Jacobs, was a billionaire. And many employees at QUALCOMM were multimillionaires because of incentive stock option plans.

With such a stunning performance, it is no wonder that investors are trying to find the next QUALCOMM.

And yes, the IPO market is a great place to find a home run. However, as with QUALCOMM, the home run may take some time. Also, there's a good chance that the next QUALCOMM likely will be a dud. The IPO market is a high-risk arena. In fact, even QUAL-COMM had a steep fall in 2000 (Figure 7.1).

To put things in perspective, with the Nasdaq surge and the Internet explosion, the IPO market was red hot from 1995 to 1999. But

FIGURE 7.1

QUALCOMM, Inc.

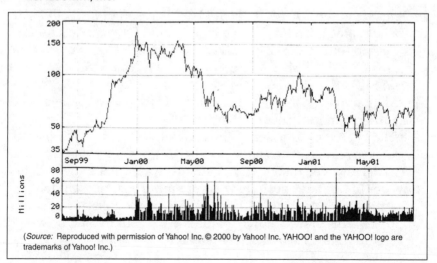

(*Source:* Reproduced with permission of Yahoo! Inc. © 2000 by Yahoo! Inc. YAHOO! and the YAHOO! logo are trademarks of Yahoo! Inc.)

all good things come to an end. By 2000, with the plunge in Nasdaq, the IPO market plunged even harder. About one-third of all IPOs fell at least 70 percent. Some of the IPOs—such as Pets.com and Jeremy's Microbatch Ice Creams—went bust. Table 7.1 provides a sample of some of the wireless IPOs of 2000.

TABLE 7.1

Past Performance of Some Wireless IPOs

Name	IPO Price	Current Price (7/31/01)
AT&T Wireless (AWE)	$29.50	$18.69
China Unicom (CHU)	$19.99	$17.32
GoAmerica (GOAM)	$16.00	$1.78
Nextel Partners (NXTP)	$20.00	$14.86
o2wireless (OTWO)	$12.00	$1.95
Novatel Wireless (NVTL)	$8.00	$1.00
OmniSky (OMNY)	$12.00	$1.18
Vyyo (VYYO)	$13.50	$1.24

This table makes you not want to invest in wireless IPOs, right? Well, this should not be the case. Actually, the best time to invest in the IPO market is when it is in a major slump. During these times, valuations are attractive, and Wall Street will focus on top-quality firms. Of course, this means that when times are good, there are likely to be many bad IPOs on the market. Thus you'll need to do your homework.

WHAT'S AN IPO?

Simply put, an IPO is when a private company issues stock to the public for the first time. The shares are listed on an exchange—in most cases either the New York Stock Exchange or the Nasdaq.

There are two main ways to take companies public:

■ *Underwritten.* This is when an investment bank backs a company's IPO with its own capital. Thus, on the day of the IPO, if there are not enough buyers, the company still gets its cash. In exchange for this, the investment bank wants hefty fees, as well as the opportunity to engage in extensive due diligence. In other words, the investment bank wants to make sure that the company is a good bet.

- *Self-underwritten (also known as direct IPOs).* This is when a company does not use an investment bank for its IPO. This is a huge red flag. In most of these cases, a company is *unable* to get an investment bank to believe in the prospects of the company.

There are other problems. First of all, there is no due diligence. Rather, you merely trust the company that everything is okay. Next, the company is likely to have little or no analyst coverage. There is no incentive for an investment bank to follow the stock because there is little likelihood of getting fees from the company. Without such coverage, it is extremely difficult for the company to get investors to buy the stock. After all, when a top analyst says that a company is a "strong buy," there is usually a pop in the stock price, and a new stream of investors come in.

Next, many self-underwritten companies raise small amounts of money—say, less than $10 million. In other words, there is not likely to be enough capital to pursue the potential business opportunities, and this will hinder the growth rate.

However, even if an investment bank is involved, this does not imply that the IPO will be a success. Sometimes an investment bank will not be committed to the IPO. Instead, the offering will be *best efforts.* This means that the investment bank will try to do its best to raise money. Of course, the investment bank is not taking on much risk. This should be another major red flag for investors.

Or a company may have a small investment bank. Even if the investment bank is committed to the offering, there could be problems. Small investment banks have a difficult time getting analyst coverage in a stock. Also, small investment banks have difficulties raising sufficient amounts of money for companies. It is a good idea to stick with the well-known investment banks, such as

Morgan Stanley
Goldman Sachs
CS First Boston
Merrill Lynch
Lehman Brothers
Robertson Stephens
Deutsche Banc Alex. Brown
Salomon Smith Barney

Chase H&Q

UBS Warburg

A good way to understand the IPO process is to take an example: David Oros has had a strong history in the wireless industry. He was president of the Wireless Data Group for Westinghouse Electric, where he managed large-scale programs for advanced airborne radar development. In fact, he holds the U.S. patent for the multifunction radar system.

In 1996 he founded his own company, called Aether Systems. He wanted to quickly establish Aether as a dominant player in the wireless world, focusing on providing data to handheld devices.

Within a year, Aether launched its first product, called AirBroker, a provider of real-time stock market information. The next product was MarketClip, which involved a partnership with Reuters. The product was available for Palm and Windows CE devices. Incidentally, Oros was even able to convince Reuters to invest in his company.

Oros was successful in signing top customers like Morgan Stanley, Charles Schwab, and Merrill Lynch. He even helped to found OmniSky, a wireless Internet service provider, which went public in 2000.

However, Aether's revenues were erratic. In 1996, the company generated revenues of $1.4 million (although this was mostly from consulting fees). A year later, revenues were $1.8 million, and then revenues dropped to $1.5 million in 1998. For the first half of 1999, revenues were $787,000. Moreover, losses were increasing significantly. They went from $417,000 in 1996 to $4.3 million for the first half of 1999. Since inception, the company racked up losses of $12.2 million.

Nevertheless, Oros had a way to bump up revenues: acquisitions. In September 1999, Aether purchased Mobeo, a provider of real-time financial information to employees and customers of financial institutions. With the acquisition, Aether was able to show $5.8 million in revenues for the first part of 1999. Aether gained about 3,300 new subscribers with the deal.

In 1999, Oros was able to hire Merrill Lynch as its investment banker. Merrill Lynch performed due diligence on Aether and determined that it was a good candidate for an IPO.

The IPO process was expensive—about $1.5 million. Expenses included (and these amounts are fairly typical)

Securities and Exchange Commission (SEC) fees: $31,171

National Association of Securities Dealers (NASD) filing fee: $8,000

Nasdaq national market listing fee: $95,000

Accounting fees and expenses: $400,000

State law filing fees (blue sky): $10,000

Legal fees: $500,000

Transfer agent and registrar fees: $25,000

Printing and engraving: $250,000

Officer and director liability insurance: $190,000

Miscellaneous fees: $30,829

The management of Aether, Merrill Lynch, and the law firm Wilmer, Cutler & Pickering helped to draw up the prospectus (also known as the *S-1 filing*). A prospectus is a long document—which can be several hundred pages—that contains all the necessary disclosure information for a company's potential investors. Contents include industry background, major contracts, management biographies, financial statements, and risk factors.

The prospectus was filed in August 1999. After this, Aether and the SEC went through several rounds of revisions of the prospectus.

A few weeks before the stock was issued to the public, key officers of Aether went on a road show. A *road show* is a presentation to key institutional investors. Most road shows hit the major financial locations, such as New York and Los Angeles, as well as certain countries. During these meetings, investors fill out indications of interest (IOIs). While these are not committed offers to buy the stock, they are nonetheless a good indicator of the demand for the IPO.

The night before the IPO, on October 20, 1999, the management of Aether and Merrill Lynch had a pricing meeting. Based on the IOIs and current market conditions, the offering price of the IPO was set at $16 per share.

In all, Aether sold 6 million shares, raising about $96 million. However, Aether only kept $89.3 million. Why? Well, Merrill Lynch got $6.67 million for its efforts (basically, investment bankers get paid a percentage of the amount raised, which is about 7 percent).

With the money Aether used about $12.3 million to repay the debt for the acquisition of Mobeo. There also was a $2.5 million payment for ownership in OmniSky. The remaining amount would be used for general corporate purposes.

When the IPO hit, the stock priced opened at $50 per share. By the end of trading day, the stock hit $48.44. By March 2000, the stock would be over $300 per share. According to *Forbes* magazine, Oros was number 260 on the magazine's ranking of the 400 richest Americans (at about $1.1 billion).

With the high valuation, Aether used its stock as currency to buy other companies. In February 2000, Aether purchased Riverbed Technologies, a developer of mobile data-exchange and device-management software. With the acquisition, Aether would be able to expand into other markets beyond financial applications, such as trucking. In the deal, Aether issued 4.5 million of its shares for all the shares of Riverbed. This amounted to about $1.2 billion. Also, 900,000 shares were set aside for an option plan for existing employees of Riverbed.

There was something else Aether did when its stock was high: It raised more capital. This was done in a secondary offering. The company sold 5.4 million shares of common stock, raising about $1.1 billion. The company also did a convertible debt offering. The notes paid 6 percent interest and were convertible into Aether stock. The notes had a maturity due date of 2005. With the notes, Aether raised about $311 million.

The money would allow Aether to make more acquisitions. Other uses of the proceeds included a $100 million investment in a strategic alliance with Reuters, $25 million to fund Aether's advertising campaign, $19 million to repay debt for the acquisition of LocusOne, and $10 million to invest in a new company known as Inciscent.

No doubt the offering was very smart. Basically, wireless stocks—and the stocks of most high-tech companies—had reached a high. Within a few months, it became exceedingly difficult for high-tech companies to raise money. Now, Aether had a nice war chest.

However, as high-tech stocks fell, so did the stock price of Aether. By early 2001, the company's stock hit a low of $8.87.

The company was experiencing a slowdown in its core business. In a conference call with Wall Street, Aether declared that its losses would be much greater than estimates. A number of analysts downgraded the stock. There also were concerns that the company was having difficulties integrating its 10 acquisitions (all done within 2 years). Analysts did agree, however, that Aether should be able to weather the storm because it still had about $900 million in cash in the bank.

ON THE GROUND FLOOR

Despite the fact Aether's stock price fell substantially, it would have been a very lucrative IPO—had you bought shares early. The problem is that it is extremely difficult to get shares at the IPO price.

For the most part, IPOs are deliberately underpriced. This is to compensate investors for the risk of taking a bet on a new company. However, not all investors get this juicy price. Rather, just like all good deals, the hot IPOs go to investors who bring lots of commissions to brokers. These investors usually are institutions or very wealthy people.

True, you can buy the shares in the aftermarket. Of course, the shares already will have zoomed. In fact, buying in the aftermarket is typically a high-risk activity. Rather, this should be left to savvy professional traders. But there are some strategies for individual investors to use, as the following subsections demonstrate.

LOCKUPS

Patience is a virtue with the IPO market. Over time, the hype tends to filter out of the valuation of IPO shares. There is also a *lockup period*. This is a clause in most IPO deals. Basically, it prevents employees of a company from selling shares within 6 months of the IPO. The main purpose is that if these shareholders sold during the time of the IPO, the stock price likely would tank.

Interestingly enough, by the time the lockup expires, the employees do, in fact, sell their shares. And the stock may tank. This is good for you if you want to get a better valuation on the stock.

Keep in mind that the lockup period is not foolproof. In some cases, the stock price may even go up! This may be the case if the company reported a strong quarter or a big deal.

ONLINE DISTRIBUTION

This has become a normal part of the IPO distribution process. Interestingly enough, it started with beer. How? A former IPO attorney, Andrew Klein, left the law industry to start a microbrewery called Spring Street. He had a difficult time raising capital, so he had a bright idea: Why not issue shares using the Internet as a distribution channel? It worked wonderfully, and he raised $1.6 million for his company in 1995.

As the IPO market heated up, Klein thought that there was more money to be made distributing IPOs than beer. As a result, he founded the online investment bank Wit Capital. Since its founding in 1996, Wit Capital has distributed shares in more than 100 IPOs.

To participate in a Wit Capital offering, you must fill out an eligibility profile online. As stated earlier, IPOs are very speculative. Thus a brokerage firm wants to get an indication that you understand the risks. Basically, if you are willing to potentially lose lots of money, you qualify.

Next, Wit Capital will send you the preliminary prospectus. This is a federal requirement. If your broker does not do this, then there is a violation. Stay away from this offering!

If the offering looks like a good investment, then you make a conditional offering (which means that you are interested in buying shares but not obligated to do so). This shows that you are interested in buying the stock—and you specify a quantity and a maximum price. In many cases, the stock price will change before the IPO hits the markets. Thus Wit Capital will notify you of this and see if you still want shares.

When the IPO is ready to be priced, Wit Capital randomly distributes the shares. This is not to imply that you have a good chance of getting shares. This actually can be difficult, especially when an IPO is red hot.

But there is something else that hinders your chances of getting IPOs: *flipping*. Flipping occurs when you buy and then quickly sell shares, gaining a nice short-term return. Wit Capital frowns on this because flipping makes it more difficult for Wit Capital to get allocations of shares. Wit Capital's recommendation is to keep the shares at least 30 days (this is fairly standard). Also, you must have enough cash in your account to purchase at least 50 shares.

Some of Wit Capital's wireless IPOs include GoAmerica, Research In Motion (RIM), and Allscripts.

DUTCH AUCTION SYSTEM

In 1968, William Hambrecht founded a boutique investment banking firm, Hambrecht & Quist. By setting up in San Francisco, he was able to become a leader in high-tech IPOs.

Of course, he had firsthand knowledge that the IPO process was unfair to individual investors. It also was unfair to companies raising money. After all, do the IPOs necessarily need to be under-valued? Doesn't this mean less capital for the firm and a competitive disadvantage?

With the emergence of the Internet, Hambrecht developed a new model—called *OpenIPO*—for the distribution of IPOs. Hambrecht went to economist William Vickrey, who had won the Nobel Prize. Vickrey used the Dutch auction model to distribute IPOs over the Internet.

With this new proprietary technology, Hambrecht founded a new investment bank, WR Hambrecht, in 1998 (apparently, H&Q did not want to pursue the system).

Here is how it works: Suppose that XYZ Wireless wants to go public. WR Hambrecht does the due diligence and prepares the prospectus. The IPO is then posted on the WR Hambrecht Web site.

The company wants to raise $20 million. Well, all investors have an opportunity to bid on the offering—whether you are a deep-pock-eted institution or a lowly individual investor. You place your bid by opening a brokerage account with WR Hambrecht. The OpenIPO computer system will process all the bids. It will determine the price at which the company will raise the $20 million. If this price is, say, $10 per share, then anyone who made a bid of $10 or higher will get their shares at $10 a piece.

So how has OpenIPO performed? Keep in mind that the system is still very new and that it is too early to handicap it.

There have been some problems, however. One is that it has been difficult for OpenIPO to attract major companies. For the most part, OpenIPO has participated in the IPOs of smaller companies, with raises of about $20 million to $40 million. In fact, many of the companies are in traditional industries, such as Ravenswood (a win-ery) and Peet's Coffee.

Why the difficulty in attracting major companies? Well, the fact is that the big firms, such as Goldman Sachs and Morgan Stanley, have tremendous resources and teams to do successful IPOs. There is also a factor of prestige for a company using a top firm. Somehow, it instills confidence in potential investors.

RISK FACTORS

A great benefit of the IPO process is that a prospectus must state a company's risk factors. Keep in mind that it is conservative corporate attorneys who write these things, so many are routine boilerplate. In some cases, the risk factors can be downright hysterical. Take a look at this risk factor from World Wide Wireless communications (the company provides high-speed broadband wireless Internet service):

> We anticipate that a substantial percentage of our revenues will be derived from operations outside of the United States. Our reliance on international operations to obtain consents of local regulatory authorities, some of which may significantly delay or deny permitting us to operate in those jurisdictions, might inhibit our efforts in certain markets. For example, we will not be able to generate revenues from our operations in Argentina if and until such time as the governmental regulatory authority, the CNC, reinstates some or all our subsidiary's licenses. In early 2000, the government of Argentina announced that it was placing a freeze on all license transfer applications, which has effectively delayed consideration of our application. In September 2000, the government of Argentina revoked licenses for certain lower transmission frequencies, for all communication carriers, including those of the Company's subsidiary, Infotel Argentina, S.A. Although we have resubmitted the necessary paperwork to reinstate licenses in Argentina, it is unclear at this point when and if the licenses will be reissued. A denial of our most recent application or a significant delay in consideration of our application could either prevent us from conducting our planned operations in Argentina or materially adversely affect our ability to do so. Our prospective operations in other jurisdictions are also subject to receipt of government approval, which we cannot ensure that we will receive.

Hmmm. . . .

Risk factors definitely can provide crucial investment information. Here are some to focus on.

LITIGATION

In the high-stakes world of wireless, litigation is very common—especially with disputes over intellectual property. True, a good amount of the suits are without merit. However, they still can have a negative effect in terms of slowing down a competitor. Lawsuits not only are expensive, but they also divert management time away from the business.

Litigation is always a wild card. What might a jury award? Besides, juries may not necessarily understand the complexities of wireless technologies. A courtroom can become a lotto game for the parties in dispute.

However, this does not mean that you should refrain from investing in a company that is involved in litigation. This would be counterproductive because the industry is rife with these disputes. Rather, it is a good idea to look at what issues the suit covers. Does it go to the heart of the technology? As stated earlier in the case of QUALCOMM, the lawsuit from Ericsson had a significant effect on the stock price.

CUSTOMERS

A risk factor might indicate that a company has only a few customers that represent a significant amount of business. Thus, if one or two of these companies leaves or goes bust, the consequences can be devastating.

In addition, the nature of a company's business may lend itself to volatility in the customer base. Say that a company has a high-priced item. If the economy falters, such items usually are the first things to go.

A case in point is o2wireless. Stephen Johnston cofounded the company in 1991. At that time, the company was called American Communications Construction, which developed cell phone systems in Kentucky and West Virginia. By 1997, Johnston merged his company with several cell phone providers.

o2wireless evolved into a full-service outsourcing company for the telecom industry (with about 600 employees). Services ranged from business planning to design, deployment, and maintenance of telecom networks. The company had implemented more than 50,000 communications facilities in all 50 states and 35 countries.

By August 2000, the company went public at $12 per share. The stock went as high as $16.59 and settled at the end of the day at $13.38. In all, the company raised $73.2 million.

The company was not burning lots of money. In 1999, the company posted sales of $48.6 million and a loss of only $949,000. Sales were $24.5 million in 1998, and losses stood at $2.8 million.

However, looking at the risk factors section, there were some interesting tidbits:

> The wireless telecommunications industry has experienced a dramatic rate of growth both in the United States and internationally. If the rate of growth slows and carriers reduce their capital investments

in wireless infrastructure or fail to expand into new geographies, our business and results of operations would suffer. To date, the pace of network deployment has sometimes been slower than expected, due in part to difficulties experienced by holders of licenses in raising the necessary financing, and there can be no assurance that future bidders for licenses will not experience similar difficulties.

We generate a significant portion of our revenues from a limited number of customers, and we expect that this will continue for the foreseeable future. For example, for the year ended December 31, 1999, revenues from each of our three most significant customers, Nortel Networks, Sprint and Carolina PCS, accounted for more than 10 percent of our revenues, and collectively these customers accounted for approximately 36 percent of our revenues. Further, our contracts with customers are for limited terms, and our customers may discontinue use of our services upon short notice. If we lose any of our large customers, or if we are unable to add new large customers, our revenues will not increase as expected.

Some of our customers and potential customers have limited operating histories and financial resources. These customers often must obtain significant amounts of financing to fund their operations and deploy their networks. We frequently work with such companies prior to their receipt of financing. If these customers fail to receive adequate financing and therefore fail to make timely payments to us, we could lose expected revenues and our results of operations would be harmed.

At first, these risk factors seem to be inconsequential. For the fourth quarter of 1999, o2wireless had a solid performance. Revenues increased 97 percent to $45.7 million. There was even a profit of $1.9 million. For 1999, revenues were up a stunning 189 percent to $140.3 million.

Johnston said to shareholders: "o2wireless is well positioned to continue to capitalize on the significant growth within the global telecommunications sector, particularly the trend toward outsourcing. Outsourcing network design and deployment allows our customers to focus on their core competencies. Thus, o2wireless provides the expertise carriers and customers need to implement new products, services and technologies that will drive market share and reduce churn." The stock reached a high of $24.

However, the telecom market deteriorated quickly. By March 2001, o2wireless was singing a different tune. The company warned that it was lowering its revenue and earnings-per-share expectations for the first quarter of 2001. According to Johnston, "In line with many other telecommunication providers, we expect overall market growth to slow in 2001 as a result of longer spending lead times due to this challenging economic environment."

In May 2001, the company reported its earnings. Revenues were $30.4 million, which constituted a 16 percent increase from the same period a year earlier and a 33 percent decrease from the fourth quarter. The company showed a loss of $6.6 million. The company's top customers—Nortel, Sprint, and Carolina PCS—were experiencing major troubles. This meant the delay of large up-front commitments to fund expansion of wireless networks. The stock price of o2wireless sank to $2.50 per share.

By looking at the risk factors, you would have been better able to anticipate the company's problems when the economy began to falter in early 2001. For example, from January to March, the stock had a range of $10 to $13 per share. By selling then, you would have avoided the big drop in the stock when it hit below $2 in April.

SHIFTING BUSINESS MODEL

Beware of companies that have a pattern of changing their business model. Why didn't it work in the first place? Are any of the prior investments of any use?

Also, with a shift in business model, is the company entering a market that is competitive? In a way, the company will be transforming itself into a start-up, representing high risk to the investor.

CONFLICTS OF INTEREST

These must all be disclosed in the risk factors. However, in order to remain competitive, it is often necessary for companies to collaborate—even with competitors. Thus, while traditionally conflicts of interest were considered a danger sign, this is less likely to be so now.

In fact, one of the nation's top venture capitalists, John Doerr (who funded such companies as Netscape, Handspring, and Intuit), believes the following: "No conflict, no interest." He strives to find opportunities to partner so as to accelerate the growth rate of his investments.

In the Aether IPO, there was a risk factor outlining the conflicts that Oros had, as well as other officers and board members. After all, Oros is on the board of OmniSky, a company that is in some senses competitive with Aether. However, Aether has a strict procedure that requires its officers and directors to recuse themselves from votes that pose direct conflicts.

TAKING ON THE GIANTS

The telecom carriers have never been known to be quick-footed or innovative. However, they have tremendous capital and distribution. If the carriers decided to enter a market, this can spell doom for upstart companies.

A classic example comes from the digital line subscriber (DSL) companies that went public in 1999. One of the highfliers was Covad.

The cofounders of the company responded to the opportunities opened up by the Telecommunications Act of 1996 and launched its service in late 1997 (called *TeleSpeed*). It was not difficult to obtain venture funding. By March 1998, Covad raised a stunning $152 million. However, it was greatly needed because the company offered its service in a variety of metropolitan areas. By 1999, the company entered strategic relationships with AT&T, NEXTLINK, Qwest Communications, and Concentric (all made equity investments).

In January 1999, Covad went public, raising $161.4 million. Priced at $18, the stock surged to $30.25 on its first day of trading.

However, in the company's prospectus, there was this ominous risk factor:

> All of the largest ILECs present in the Company's target markets are conducting technical and/or market trials or have entered into commercial deployment of DSL-based services. The Company recognizes that each ILEC has the potential to quickly overcome many of the issues that the Company believes have slowed wide deployment of DSL services by ILECs in the past. The ILECs currently represent and will in the future increasingly represent strong competition in all of the Company's target service areas. The ILECs have an established brand name and reputation for high quality in their service areas, possess sufficient capital to deploy DSL equipment rapidly, have their own copper lines and can bundle digital data services with their existing analog voice services to achieve economies of scale in serving customers. Certain of the ILECs have aggressively priced their consumer asymmetric digital subscriber line ("ADSL") services as low as $30 to $40 per month, placing pricing pressure on the

Company's TeleSpeed services. The ILECs are in a position to offer service from COs where the Company is unable to secure collocation space and offer service because of asserted or actual space restrictions, which provides the ILECs with a potential competitive advantage compared with the Company. Accordingly, the Company may be unable to compete successfully against the ILECs, and any failure to do so would materially and adversely affect the Company's business, prospects, operating results and financial condition.

The ILECs? This stands for *incumbent local exchange carriers*. These are the megacarriers that own the access lines to consumers and business (the *last mile* of the telecom network). As the risk factor states, the ILECs certainly have many advantages. And they used the advantages, bankrupting many of the DSL upstarts in the process. Essentially, the ILECs had the cash flow to reduce the prices enough to kill competition. Also, the costs of installing DSL remained high. After all, there was still the requirement of having a technician come on site.

By the first part of 2001, Covad was losing huge sums of money. In fact, the company was unable to file its annual report on time, and the stock was in jeopardy of being delisted.

ANY PROFITS?

In the early stages of a company's history—especially in the wireless industry—there is a grace period in which there are expected to be losses. But how long should this be? There are no steadfast rules. However, a good rule of thumb is 5 years. If a company is not in the black by then, there is a good chance that the company never will be profitable.

For example, Stephen Maloney cofounded i3 Mobile in 1991 from a basement office (the original name was Intelligent Information). The first product was Quote Alert Service, a wireless device for stock information. Until 1996, the company distributed its products through paging carriers. Then i3 Mobile began selling its products and services through wireless network operators (the first deal was with Omnipoint). Other deals included PrimeCo PCS, Bell Mobility, US Cellular, SBC Communications, Pacific Bell, and AT&T.

As a result, the user base for i3 Mobile started to accelerate. Table 7.2 shows the results.

TABLE 7.2

Number of i3 Mobile Users

1997	29,000
1998	107,000
1999	450,000

Despite this growth, the company had not generated any profits since 1991. And the prospectus stated that the losses would continue "for the foreseeable future."

Net losses were $10.2 million in 1999 and $2.8 million in 1998. The accumulated deficit was $45 million.

However, this was not a concern for investors. In April 2000, the company raised $81.6 million from its IPO. The offering price was $16, and the stock ended its first day of trading at $25.

Now the stock is trading at $2.50. In April 2001, the company reported its first-quarter results. Net revenues were only $1.3 million, which was up from $900,000 the same period a year earlier. Losses were $4.7 million, which was up from $3.6 million a year earlier.

However, the company had the advantage of doing a recent IPO, so it still had $80 million in the bank and could weather the storm for some time. The chief executive officer (CEO) then announced that once again the company would change direction: "The focus of i3 Mobile is changing from being an enabler of wireless data to a developer and marketer of premium mobile products and consumer subscription services. We see strong interest from wireless network operators for a suite of premium wireless data products and services that will provide significant incremental revenues."

The big question is: Will the company ever make money? So far, things do not look great. Yet again, investors will have to wait and see.

The case of i3 Mobile points out that a company needs more than just cutting-edge technology. Rather, a company needs to eventually prove to Wall Street that there is, in fact, a market for its products.

OTHER KEY SECTIONS OF THE PROSPECTUS

Of course, there are more than risk factors in the prospectus. In fact, the prospectus offers a wealth of information. At first, it is intimidating reading. After some time, however, you will be able to spot the key areas. Here are some suggestions for what to look for.

SELLING STOCKHOLDERS

Major investors, directors, and officers must disclose if they are selling stock in their IPO. It is not necessarily bad if, say, the top executives sell some stock. They should be allowed to get some liquidity for their time and effort. Taking a company public is a great achievement and should be awarded.

However, as with anything, moderation is essential. Does it look like the officers are bailing out? Be careful if they are selling 20 percent or more of their holdings.

USE OF PROCEEDS

In many cases, this is quite vague. It will say that, basically, the company will use the IPO funds for whatever uses management deems important.

However, sometimes a company will use the money to pay off debt. True, this reduces the outstanding debt, but there is also less money for the company to devote to operations, research, and new products.

Also, if the transaction is a spin-off (described below), the parent company may take a substantial amount of the cash from the offering. This could be debilitating for the spin-off.

MANAGEMENT COMPENSATION

It may look like management is taking large salaries. The fact is, however, that it is difficult to find qualified managers. Therefore, look at the biographies of management. What has been their track record? Have they taken companies public before? Do they have a successful track record in wireless? Have they been part of fast-growing organizations? If so, then they should get large salaries. Of course, the compensation should not be out of whack with that of similar companies as well.

Moreover, make sure that management is part of an employee stock option plan. If the company's stock soars, so will their compensation. It's a win-win. In fact, it would be a danger sign if a company does not have an option plan. What is the incentive to improve the stock price? Instead, members of management may be more concerned about increasing their salaries.

BOARD OF DIRECTORS

This is a group that meets typically once a month to oversee the strategic direction of the company. Actually, the board has a fiduciary responsibility on behalf of the shareholders to make sure that the company is headed in the right direction. A board is also instrumental in providing advice, as well as contacts for potential customers or partners.

Here are the outside board members of Handspring (before the company went public):

- Dr. Kim Clark, dean of the faculty and George F. Baker professor of administration at Harvard Business School. He researches on modularity in design and the integration of technology.
- John Doerr, general partner of Kleiner Perkins Caufield and Byers. He serves on the boards of such companies as Amazon.com, Martha Stewart Living Omnimedia, and Sun Microsystems.
- Bruce Dunlevie, managing member of Benchmark Capital, a venture capital firm. He also serves on the boards of Wink Communications and Rambus.
- Mitchell Kertzman, CEO of Liberate, an interactive TV software company. He also has held high-level executive positions at Sybase and Powersoft.

GOING CONCERN

This sounds like a harmless phrase, right? Far from it. If you see this, you definitely should be very concerned.

A "going concern" statement is provided by the company's auditors and essentially indicates that the company is likely to go bust unless there is an IPO. Your investment dollars are being used to bail out the company. Stay away!

IPO STRATEGIES

The IPO market is no doubt quite unique. For example, an under-writer is allowed essentially to manipulate the stock for a few months after an offering. This would be illegal otherwise, but regulators understand that a newly minted IPO certainly needs support. If not, the stock could go to pennies.

Here are some tips and strategies for dealing with the unique aspects of the IPO market.

BEWARE OF MARKET ORDERS

Simply put, do not put in a market order on the day of an IPO. You are playing a dangerous game. On the day of an IPO, the stock price can be extremely volatile.

A classic case is the Palm IPO. In March 2000, the company priced its IPO at $38 per share, raising about $874 million. Suppose that you thought to yourself—"I'll buy 100 shares at the market."

When Palm opened, the stock hit $150. If the market order hit at that price, the purchase amount would be $15,000, not $3,800. Then, the stock began to fall. By the end of the day, it was trading at $95.06. In other words, you could have lost 36 percent in a matter of hours.

Instead, it is better to set limit orders, in which you can establish the maximum price you will pay for the stock.

TAKING THE BAD DEALS

A broker may say that in order to get the hot IPOs, you'll need to take some of the bad ones. If you hear this, get another broker. The problem? Actually, there are a couple of problems. First of all, why do you want bad deals? Second, the practice is illegal. A broker cannot tie one deal to another. Third, you probably will not even get the good deals anyway (there probably are none).

QUIET PERIOD

An underwriter cannot publish a research report within 25 days following an IPO. Of course, after this time limit, the firm's under-writers—those which have research departments—will have research reports ready to be distributed to investors. Why the need for the silence? Basically, regulators do not want there to be overhyping of an IPO. The quiet period allows people to make their own investment decisions.

No doubt the underwriters' research reports typically will be positive—with many "strong buy" recommendations. In fact, some investors will play the quiet period, that is, by buying shares in the IPO a few days before the positive reports come out.

Although this is not foolproof, there tends to be a pop before the expiration of the quiet period. For example, Microtune (Nasdaq: TUNE) went public in August 2000. On the first day of trading, the stock surged 136.8 percent. The company develops radio frequency (RF) tuners that are used for cable modems, set-top boxes, and automotive entertainment systems.

When the quiet period expired, Chase H&Q and SG Cowen placed "strong buy" recommendations on Microtune. The stock increased by about 10.9 percent. A day later, Goldman Sachs and Bear Stearns produced positive research reports, and the stock increased by a nice 33.3 percent.

PUMP AND DUMP

While the movie *Wall Street* was about greed from insider trading, the year 2000 movie *Boiler Room* was about the greed of IPOs. In *Boiler Room*, young brokers would peddle shell companies to gullible investors who wanted to make quick money.

In the real world, there are "boiler room" brokerage firms (they are also called "chop shops" or "bucket shops"). They deal in so-called microcap stocks—those with market capitalizations below $100 million. The brokers use high-pressure cold calls to get investors excited in investing in hot areas. Of course, because of the nature of wireless, the industry is susceptible to boiler rooms.

These firms will then do a pump-and-dump scheme. That is, the brokers will get shares in shell companies at very cheap prices and then hype the offerings. The stock prices will soar as retail investors spend more and more on the stock. Eventually, the stock price collapses. In the end, the brokers will have sold the stock at higher prices and also generated hefty commissions.

Interestingly enough, boiler rooms are often named after well-known underwriters so as to confuse investors. For example, in *Boiler*

Room, the broker is called J. T. Marlin. Kind of sounds like J. P. Morgan.

The SEC has been trying to crack down on boiler rooms. Keep in mind, though, that the SEC is also understaffed and boiler rooms can be extremely crafty. Thus the rule for investors is: Buyer beware! Here are some tips:

- *Check out the firm.* Call the NASD to see if there is a history of the firm.
- *What is the offering price of the stock?* If it is $5 or $6 per share, this should be a warning sign. If a stock is priced below $5, then the company must abide by penny stock rules, which are rigorous.
- *Does the broker say that the investment is "guaranteed" or use inflammatory language such as "This will be a home run"?* Such statements are prohibited in the securities industry.
- *Remember that a stockbroker is mostly a salesperson.* True, he or she must take an exam—called the Series 7—but it is fairly general. A broker gets paid by generating commissions, not by being a smart researcher. Thus, if you hear a broker talk about wireless technologies, take it with a big grain of salt. He or she is likely pulling the information from a research report. Simply put, a broker does not have the time to do independent research.
- *Seminars are another popular way to get clients.* The presenters will have slick visuals and talk about the big opportunities. But again, the firm is out to make commissions. The presenters are not providing neutral, third-party information.
- *Wireless is a worldwide phenomenon.* This makes the industry prone to frauds that involve offshore deals. If you get a pitch about a foreign wireless deal that provides a big upside as well as great tax advantages, be wary.

SLICE 'EM AND DICE 'EM

As companies get bigger and bigger, it gets much harder to maintain high growth rates. Sure, some companies will enter new markets. Yet this may have minimal impact because the company will already have substantial revenues.

Another approach is a *spin-off*. In this transaction, a company will issue stock in a division to shareholders. Hopefully, this will unlock shareholder value in the division that is being swamped by the slower-growth businesses of the parent. By spinning off a faster-growing division, that division should garner a higher price-earnings (P-E) ratio. For the most part, Wall Street likes pure plays. It makes it easier to analyze the investment decision.

Be careful, though. In some cases, a spin-off is intended to get rid of a badly performing division. Perhaps the parent company does not have the necessary expertise or capital to make the division run right. By making it a separate company, the parent can wash its hands of everything.

This does not mean that this type of spin-off is a bad investment. In fact, it could mean an opportunity to invest in a turnaround situation, which can be quite lucrative.

Or the reason for the spin-off may be the result of a regulatory requirement. For example, in the early 1980s, the federal government won its antitrust case against AT&T. Consequently, AT&T had to spin off a variety of divisions, known as the Baby Bells.

Actually, spin-offs are quite common in the wireless industry, which involves megacompanies with far-flung operations. Let's take a look at some of the other reasons a parent company may do a spin-off:

- *Taxes.* If structured properly, a spin-off can be a tax-free transaction for both the parent and the shareholders who receive equity in the spin-off. In other words, this can be more beneficial then selling off the company (which is likely to trigger a capital gains tax). To get the tax advantages, however, the parent must spin off at least 80 percent of the division, and the division must have been in existence for at least 5 years. If the parent is denied the tax-free status, then the shareholders will be taxed as if they received a dividend.

- *Analyst coverage.* Overall, there should be more coverage for spin-offs in general. For example, even though AT&T traditionally has had a large number of analysts, the coverage expanded greatly when Lucent was spun off. Before the spin-off, the Lucent division was only one part of a massive company. As a separate entity, however, it made more sense for an analyst to cover Lucent.

- *Management incentives.* Taking the preceding example, suppose that you work at the Lucent division and it is performing extremely well. However, your compensation is
  tied to the stock price of AT&T, which as a whole is performing subpar. Well, in this case, you will not be getting
  sufficient rewards for your hard work. With Lucent spun
  off as a separate company, however, the compensation can
  be tied much more clearly to your performance.
- *Acquisitions.* The spin-off often will raise money in the
  transaction. Also, with the new currency from the public
  offering, the spin-off can use its cash and stock to purchase
  other companies.
- *Strategic flexibility.* A division of a massive company often is
  presented with this problem. For example, while Lucent was
  a division of AT&T, the company had difficulty signing deals
  with global telecom companies. The reason was that it did
  not, in effect, want to help out a competitor, AT&T. However,
  as the spin-off, Lucent could now close these deals.
- *PR event.* A spin-off likely will get some good press. It's
  kind of like an IPO, in which investors—hopefully—will
  get excited and send the share price northward.

In addition, there are different types of spin-off structures:

- *Traditional spin-off.* The parent company spins off the division to existing shareholders on a pro rata basis. No money
  is raised, and the spin-off is a completely separate entity.
- *Equity carve-out.* A certain amount—usually 20 percent—of
  the division is sold to the public in an IPO. After about 6
  months (in most cases), the rest of the shares will be distributed on a pro rata basis to shareholders of the parent.

GOOD INVESTMENTS

Several studies point out that spin-offs can be profitable for shareholders. A study from Penn State—which covers 25 years of spin-off
activity as of 1988—shows that spin-offs outperform the Standard &
Poor's (S&P) 500 by about 10 percent each year. What's more, the
parent companies did well, too, garnering returns of about 6 percent above the S&P 500.

A study from McKinsey—which looked at 300 spin-offs from 1988 to 1998—shows that the 2-year return was an average 27 percent, which compares with 17 percent for the S&P 500.

Remember that these are averages for investing in spin-offs. This does not mean that you should rush out and invest in any spin-off that comes your way. In fact, there are certain things to keep in mind:

- *Shareholder base.* The shareholders of the parent have invested in the company obviously for the business of the parent. For example, suppose investors own stock in a conglomerate telecom company because it provides consistent growth and has a nice dividend. Then the telecom company decides to spin off its upstart, money-losing, no-dividend division. What might the shareholders of the parent do when they receive their shares? Well, in many cases they dump them. In fact, it is common for the value of the spin-off division to fall during the time of the distribution of shares. This can be an opportunity for investors to get a good valuation—that is, by waiting a bit.
- *Index fund phenomenon.* Index funds have strict policies. Simply put, they must mimic the performance of an index. However, if they receive shares in a spin-off that is not part of the index, then the fund managers have no choice but to sell these shares—whether or not they think it is a good company.
- *Information inefficiency.* Initially, the analyst coverage will be small—but it will grow. It will take some time for the analyst to gain an understanding of the spin-off. Actually, it will be difficult to estimate the earnings. So expect volatility.

TRACKING STOCKS: ON THE RIGHT TRACK FOR INVESTORS?

A *tracking stock* is common stock—which trades on its own—that tracks the financial performance of a specific division of a company. If the division does well, so will the tracking stock. This is the case even if the parent company does not perform well.

Tracking stocks can be good deals—that is, for the company issuing them. As for investors, you should avoid these contraptions.

Perhaps the main reason is that even though you are using hard-earned dollars to buy the shares, you have absolutely no ownership in the company. That's right. None.

It's actually kind of hard to believe, but it's true. Essentially, as the name implies, a tracking stock merely tracks the performance of a certain part of a bigger company.

Interestingly enough, this means that there is no takeover value to tracking stocks. After all, how can you take over the company if the current shares do not represent ownership in the company? It's impossible.

However, there are more problems. Here's a laundry list.

WHO'S LOOKING OUT FOR YOU?

The board of directors may not have your interests in mind. You see, the tracking stock does not have its own board of directors; rather, the board is from the parent company. Therefore, is this board representing the parent or the tracking stock? For example, will the board vote to spend money on a project for the parent or instead fund a project for the tracking stock?

A classic example comes from the first tracking stock, EDS. EDS is a large computer consulting firm that was part of General Motors. Shareholders of EDS felt that their interests were not being served and sued GM. However, the Delaware Supreme Court ruled against the shareholders. The court believed that the ultimate duty of management was to the parent company, not the tracking stock.

IS THE MARKET AT CRAZY VALUATIONS?

If anything, the popularity of tracking stocks is likely to indicate a market top. It should be no surprise that tracking stocks emerged in the late 1990s as traditional bricks-and-mortar companies wanted to highlight their upstart online assets.

This is not to imply that it is impossible to make money in tracking. Rather, if the market is red hot, just about anything can go up. Of course, you want to make sure that you get out of the stocks when things begin to turn—which is certainly no easy task.

An example of a high-flier tracking stock is the wireless division of Sprint, which is called Sprint PCS. In November 1998, Sprint PCS issued shares to the public, raising a hefty $842 million. By March 2000, a $10,000 investment would be worth about $70,000. With the slowdown in telecom, however, Sprint PCS also suffered. However, a $10,000 investment would still be worth about $25,000 today.

SUMMARY

At this stage of the wireless industry, many companies are using tracking shares. There are also many huge corporations around the world spinning off their wireless divisions. Many analysts also agree that wireless companies will make up a substantial portion of the next IPO wave.

For instance, the recent trend is for giant telecom companies to launch IPOs for their wireless divisions. This gets the parent company much-needed cash to handle debt and other expenses while freeing up the faster-growing wireless business.

While the large IPOs tend to be tamer in terms of volatility, smaller companies also will be using strong markets to their advantage.

Investors should approach this entire area with caution. For sure, the allure of hot wireless companies will cause quite a stir in the market for years to come. Don't be entranced by the siren's song of guaranteed wealth—research companies thoroughly, and understand the risks.

In a nutshell, follow these rules:

- If you're looking at a public stock, look at its history and how it is capitalized. Is it a tracking stock? A recent spin-off? Make sure you understand the ramifications of each scenario.

- If you're looking at an upcoming IPO, be very careful. In general, it's best to stay away from IPOs completely for the first few months of their public life, especially for novice investors. Unless you're willing to tolerate the risk of a significant loss, it's better to wait until the quiet period expires and things settle a bit.

- Read through company filings for important information. It may be good to compare the reports with past successful or destitute companies for reference. Remember that all companies have risks going forward.

- Rather than just crunching numbers on a wireless company, look at the story. Check out the background of its management as well as partner companies and even customers. A company with great numbers but shoddy management and a poor customer list should raise some flags.

ONLINE RESOURCES

Keeping track of lockup periods, risk factors, quiet periods, and financials definitely can be time-consuming. However, there are several good Web sites that help out:

- *IPOPros.com.* This is part of theStreet.com. A noted IPO analyst, Ben Holmes, writes great commentary on the site. On the site there are lists for upcoming quiet period and lockup period expirations (as well as some analysis of each deal). One neat feature is "IPO eyeballs." This shows the top 10 most looked-up deals in the IPOPros.com database. This can be a great indicator of investor sentiment. The site will make recommendations on stocks. One section is entitled "Buy and Hold," in which IPOPros.com tries to locate IPOs that are market leaders and represent good long-term investments. Unfortunately, with the downdraft in the IPO markets, the picks have not been great. In terms of wireless, IPOPros.com selected AdvantGo and Palm, both of which plunged substantially in value. Remember that IPO sites will provide you good fundamental information, but an IPO analyst is usually a generalist and likely does not have the necessary specialized knowledge in such areas as wireless.

- *IPO.com.* This is a very comprehensive site. You have daily commentary. You also can customize alerts based on the types of deals that interest you (say, wireless). You can even get these alerts through your cell phone, Palm, or RIM device. IPO.com has an extensive IPO database, in which you can search deals based on a myriad of criteria (industry, underwriter, size, and so on). In fact, the database goes beyond IPO data and also includes venture capital, American Depositary Receipts (ADRs), secondaries, and private placements.

8

Red Flags: When to Sell Your Wireless Stock

Only three months ago you bought an upstart wireless company for $5 per share. Now the stock is trading for $35 per share. By all accounts, the company seems to be on track still. All major brokerage firms have "strong buy" or "buy" recommendations on the stock. The last earnings report exceeded expectations by a big amount. Yet you are wondering if you should sell or hold on. Also, in a few days the company will be announcing its quarterly earnings report. What should you do?

The famed investor Warren Buffett is a strong believer in holding a stock for the long term. In fact, he says that he would prefer to hold a stock even until he dies.

Then again, Buffett does not invest in wireless stocks. And in the emerging wireless world, it could be deadly not to sell out a position when you have a profit.

Much of the decision to hold or sell a wireless stock depends on the individual investor and his or her own financial goals. For instance, if your investment time frame is only a few years before you intend to buy a house, you may be more inclined to sell a company once you've made a profit (or cut your losses short). However, if you are looking to find a long-term winner that eventually will dominate its market segment, you are going to have to weather some more bumps along the way as you hold through the ups and downs.

It would be a good idea for individuals, then, to assess their own personal situations before addressing other factors concerning sell decisions. Since the best time to sell a stock varies depending on personal risk tolerance, it doesn't make much sense to explore sell indicators without this context.

Of course, the best thing to do is to pick the very best companies so that you don't have to worry so much about selling them—just take your profit when you need the cash. In reality, though, all investors—even the best—have to determine when to sell a stock.

In this chapter we will look at some of the early danger signs that can spell disaster for a wireless stock. Often there are red flags that appear well before a downturn in the price of a stock.

JUNK BONDS

Despite the name, *junk bonds* are not evil. In fact, they were critical for the formation of various cutting-edge businesses in wireless. For example, McCaw Cellular was a heavy user of junk bonds. It was in 1986 that McCaw met the mastermind behind junk bonds, Mike Milken. In fact, during the past 15 years, Milken has raised a stunning $26 billion for such companies as MCI, Time Warner, Turner, News Corp, Viacom, and Metromedia. Milken clearly understood the high growth potential of the communications industry and knew how to structure deals for the companies to get the capital they needed to execute on their business plans.

With Milken, McCaw was able to raise about $2 billion from 1986 to 1989. It certainly was a major catalyst for growth. He was able to buy cellular licenses and companies. It was a high-risk strategy because the interest payments were substantial. In fact, it was not uncommon for McCaw to be on the verge of bankruptcy. No doubt, the stock price was quite volatile. McCaw's vision was correct, however: Wireless would become a huge business. In 1994, he sold his company to AT&T for $12.6 billion.

In essence, junk bonds are bonds that have a higher risk of default, that is, according to two major agencies that judge the riskiness of bonds: Standard & Poor's (S&P) and Moody's (Table 8.1).

TABLE 8.1

Bond Investment Rating Systems

Low Risk ◄————————————————————————————►									High Risk	
Moody's Rating System										
Investment grade:	Aaa	Aa1	Aa2	Aa3	A1	A2	A3	Baa1	Baa2	Baa3
Speculative grade:	Ba1	Ba2	Ba3	B1	B2	B3	Caa1	Caa2	Caa3	Ca	C1
S&P Rating System										
Investment grade:	AAA	AA+	AA	AA–	A+	A	A–	BBB+	BBB	BBB–
Speculative grade:	BB+	BB	BB–	B+	B	B–	CCC+	CCC	CCC–	CC	D

Any bond that is considered "speculative" is considered a junk bond. To compensate for the risk, junk bonds will carry a higher yield than risk-free U.S. Treasury bonds, although the gap between these two types of bonds varies. On average, the gap is 4 to 5 percent. However, when the economy suffers—such as during the early 1990s or the late 1990s—the gap can be more than 10 percent.

So how can junk bonds help you with your wireless investment? Actually, they can be a leading indicator. Here are two ways:

- *Danger.* If you own a wireless stock that has outstanding corporate bonds, make sure you monitor the price regularly. Many financial sites, such as Yahoo! (bonds.yahoo.com), allow you to do this. The price of a bond is expressed as a percentage of the face amount. The face amount is the price at which investors initially purchased the bond. If the bond is selling at 100, then it has maintained its price. If the bond is selling at 110, then it has increased 10 percent. If the bond is selling for 70, then it has fallen 30 percent in value. When following corporate bonds, be wary if they fall below 70— or more than 30 percent of face value. Such a decline could be an indication that bond investors are sensing that company problems are getting worse.

  Remember: If you own stock in a company, you are last in line for the liquidation of assets if there is a bankruptcy. The creditors, such as the corporate bondholders, will get paid off before the stockholders. During 2000–2001, such telecom companies as ICG and Teligent went bust. Shareholders lost everything. As for the bondholders, they got anywhere from 10 to 20 percent on the dollar.

■ *Hope.* Suppose that you are interested in buying a telecom company. You check the corporate bond prices, and they are at about $65 (which means the company is in the danger zone). During the next few months, however, the bonds have increased to $80. This is a sign that the company is on the mend and may stage a turnaround.

CONVERTIBLE FINANCING

The playwright George Bernard Shaw once said, "The lack of money is the root of all evil." During 2000–2001, this certainly has been true for the worldwide telecom industry. After about 6 years of seemingly unlimited access to capital, it finally ground to a halt.

Even such major companies as Nortel and Lucent were not immune. In fact, during 2001, Nortel posted a stunning loss that exceeded $19 billion.

In a way, though, Nortel is lucky. It has lots of assets and a long history of success. For Nortel, gaining additional financing is not really a huge problem. What about smaller companies? The story there is much different.

The financial structure that should raise big concerns to individual investors is the *private investment in public entities* (PIPE). Simply put, this is when wealthy individuals or institutions (known as *accredited investors*) agree to invest in an existing public company.

In fact, a number of traditional U.S. buyout firms jumped into the telecom PIPE game in the middle of 1999 just when things were beginning to reach a market top.

No doubt, these buyout firms were savvy investors. Forstmann Little was one of the first buyout firms (started in the 1970s) and backed such deals as Gulfstream, General Instrument, and Ziff-Davis Publishing. Kohlberg Kravis Roberts was behind the famous RJR Nabisco $30 billion buyout in 1988. Although this deal had problems (at one point the deal almost went bust), Kohlberg Kravis Roberts had many major successes, such as the buyouts of Beatrice, Safeway, and Duracell. As for Hicks, Muse, Tate & Furst, it saw great success with Dr Pepper and Seven Up.

Unfortunately, there is a big difference between high-flying telecom companies and cookie and soft drink companies. In all, buyout firms have invested about $10 billion in telecom PIPEs since 1999.

Table 8.2 presents a chart of some of the high-profile deals (Beware: It's ugly).

It's hard to believe, but none of the telecom PIPEs are above water. Most are in critical condition or dead.

In light of the disastrous results, the major buyout firms are likely to stay away from telecom PIPEs. However, this does not mean that PIPEs will go away. Rather, expect many more. This is especially the case when financial markets are tight—which is what happened during 2000–2001. With the fall in the Nasdaq, investors did not want to take a big bet. Yet there are many upstart companies that still need cash to finance their operations. Thus it becomes a question of either going bankrupt or taking money on very harsh terms. This is usually done in the form of PIPEs.

However, the major buyout firms will not do such deals with PIPEs that have harsh terms. They want to maintain a pristine reputation. They do not want to structure deals that ultimately are meant to destroy companies. But there are many smaller financial firms that will.

Although most hedge funds are legitimate operations, some specialize in PIPE financings. Basically, these firms are only looking for a quick buck. They have really no concern for the long-term prospects of a company. These PIPE firms have managers who are very convincing and make offers that look almost "too good to be true." Such deals often involve investments of $10 million to $50

TABLE 8.2

Big Deals Gone Bad

Company	Buyout Group	Amount Invested	Price of Investment	Current Price
ICG	Hicks, Muse, Tate	$700 million	$28.00	Bankrupt
Teligent	Hicks, Muse; Chase Partners	$500 million	$57.50	56 cents
Rhythms NetConnections	Hicks, Muse	$250 million	$37.50	10 cents
Winstar	First Boston	$900 million	$45.00	Bankrupt
XO Communications	Forstmann Little	$850 million	$31.63	$1.60
McLeodUSA	Forstmann Little	$1 billion	$12.17	$3.00
RCN Corp.	Hicks, Muse	$250 million	$39.00	$3.80

million, which can be enough to save a company. Moreover, PIPEs do not involve much paperwork (because there are no individual investors) and can take, say, a couple of weeks to close.

Let's take a look at the problems. PIPE investors do not get common stock; instead, they get preferred stock. The preferred shares will carry a dividend, perhaps 10 percent per year. And the preferred stock typically will be considered *participating* and *supercharged*.

Suppose that your company, ABC Wireless, gets a PIPE for $10 million, which gives the investors 30 percent of the company. The preferred shares are supercharged by a factor of 2 (the factor is negotiable, but this is a typical number for a PIPE deal).

Then, in a year, the company is sold off. The PIPE investor gets $1 million in dividends, $20 million for the repayment of the preferred stock ($10 million times the supercharge factor of 2), and 30 percent of the price of the buyout, or $30 million. A very nice payday indeed! Then again, the company did get the capital it needed to fund its business (when no one else had faith).

Unfortunately, in most PIPE deals, the reverse happens—that is, the stock price collapses, and the company goes to nothing. With an Excel spreadsheet, a crafty financier can easily figure out how to siphon money from a desperate company.

Interestingly enough, the financial structure is called a *death spiral*. Of course, a PIPE investor will not call it this. Rather, it will have a nicer-sounding name, such as a *convertible with a reset provision*. It is almost a "can't lose" for the PIPE investor.

The convertible preferred option gives the PIPE investor the right to exchange the preferred stock for common stock depending on the stock price. And if there is a reset provision, the PIPE investor actually gets more and more shares as the stock price declines. Thus the PIPE investor will short the stock (this means that the investor will make money as the stock declines). This puts selling pressure on the stock, which gives the PIPE investor the right to get more common shares. The PIPE investor then shorts the stock again and gets more shares. And on and on. The PIPE investor makes greater profits as the stock price plummets.

True, some deals will have "no short" provisions. But this means very little. It is not difficult to set up offshore hedge funds to get around the no-short-sale provision.

Now this is not to say that all PIPE deals are, well, pipe dreams. Some deals have, in fact, worked well for all investors. For such a deal to work, however, a company must have a solid business model. Also, look to see if the investor is strategic, that is, a company that can benefit from the other company's products, technology, or sales force. In other words, a strategic investor does not have the incentive of destroying the company. However, if you see that the investors are mostly financial players—such as hedge funds—then watch out.

When on the outside looking in at PIPE deals, an investor needs to be aware of the business/financial environment both within the company and in the general market. If the company is in a dire position and is bleeding cash, a PIPE deal may foretell the last gasp for air. Make sure that the cash coming from the deal serves a very specific business need and is not just there to keep the ship from sinking faster.

INSIDER SELLING

In Chapter 5 we learned the power of insider buying. On the other hand, insider selling is less conclusive and may or may not indicate that a company is in trouble. However, this does not mean that it should be ignored. Here are some factors to look at:

- *Cluster selling.* The more insiders who are selling the stock, the more convincing is the signal that there may be problems with the company. One good rule of thumb is that when there are three or more sellers, there may be trouble.
- *Industry selling.* If many wireless companies are experiencing insider selling, this indicates that the industry may be slowing down.
- *Selling at new lows.* This is definitely troubling. It looks as if insiders are bailing out at any price.
- *Percentage of holdings.* If executives are selling off large stakes—say, 50 percent or more of total holdings—this is a bearish signal.

As stated previously, insiders often sell shares for personal reasons—reasons that really don't have anything to do with the company's prospects. In general, though, an insider who has faith in the eventual growth of his or her company will be very reluctant to part with shares. Still, since stock is the primary compensation for many insiders, some selling is expected.

It's best for investors to balance selling activity with events in the company. For instance, you may notice several officers of the company selling shares within days of each other. This may alarm you at first and even lead you to sell the stock prematurely, but it may not be such a bad sign. If the officers are all selling only minor stakes (less than a few percent of their total holdings), then this is not such an unusual circumstance.

Such cluster selling may be coincident with a company event, such as the expiration of a provision in their stock option plan. Senior officers often are very limited in the times when they can sell stock. Many sell some shares at the few opportunities they have, regardless of the state of the company. Taking the time to review the details of insider sales is important in these cases.

Another benign sign is when insiders declare stock gifts. Obviously, most people would not give a stock that is going to tank as a gift—at least not to someone they care about. While it does open up the opportunity for the recipient to sell the shares, putting downward pressure on the price, this is usually not a concern. It is done most often for tax reasons and is reported simply because it has to be.

There are a few cases of insider selling that should be a warning sign, though. As stated earlier, selling at new lows is never really a positive sign. Even though it may be a desperate move by an insider who is strung out on debt, the fact that an insider would be leveraged like this should cause some concern.

The worst case, though, is when an insider sells a significant portion of his or her holdings. Especially if this is tied to selling during new low points of the stock—watch out. Most people will not sell a majority stake in a company unless they're ready to move on. This move may be to a better opportunity, or it may be because sitting on cash is safer. In these cases, an investor needs to know the reason behind major sales—especially if they are from senior management.

Sometimes, when a senior officer sells a majority of his or her stake, he or she will make a public statement as to why he or she is doing it. If the officer doesn't make such a statement, it is safer to assume that the reasons aren't good. For instance, a chief operating officer (COO) may sell out his or her stake in a company to go on and start his or her own company, where he or she wants to be chief executive officer (CEO). With the ceremonial blessing of the CEO, this departure may be under amicable circumstances and shouldn't worry Wall Street too much.

BUILDING A WIRELESS NETWORK

Building a nationwide wireless network is not only incredibly expensive but also time-consuming and a complex technical challenge. For the most part, it is the major service providers, such as AT&T and Sprint PCS, that build nationwide networks. On some occasions, however, upstart companies will try it as well. Unfortunately, for these companies, this could spell disaster.

A case in point is Metricom. Founded in 1985, the company has a long history. Originally, the company developed technologies that would read gas and electric meters. In the mid-1990s, though, the company dumped this business and set out to develop modems—called *Ricochet*—that would allow high-speed wireless Internet access to laptops.

To do this, Metricom needed to develop its own nationwide wireless network, which would cost a huge sum. The company decided to start with regional service in cities and raised money from WorldCom and Paul Allen, the cofounder of Microsoft. Even the company's regional plan was enormously expensive—in 2000 alone, Metricom spent $645 million on its network.

By 1996, the service was launched in three cities. Actually, a big problem was that Metricom targeted highly competitive cities, such as Seattle; Washington, DC; and San Francisco. After all, these cities had many alternatives to high-speed access, such as cable modems and digital subscriber lines (DSL). Perhaps a better strategy would have been to focus on smaller cities that did not have many alternatives.

Moreover, the Metricom service was pricey, at about $75 per month (the modems cost up to $300 each). Despite spending millions on marketing, public relations, and advertising, the company was able to obtain only 40,900 subscribers.

Metricom wanted to provide service in 46 cities, which would make it truly a nationwide system. By the middle of 2001, however, only 13 cities were covered due to an overly ambitious expansion plan. Soon the company was in a cash crunch and could not afford to expand the service to any new markets without additional capital. In late June 2001, the company had no choice but to declare bankruptcy. Metricom's stock chart tells the story best (Figure 8.1).

One lesson for investors is to understand the costs of building a network alone. Without the backing of a company that had a huge cash flow, Metricom could only bank on future subscribers to sustain

FIGURE 8.1

Metricom, Inc.

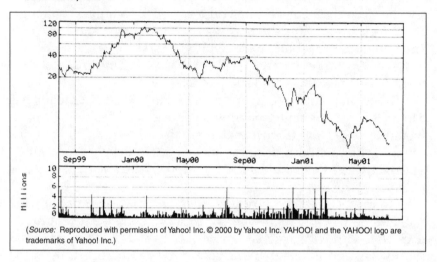

its business. Investors need to consider that the subscribers may not materialize for any number of reasons, possibly even future macroeconomic events. A plan to become a profitable regional company first may be a better step toward a national presence.

THE PRICE KNOWS

Ever notice a stock price that falls with no news? Then, a week later, the company announces that its sales have slowed down. True, it is illegal for insiders to trade on such information, but they do anyway.

As an individual investor, it's a good idea to monitor your stocks daily to see if there is any of this type of price behavior—especially if you're in volatile wireless stocks. If a stock falls 20 percent or more with no news, you probably should lighten up on the position or maybe even sell it completely. It could be an ominous sign.

True, you will take a 20 percent hit, but look at Table 8.3.

What does this mean? Suppose that you lost 20 percent on your investment. The stock would need to increase 25 percent for you to break even. If there is a 60 percent decline, you would need a 150 percent increase. And so on.

One smart strategy is to set up stop losses. For example, suppose that you buy AT&T Wireless for $20. The stock then climbs to

TABLE 8.3

Gains Required to Cancel a Loss

Percent Loss on Stock	Percent Return Required to Break Even
−20%	+25%
−30%	+43%
−60%	+150%
−80%	+400%

$30. You then set a stop loss at $25. Thus, if the stock hits $25 or below, your shares will be sold off. This provides downside protection. In fact, it's a good idea to adjust the stop loss periodically. Thus, if the stock climbs to $40, you can adjust the stop loss to $35.

PENNY STOCKS

Suppose that you come across an upstart wireless company whose stock price is 25 cents per share. You think to yourself: "It only needs to go up another 25 cents to double, right?" Yes, it does not seem like much of a leap for the stock to go up 25 cents. However, this is a trap for investors. In fact, with penny stocks, the chances are good that they will go to zero, not 50 cents.

You'll find most of the penny stocks on either the bulletin board or the pink sheets. Essentially, these are exchanges for stocks that cannot meet the minimum financial requirements (e.g., the assets of the company) to be listed on Nasdaq or the New York Stock Exchange (NYSE). Bulletin board and pink sheet exchanges have very few rules, and the volume tends to be very light (in some cases, days can go by before a stock has any volume).

Penny stocks are certainly prone to hype. You often will hear such words as *revolutionary*, *limitless*, *huge market*, and so on. However, if you look deeper at the company's financials, you probably will find some danger signs: The management team may be inexperienced (the team may, in fact, have no business experience); there may be excessive salaries or nepotism; there may be late filings with the Securities and Exchange Commission (SEC); the company may be involved in litigation, and so on.

In fact, you may find several of the warning signs we've discussed taking place within such a company. Often there are several rounds of financing where preferred stock is given to investors for cash to continue operations. More and more common shares are then issued to support these deals. Be wary of penny stocks that have several hundred million shares outstanding. At every turn, individual investors lose out because their stake is diluted.

Penny stocks are also subject to pump-and-dump schemes, which were explained in Chapter 7. There have been many stories in the recent past (many coinciding with the dot-com boom) where unscrupulous individuals manipulated penny stock shares. The best advice is this: Avoid penny stocks altogether, not just those in the wireless segment.

RESEARCH ANALYSTS

There are quite a few Wall Street firms that provide research coverage of the wireless industry. In fact, some of the firms, including the following, publish their extensive reports on the Web.

WRHAMBRECHT (WWW.WRHAMBRECHT.COM)

Peter Friedland is the analyst; he formerly covered the wireless industry for ING Barings since 1996. Interestingly enough, his degree is in English, but he nonetheless holds the Certified Financial Analyst (CFA) designation, which is a must-have for stock analysts (the CFA designation takes 3 years to attain).

One area that Friedland likes is the enterprise market. According to Friedland, "As IT [information technology] managers become more comfortable with enabling wireless connectivity to highly secure corporate networks, we believe businesses will implement solutions enabling employees to access corporate database applications on their handheld devices, such as sales inventory software." He also covers the consumer market. "We believe consumers will look to the wireless Internet to simplify their lives," says Friedland.

As of mid-2001, the stocks he covers include Aether, ALLTEL, AT&T Wireless, Comverse Technology, InfoSpace, Metricom, Nextel, Openwave, and Sprint PCS.

EPOCH (WWW.GS.COM)

The analyst that covers the wireless sector is Matthew Adams, CFA. Prior to joining Epoch, which has been acquired by Goldman Sachs,

Adams worked at Bear Stearns and Salomon Smith Barney. He has a bachelor's degree in economics from Cornell University.

As with Friedland, Adams sees much potential in the enterprise market. Says Adams, "The Internet's quick access to information and commerce has become central to our lives. Wireless data is the next step and we see it as a new medium, not just an extension of the Internet."

As of mid-2001, Adams covers Aether, Handspring, InfoSpace, Openwave, Palm, Research In Motion, and Vicinity. There is even coverage of up-and-coming private companies, such as Mobileum, ViaFone, and Wireless Knowledge.

There is no doubt that research available through these and other analysts can be incredibly useful. However, you should not rely on it completely. There are some things an investor needs to understand about how Wall Street research works (or doesn't work).

While Wall Street research can be illuminating, it also can be very wrong. Let's take an example: Winstar. It's hard to believe, but this company was once a ski apparel shop. When the telecom industry boomed in the late 1990s, however, the company had more ambitious ideas. It dumped the ski business and became a competitive local exchange carrier (CLEC) in 1996.

Winstar had no problems raising money. In fact, the company's money backers were top-notch, such as Microsoft, Lucent, Cisco, and Compaq. By March 2000, Winstar was trading at $65 per share, giving the company a hefty $10 billion market capitalization.

Despite the billions raised, it was not enough capital to deal with the high-tech recession in 2000. By the end of the year, the company had accounts payable of $457 million. Typically, the company paid its bills within 90 days. But this had surged to 370 days. Winstar was quickly running out of cash. There was about $316 left in the bank account.

Winstar's debt was at $5 billion, and the company would have to cough up $400 million in interest payments for 2001. The company's accounts receivables increased 70 percent to $230 million, indicating that customers were not paying their bills.

Yet these appeared to be nonissues for the analysts who covered Winstar. As of March 2001, Jack Grubman, an analyst with Salomon Smith Barney, had a $50 price target on the stock and thought the company's fundamentals were still sound. Mark Kaston, an analyst with CS First Boston, also was upbeat on Winstar. He had a $79 price target.

One of the few Winstar doubters was Mark Rose, who was the junk bond analyst with Goldman Sachs. He was very concerned about the debt, which was 4.2 times annualized revenues.

In early April, Winstar announced that it would delay the filing of its 10-K, which is the company's annual report to shareholders (this is typically a sure-fire sign of big trouble). A few weeks later, the company filed for bankruptcy, and all the while, analysts stuck to their "buy" and "hold" ratings.

Why did this happen? As with anything, there probably will never be a complete answer. Such scenarios are not uncommon. Actually, a big problem is how Wall Street is structured. Much of the profits for Wall Street come from investment banking activities, such as initial public offerings (IPOs), debt financings, secondaries (a secondary offering is a stock issue designed to raise money after an IPO has been completed), and mergers and acquisitions. The fees can be huge. For example, in a junk bond offering for Winstar, Salomon Smith Barney and CS First Boston earned about $50 million in fees.

The profits from the investment banking fees go to pay for the research department. This presents a potential conflict. If a research analyst is negative on an investment bank's client, the client may be inclined to, in some cases, terminate the firm's services or threaten to do so.

In fact, less than 1 percent of analysts' reports have "sell" ratings. Rather, if an analyst is negative on a stock, he or she will use a less offensive code word, such as "neutral," "market perform," or "hold."

Another problem is that analysts tend to be young and new to the industry. They may not necessarily have the experience to spot problems with companies. And analysts usually do not stay analysts for long. In fact, being an analyst can be a stepping-stone to move into investment banking or being a fund manager, where the compensation typically is higher.

Finally, analysts typically will be interviewed on finance networks such as CNBC and CNNfn. True, these are good channels—and their programs can be informative—but never buy a stock simply because an analyst says it is a good buy. The interviews are often short, and you probably will not get the whole story.

However, with the dot-com fallout of 2000–2001, Congress has conducted several hearings on the conflict issues regarding Wall Street analysts. Now many firms are requiring their analysts to indicate if they have any positions in the stocks they cover. There are also moves to have analysts clearly explain what they mean by such things as "strong buy," "buy," "hold," and "sell." The pressure from Congress is certainly good news. Hopefully, it will help to minimize the conflict problems and result in better research for investors.

BAD NEWS

There is a theory of investing called the *cockroach theory*. That is, if you find one, there are certainly many others nearby. In other words, if a wireless company makes a very bad announcement, there is likely more trouble to come.

What do we mean by *very bad*? For example, a company may not meet its earnings estimates. What if all other companies in the industry are not meeting their estimates? In this case (suppose the wireless industry is in a downturn), this does not necessarily mean that you should sell. Perhaps, on a relative basis, your company—that is, the company in which you are invested—is still growing at a faster rate than its peers and is continuing to run its operations smartly. In this case, you may want to buy even more shares. When the industry turns around, your stock is likely to lead the rally.

Here's a look at the kinds of bad news that should be big factors for selling your stock:

- The company loses a customer that accounts for 10 percent or more of sales.
- The CEO or chief financial officer (CFO) resigns. This usually indicates that a company is undergoing a serious restructuring.
- There are late filings of financial statements with the SEC. At a minimum, this means that the company is suffering from severe organizational problems. At worst, the company may be experiencing substantial financial problems or even has uncovered examples of fraud.
- The company changes its auditor. This may indicate that the auditor has found problems, but the company does not want to disclose the problems.

All this type of news is readily available. Thus make sure that you keep track of your wireless stocks on a daily basis.

CHAT BOARDS

With the Internet revolution during the 1990s, there has been the emergence of online investor chat boards. Some of the more popular ones include Ragingbull.com, Yahoo.com, and MotleyFool.com. And for the most part, investors in tech stocks dominate the chat rooms.

As for wireless companies, some have tremendous amounts of chat traffic. Look at QUALCOMM, for example. At Ragingbull.com, this company has more than 92,000 messages.

However, beware of chat rooms. Perhaps the biggest reason is that you really do not know the sources of the messages. The poster actually may be a 12-year-old kid who has lots of time on his or her hands. The allure of finding out inside information often keeps people attached to these boards. However, it also brings in frauds and individuals looking to manipulate shareholders.

Besides, reading messages on the boards can be very time-consuming. Your time is better spent reading the official news releases of the companies you are watching, as well as the financials. Many chat rooms and message boards also tend to degenerate into heated, emotional discussions of stocks rather than serious, objective analysis. No serious investor should look to chat room gossip as a valid source of information when attempting to determine when to sell a stock—wireless or otherwise.

HOT MARKETS

Through the history of wireless, there have been times when valuations have soared on Wall Street. This happened in the middle to late 1980s with cellular, as well as with the dot-com surge in the late 1990s. During these times, it is extremely easy to make money. Basically, just pick a wireless stock—almost any wireless stock—and you should do well.

A big mistake is to somehow believe that such success is purely from your research abilities. Such hubris is the downfall of most investors. When investing, be humble and realize that all good things come to an end. Thus, as you are making money on your wireless stocks, it is a good idea to start lightening up your positions and diversifying into other areas (perhaps areas that are depressed). Ultimately, when investing, you need to look at the big picture of asset allocation. It is dangerous to have a big part of your portfolio—more than 20 percent—in one sector, especially a high-risk one like wireless.

SUMMARY

Selecting the best wireless stocks to buy is a chore in itself. But it can be even more difficult to determine when to sell them. As the opportunities in the wireless market grow, investors undoubtedly will be faced with decisions of when to take a profit on certain stocks.

As stated at the beginning of this chapter, it is important to first understand your goals with your wireless investment. Since the wireless market is in a high-growth phase, the companies in this area are going to be inherently more risky than other holdings you may have (blue-chip stocks or bonds). The nature of the market makes it even more important to have a plan and to be tuned in to warning signs.

When you buy a wireless stock, watch its progress carefully. Assuming that you've researched the company thoroughly, watch the moves of insiders and the decisions made at board meetings and annual stockholders meetings. Look for the reasons behind the reasons for financing events such as bond sales or PIPEs.

Keeping in touch with the market your company plays in is also vital. If the entire market is booming while your company has anemic growth, take a hard look. You want your investment to be a top performer, but during some economic downturns this simply may mean being the best of the bad performers.

Okay, this chapter has been kind of grim. But do not let this scare you. Wireless is no doubt a powerful industry, and there are incredible investment opportunities. Before you buy a stock, however, question it hard. And this vigilance needs to continue when you own a wireless stock. It certainly will help to boost your rate of return ultimately—which is far from being grim!

9

Foreign Investing

*You have done extensive research for a wireless stock based in another coun-
try. You cannot purchase the shares in the United States but instead must
deal directly with the country's stock exchange. You buy 10,000 shares for
$50 each. After a year, the stock soars to $100. You decide to sell.
Unfortunately, the broker will not return your calls, and several weeks go
by. You learn that the brokerage firm has gone bust. It takes another month—
and a trip overseas—to get your certificates. By the time you sell your stock,
the price has come down to $50 per share.*

Sound far-fetched? Not really. The story is similar to what one of the
authors of this book has experienced in real life.

The concept of individuals investing in foreign markets is definitely new. During the 1970s, the U.S. stock exchange was the clear
leader, representing about two-thirds of the whole value of all stocks
in the world. The need to invest overseas was not as strong. Much
of the value was still in the United States.

By the late 1990s, however, the U.S. share of global stocks was
about 35 percent. In other words, by focusing only on U.S. stocks, you
are missing out on two-thirds of the opportunities outside U.S. borders. Actually, some of the most innovative and influential wireless
companies are based overseas.

In this chapter we'll take a look at some of the emerging markets that are likely to experience substantial growth from wireless. We'll also look at some of the risks inherent in investing in foreign companies.

EMERGING MARKETS

In western Europe and various parts of Asia, the financial markets are quite stable—very similar to the U.S. securities markets. And many of the companies are mature as well, such as Nokia, British Telecom, and Ericsson. This is not to say that there is not much upside in these countries. There certainly is. However, some of the biggest upside is likely to come from emerging markets. Of course, the risks are enormous. For example, Russia saw its stock market skyrocket more than 200 percent in 1997. However, by the following year, the market fell by half.

What is an *emerging market*? According to the World Bank, it is a country that has a per capita gross national product of less than $10,000. Examples include Brazil, China, India, Korea, Poland, Thailand, Mexico, and Argentina.

Many of these countries have been the victims of European and even U.S. colonization. Since gaining their independence, these countries also may have experienced socialism, dictatorships, and civil war.

With the fall of communism, however, and new visionary leadership, a number of emerging markets are poised for growth. These countries are reducing inflation, tax rates, and foreign debt; reducing impediments for foreign investment; and privatizing government-owned industries.

Keep in mind that during the 1800s, the United States essentially was an emerging market country. The United States fought for independence and instituted free-market institutions. It also helped that the United States had a talented and hard-working pool of labor and tremendous natural resources. European investors saw the opportunities and invested in such things as railroads. It was certainly a wise investment.

Interestingly enough, the emerging market countries have an inherent advantage: They are not hamstrung by legacy infrastructure. This is important for the wireless market. Why? These countries do not have to build out expensive wireline infrastructures. Instead, they can build out wireless systems.

This looks to be the case, for example, in Africa. The continent is experiencing high growth rates in cellular. In South Africa, there are about 9 million cell phone users. Estimates are that this will surge to 18 to 20 million by 2005.

Wireless technologies make sense in Africa. The continent is huge, and cities typically are separated by great distances. This has made it difficult and expensive to develop landline communications infrastructures.

In fact, mobile commerce may be widely adopted in Africa. For many, it takes a long drive to find a bank and conduct transactions. With a wireless device, however, bills can be paid quickly and efficiently. The cell phone will become, in a sense, a virtual wallet.

In fact, many citizens in Africa will make their first phone call on a cell phone rather than on a landline phone wired into their house. The concept of having a home phone will be bypassed.

Another growth area is Latin America. Take Telebras, the main telephone company in Brazil. From 1998 to 2001, the company saw its cellular subscribers explode from 5.2 million to 25 million. And yet, there is much more growth to go. Brazil has a population of 172 million. By 2005, the country is expected to have about 55 to 65 million subscribers.

True, Brazil has a large amount of poverty and low-income workers. However, Telebras has introduced prepaid phone services, which makes it much easier for consumers to afford cellular services. Also, over time, as volumes increase and competition stiffens, the prices should fall.

However, building the wireless network was not easy and involved many glitches and quality problems. When cell phones were introduced in 1990, the deposit required for each user was equivalent to US$20,000. Over time, however, the system got better and much more alluring for consumers.

PRIVATIZATION BOOM

A big part of the growth story for emerging markets is privatization, in which government-owned businesses are sold to the public in initial public offerings (IPOs). There are many reasons for this. First of all, privatization can mean billions of dollars for the government. The money can be used to help build the infrastructure of the country.

Next, by being freed from governmental control, a privatized company can make decisions based on market forces, not politics. This means better products and prices, as well as improved growth rates.

It is typically the telecom industry that is the first to be privatized. And the financial returns can be great. For example, the customer penetration rates are likely to be low initially, leaving plenty of room for growth.

But be wary. At the time of the privatization, there is likely to be much hype surrounding the offering. As discussed in Chapter 7, it is a good idea to wait for the hype to subside before buying any shares (wait a couple of months).

For example, the Brazilian phone company was privatized in July 1998, and the stock shot up to $121 per share. By September, the stock was trading below $60. If you held the stock until early 2000, the price would have been over $160.

RISKS

As shown in the example at the beginning of this chapter, you are subject to a large degree of risk when investing in foreign markets—especially those which are emerging. From political risk to liquidity issues, investors must be aware of the dangers involved.

POLITICAL RISK

In Chapter 2 we saw how the political landscape in China had a significant effect on QUALCOMM. This was not an isolated event. Expect politics to be a significant factor that has an impact on investment results in the wireless space.

Some of the political risk may include coups and even civil wars. A change in the political regime may lead to stringent restrictions on the stock exchange, currency conversions, and foreign investment. In some cases, companies could be nationalized. In this case, you lose everything. This is what happened to ITT in the 1950s, a telecom company whose assets were nationalized in Cuba.

LOCAL INSTABILITY

Many emerging markets still have very corrupt governments and areas where organized crime is rampant. If the government authority is lax or corrupt, criminals tend to have heavy influence on business. Black market systems can sap revenue from companies that attempt to sell equipment and services legitimately.

CURRENCY RISK

The stock price of a foreign stock is quoted based on the country's currency. For example, Nokia has been quoted on the Helsinki Stock Exchange since 1915 (with the stock symbol NOK1V). The stock price is expressed in the Finnish markka.

Thus, to track the value of a foreign stock, you must look not only at the stock price change in the foreign exchange but also at the change in the value of the currency relative to the U.S. dollar. In fact, the foreign stock may increase in value, but a U.S. investor still may lose money if the foreign currency loses value against the U.S. dollar.

For example, suppose that for every U.S. dollar you have, you can get 2 Finnish markkas. On the Finnish Stock Exchange, the price of Nokia is 10 markkas. If you buy 100 shares, you will need to first buy 1,000 markkas, which will cost $500.

Let's say that 2 months go by, and Nokia is trading for 12 markkas, but now a U.S. dollar can buy 3 markkas. You sell the 100 shares for 1,200 markkas and then convert this into U.S. dollars, which would be $400. You lost $100 on the trade!

Something else to keep in mind: With the establishment of the European Economic and Monetary Union (EMU), the euro has become a common currency for 11 countries in Europe. This essentially eliminates the currency risk among European countries but not those countries outside Europe.

REGISTRATION

In order to sell stock, it must be registered. Since the registration process can take a long time in some foreign markets, investors are sometimes left holding a stock they cannot sell for an extended period of time. In some countries, the company registers the stock. If the stock is falling and you request to sell the stock, do you think the company will be inclined to register the shares? Since it would put further downward pressure on the stock, the company may be inclined to drag its feet. In some cases, the company may even confiscate the stock. It could be next to impossible to undo this.

INFORMATION RISK

In the United States, we are inundated with information. If a company is public, you can make a call to the investor's relations department and get annual reports, quarterlies, and maybe even article reprints and analyst reports. Of course, you can get much of the same information for free on the Internet.

The access to financial information is much more restrained for foreign markets. Sometimes the information is in another language.

Moreover, even if you can get the information, you need to interpret it properly. For example, many countries have high corporate tax rates. Thus companies will intentionally try to reduce the reported earnings. Or the nation's accounting rules might be different. In fact, many countries do not even have quarterly reports; everything is done annually.

However, over time, the informational problems should lessen. The Internet is a global phenomenon, and it should help bring about more availability of information investors can use. In addition, foreign countries want to attract outside investment. To do this, there must be clear and consistent accounting standards and financial information that makes investment decisions easier to make.

MARKET RISK

Expect more volatility than you are accustomed to seeing in U.S. markets. The stock markets in countries with emerging private industries tend to go through extensive periods of turmoil. As the country and industries attempt to stabilize, investors rush in and out of stocks at every major turn of events. A perfect example is the Russian stock market, as mentioned earlier.

COMMISSIONS

The heavily discounted trades that are common in the United States are rare overseas. However, finding the lowest-cost trade may not be the best approach. Rather, it is perhaps more important to find an experienced broker who can, well, be trusted with your money and also will be helpful in understanding the nuances of the country's marketplace.

STOCK EXCHANGE RULES

Some foreign exchanges may make it difficult for outside investors to invest directly. Or the government may have tremendous influence over the stock exchange. When global markets collapsed in October 1987, governmental authorities pressured the Hong Kong exchange to shut down for 3 days. Needed to sell stock? Tough luck. Of course, when the market opened, prices were down more than 30 percent on average.

SHAREHOLDER RIGHTS

In the United States, the responsibility of management and the board of directors is to the shareholders. Actually, it is common that shareholders will sue if they feel that managers are not upholding their duty.

However, shareholders' rights are not necessarily paramount outside the United States. Countries such as Japan have regulations that make it difficult for hostile takeovers or buyouts from foreign companies.

Some countries may have two types of stock. There is the stock for citizens and the stock for foreign investors. Of course, the latter will have fewer rights.

Moreover, many countries do not have the extensive regulatory system that exists in the United States. For instance, insider trading is likely to be allowed in many countries outside the United States.

LIQUIDITY

This is how easy (or difficult) it is to find a buyer or seller for shares of a stock. Many emerging market stock exchanges do not have much liquidity. Some exchanges may be open for only a few hours every day because the trading activity is light. Weeks can go by without a stock having any trading.

However, low liquidity is not necessarily bad. After all, it does not take much buying power to move the stock price upward. On the other hand, it does not take much selling to tank stock prices either.

AMERICAN DEPOSITARY SHARES

While you can invest directly in other countries, this often proves very difficult. You need to find a qualified broker and also have access to timely (and understandable) information in the area in which you wish to invest.

There is another approach that is better suited to individual investors: *American depositary shares* (ADSs). These are foreign companies that are sold on U.S. stock exchanges. One example is the German telecommunications giant Deutsche Telekom (NYSE: DT), which is foreign-owned but listed as an ADS on the NYSE. You also will hear about *American depositary receipts* (ADRs). Essentially, this is the physical stock certificate showing that you own an ADS.

There are also *global depositary receipts* (GDRs). These are ADSs that are listed on more than one exchange. An example of this is the company Vodaphone, which is listed on multiple exchanges around the world.

However, even though an ADS is denominated in U.S. currency, this does not mean that there is no currency risk. Instead, you have the same currency risk as if you had purchased the stock directly.

There are also clear advantages for ADSs for individual investors:

- You can buy the shares from a U.S. broker (as well as a discount broker).
- All dividends are sent to you in U.S. dollars.
- You receive annual reports, quarterly statements, and proxy statements in English and converted into U.S. dollars.
- Your taxes are the same as if you bought a U.S. stock.

There are drawbacks, too. Keep in mind that ADSs typically represent the blue-chip companies of a given country. In other words, you are likely to miss out on the up-and-coming companies that may offer more growth opportunities.

Moreover, even though the ADSs are established companies, this does not mean the risk is lessened. These stocks, in fact, can be quite volatile. This is especially the case with companies that are transitioning their systems to new generations of wireless standards, such as third generation (3G).

Look at SK Telecom (NYSE: SKM), which is the top wireless company in Korea. It has about 58 percent of the mobile market (which is 16 million subscribers). Sales surged from $2.2 billion in 1996 to $3.9 billion by 2000. During this time, the stock price went from $15 to $39.

In 2000, the company announced that it would offer data services at 56 kilobits per second (kbps), which is more than the 28.8 kbps of DoCoMo. The company also announced that it would offer 3G services to 10 million customers in mid-2002. However, rolling out 3G was more difficult than expected, and the company extended the deadline by about a year. The stock price fell to $15.

The company had already spent $1 billion to build the 3G network and would have to spend at least another $3 billion.

UNITED STATES: A DROP IN THE BUCKET?

For many investors, an ADS is the best way to capitalize on growth opportunities in foreign wireless markets. While most of the companies sponsoring shares on U.S. exchanges are the larger bellwether stocks of the industry, there is still substantial room for growth. This is so because the largest markets for wireless are outside the United States.

As we saw in Chapter 1, the growth of wireless subscribers in the United States has lagged Europe and Asia in sheer numbers for several years now. The booming success of Global System for Mobile Communications (GSM) wireless services around the world means that a large portion of the market is outside the United States, and this trend is expected to continue. Even the most popular U.S. wireless stocks are heavily dependent on revenues from foreign customers.

With most of the wireless market overseas, foreign companies have ample opportunities in their own backyards. Figure 9.1 shows a breakdown of wireless subscribers by region for the end of 2001 and the forecast for the end of 2005.

From this graph it is not surprising that many global wireless companies consider the United States a minor market, even in the future. With many other regions dwarfing the United States, coupled with our fragmented networks, many companies put more effort into fertile GSM markets in Europe and Asia.

This is not to say that the U.S. market is insignificant to global players. It is a very lucrative market on a per capita basis and should grow substantially in the future. However, the competing technologies spread across the nation make it a complicated field with numerous players. With a limited GSM market currently, the U.S. market is often secondary to foreign companies that have little competence in other technologies such as Code Division Multiple Access (CDMA).

FIGURE 9.1

Breakdown of Major Cellular Markets

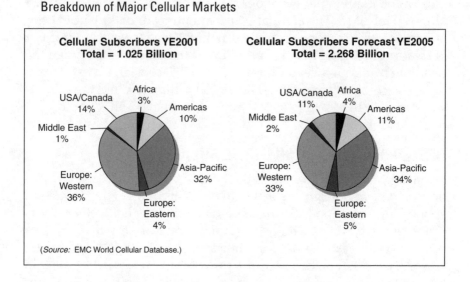

(*Source:* EMC World Cellular Database.)

Another differing aspect of many foreign markets is the penetration rate of wireless devices. This number, stated as a percentage, represents the number of wireless subscribers as a portion of the population. At the end of 2000 in the United States, the penetration rate was just below 40 percent. In contrast, many European nations have penetration rates of over 70 percent.

These higher penetration rates mean a number of things. Not only do they mean that there are more subscribers per capita, but they also mean that more of the population as a whole has adopted wireless technology as an important part of life. This breeds a mobile culture in certain regions that differs very much from other areas.

In the United States, many people still view cellular technology and wireless in general as an intrusion. Some scoff at others who talk on their phones at inappropriate times—such as in meetings or while driving. In general, it is simply a nuisance that a relatively small population of people choose to make use of. Even the media is generally biased against wireless devices, choosing to highlight possible health risks, excessive costs, and customer service horror stories.

By contrast, a country such as Finland that has a vast majority of the population using wireless devices has a notably different outlook. Those without cellular phones are seen as living in the past.

People in these areas are genuinely surprised when you tell them you're not unwired. It's almost expected.

These mobile cultures are also much more accepting of new applications for wireless devices. Since their cellular phone is a part of their daily life, it is an indispensable tool that can be improved to do even more. Short Messaging Service (SMS) services have boomed in these areas partly because everybody has them—you don't have to ask what the best way to reach them is. Just get their number. In the United States, you'd have to make sure that they've got the right type of phone, the right level of service, and the same service provider as you. This is a significant impediment to wireless growth in the United States.

The United States may get to this point someday as well, but it will be a while before we have a strong mobile culture. Until then, the best markets are going to be abroad, mostly in western Europe and Asia. This gives foreign companies a slight edge in the global wireless market.

With a large pool of investment capital in the United States and great wireless markets abroad, an ADS is a perfect fit. Investors will find at least a few ADSs that represent companies from almost all major markets of the world. Here are a few examples:

- *Vodafone AirTouch plc (NYSE: VOD).* Vodafone is currently the world's largest mobile communications company. With interests in virtually every major cellular market in the world in 22 countries, Vodafone is a global industry bellwether. Vodafone bought out AirTouch Communications in 1999 and also owns 45 percent of Verizon Wireless, currently the largest provider in the United States.
- *Alcatel (NYSE: ALA).* Based in France, this company has a diverse product base in many areas of telecommunications, not just wireless. It has operations in over 130 countries yet derives most of its revenue from Europe.
- *Cable and Wireless plc (NYSE: CWP).* Based in the United Kingdom, Cable and Wireless is a provider of integrated communications and a global carrier of communications traffic, including Internet, data, voice, and video. Services include data and Internet Protocol (IP) services such as Web hosting, e-commerce solutions, and integrated communications services.

- *Deutsche Telekom (NYSE: DT).* With its base in Germany, Deutsche Telekom AG is Europe's largest telecommunications company and the third largest carrier worldwide. The company offers traditional telephony services as well as mobile services through T-Mobil. In 2001, the company acquired VoiceStream Communications in the United States.
- *China Mobile (NYSE: CHL).* Based in Hong Kong, China Mobile is one of the largest cellular service providers in China. The company dominates many of the more developed provinces in China, such as Guangdong and Zhejiang. This ADS is more of a pure wireless player than other companies diversified in telecommunications.
- *Telecom Italia (NYSE: TI).* Based in Italy, the mobile division of Telecom Italia is called Telecom Italia Mobile (TIM). TIM is also one of the largest mobile telecommunications operators in Europe and the third largest in the world. The company provides a wide variety of telecommunication equipment and services to a global market. TIM is particularly active in expanding wireless networks in emerging markets such as Brazil.
- *NTT DoCoMo (NYSE: NTDMY).* A company based in Japan, DoCoMo was established in 1991 and is the wireless communications portion of Nippon Telegraph and Telephone (NTT). NTT DoCoMo is the largest provider of cellular telephone services in Japan and claims the most mobile Internet subscribers with its i-Mode service. The company also has been investing substantially abroad, even taking a 16 percent stake in AT&T Wireless in the United States.

And of course, one of the most popular ADSs in the world is Nokia (NYSE: NOK).

THE FINLAND FACTOR

Finland. It's a tiny country, with a mere 5 million people. And of course, the weather is extremely cold. Then again, perhaps this explains why the country is a technology powerhouse (not much to do but sit indoors and program software).

Finland has become a vision of the future of wireless. Close to 4 million Finns have mobile devices. Basically, the high penetration rate means that wireless has become an integral part of Finland's culture. If you take a trip to Finland, you will immediately see the impact of wireless:

- A teenager will send a text message to a friend to meet at a dance club tonight.
- Several people at a coffee shop exchange business cards virtually through their cell phones.
- A businesswoman reads an e-mail from a top customer.
- A small boy will be playing a wireless game.
- A shopper makes a purchase by pressing a few buttons on his or her cell phone (yes, credit cards and checks are becoming a rare thing in Finland).

Wireless is everywhere. It's a part of Finnish life.

Why the innovation? A big part is the deregulation of the telecom industry in the 1950s. The competition has led to new innovations and a robust wireless market. Also, Finland does not auction off spectrum, as is frequently done in the United States and many other countries. Rather, it gives it away—in the hope that companies will provide new technologies and services.

Just as the success of Hewlett-Packard spawned many companies in Silicon Valley, Nokia has been playing the same role in Finland. Interestingly enough, Nokia has been in existence for about 135 years. The company's original business was paper manufacturing. Now it is the leading wireless handset manufacturer, with about a 35 percent worldwide market share.

While Nokia has a $500 million venture fund, there has been little investment in Finnish companies. Rather, Nokia prefers to engage in strategic relationships with wireless Finnish start-ups. Nokia will keep its partners abreast of the latest products and the direction of the company. This gives the start-up an edge when developing new applications for Nokia headsets.

It's a virtuous cycle. The start-ups make better products, and Nokia's devices are more valuable because there are more services for consumers. However, by being selected by Nokia, a start-up usually will have a much easier time getting funding from venture capitalists.

Another critical part of the wireless success of Finland is the Helsinki University of Technology. The university is playing the same role that Stanford and Berkeley have in Silicon Valley: new technologies and start-ups. In fact, the university will incubate emerging companies, as well as provide contacts, such as from Ericsson, Nokia, and Sonera. Moreover, the start-ups also are receiving money from U.S. strategic investors and venture capitalists.

There are hundreds of wireless start-ups in Finland, and no doubt many will either fail or merge. Ultimately, however, some will become powerhouses, which may first list on the Helsinki exchange.

EXAMPLE OF A FINNISH START-UP

Back in the 1970s and 1980s, computer game programmers had to be quite efficient. After all, they were writing programs for machines that had small amounts of memory. Yet game players want fancy graphics and quick action. Well, the game programmers were able to test the limits of personal computers (PCs).

The same predicament is facing the wireless gaming industry. How do you make games fun when the available screen space and memory are not great? Well, this is an opportunity for upstart companies such as Springtoys, based in Helsinki, Finland.

The founder of the company, Panu Mustonen, actually hired programmers who developed games for the old machines, such as the Ataris, Commodores, and Amigas. In the wireless gaming industry, it is back to the future.

And the games certainly are creative. Titles include "Hanoi Towers," "Anomalous Experiences," and "Of Humans & Trolls and Beer." For example, in "Anomalous Experiences," you deal with the unbelievable: a thumbless hitchhiker and even a horseman without a body.

Since graphics are limited, Springtoys' games rely heavily on storytelling. Much is left to the user's imagination.

The company has been on the fast track and has signed distribution deals with KPN Mobile, Terra Mobile, Orange, and Sonera. The company also received equity investments from Sonera, Eqvitec Partners (a top venture firm in Finland), Wellington Partners (a venture firm based in Germany), and Shamrock Capital Advisors (which is the venture firm of Roy Disney, the cofounder of Disney).

ASIA

Asia is another powerful force in wireless development. Hong Kong has the world's highest penetration rate for wireless subscribers with about 83 percent. Other big areas include

- Singapore—70 percent
- Japan—77 percent
- Taiwan—79 percent
- Australia—69 percent

It is interesting that the penetration of all Asia—which represents 3.3 billion people—is only about 5 percent. A big part of this is the low penetration rate in China. This should change quickly, however. Like Africa, China is a large country without substantial wireline infrastructure. Building a wireless system would be cheaper and faster.

A huge beneficiary from the wireless growth in China has been China Mobile (CHL). In 2001, the company was adding 5 million users per month and will have more cell users than in the United States. In addition, there are currently more wireless phone users than landline users in China.

From 1996 to 2000, revenues increased from $10.3 billion to $64.9 billion as profits went from $4.5 billion to $18 billion. Since the company's IPO in October 1997, a $10,000 investment would now be worth about $35,000.

Of course, foreign companies are attempting to make inroads into the China wireless marketplace. But this can take a long time. Motorola started the process in 1986 and has spent over $1.5 billion in investments. Motorola also had to learn about the unique aspects of China: The legal system is very different from the U.S. or European model; and politics and culture are critical. For instance, the CEO of Motorola had to eat deep-fried scorpions (which is a delicacy in China).

China is also a country with deep religious and superstitious beliefs. A phone number that ended with 54-7424 would not sell in China. Why? Because it sounds like "I die, my wife dies, my child dies." The number 4 means death.

Just as in much of the rest of Asia, China has a strong cultural belief in family, not necessarily the individual. Family communication is very important, and wireless technologies can help promote this. Moreover, decisions usually are made by consensus.

Japan is also a glimpse into how wireless can be hugely profitable, as seen with its NTT DoCoMo service. First of all, the company dominated the traditional cellular phone market with about 32 million subscribers. Then the company offered data services to customers. The technology was i-Mode and, ironically enough, was not cutting edge. However, it proved to be in high demand in Japan. The content was strong (there were even karaoke rooms), and the connection to the Internet was always on.

In about 2 years, the service garnered more than 20 million subscribers. With its growing profits, NTT DoCoMo decided to use its cash hoard to buy stakes in overseas telecoms. In all, the company has invested about $15 billion to acquire positions in KPN Mobile, Hutchison 3G UK, KG Telecom, and AT&T Wireless. This inevitably will help to spread the i-Mode technology.

SUMMARY

Wireless is certainly global and is bringing the world closer together. It can even help some countries—which lack infrastructure, such as in Africa—to boost growth. Yes, foreign investing represents great opportunities. Of course, the risks also are great. Such investments should constitute a small portion of portfolio. However, if a foreign investment pans out, it can have a substantial impact on your portfolio.

Even if you choose not to invest in a foreign company, the influence of global players is still important to recognize. With wireless technology and services being driven largely by markets and companies outside the United States, investors should keep an eye on trends and events abroad. What's happening in key markets in Europe or Asia today can provide ideas about where the wireless world is headed.

10

Wireless Mutual Funds

Let's face it. Some investors don't want to put too much time into researching individual wireless stocks. For some investors, finding good stocks may take more time than they want to spend or may be too stressful. Since it's a good idea to be diversified in several stocks, the chore of tracking all these businesses can be of little interest to some as well.

However, suppose that you want exposure to wireless. You think it is going to be huge, yet you do not have the time or discipline to pick the stocks? A solution: You can let others pick wireless stocks for you through mutual funds.

For this you will pay a management fee—which can range from 1 to 3 percent—but this is the price you pay for professional managers who specialize in the complex world of wireless. The fees can get complicated. Let's take a look.

EXPENSE RATIO

This is composed of a number of fees. First of all, this ratio includes administrative costs, such as for keeping records, mailings to shareholders, customer support, and so on. These fees range from 0.2 to 0.5 percent.

Next, there is the management fee. This is what the portfolio managers get. This can range from 0.5 to 1.5 percent. On a big fund—say, over $1 billion—this fee can add up. This is why many portfolio managers are fairly wealthy. Of course, hopefully, they will make you wealthy, too.

Then there is the 12b-1 fee, which can range from 0.25 to 1 percent. This is a general fee to help with marketing and distribution of the fund.

For wireless and telecom funds, the expense ratios can be high—say, over 1 percent. In other words, every year, you must pay at least 1 percent of your gains in fees. Over several years, this can eat into your return.

There are other types of fees you should avoid entirely.

LOAD

Essentially, this is a commission you pay to the broker who recommends a fund to you. If you select your own funds, then make sure that you do not select a fund that has an automatic load. In fact, the loads can be high. In some cases, they can be 3 percent or more on the initial amount you invest.

REDEMPTION FEES

If you sell the fund, you must pay a fee—which can range from 0.25 to 2 percent.

LEVEL LOADS

This is also known as *C shares*. It may charge a load of, say, 5 percent but charge it over a 5-year period.

There are also hidden costs. One is the turnover rate. This is the percentage of the portfolio that has been sold during the year. It is normal for wireless and telecom funds to see turnover rates over 100 percent. Basically, this adds to the overall cost of the fund (in terms of commissions). It also can potentially result in higher taxes. That is, at the end of the year—assuming there are gains—you may get a capital gains distribution. Thus it is a good idea to wait until after the distribution has been made before investing in one of these types of funds. You can find out about the distribution date by calling the fund.

TIP

Before buying a wireless or telecom mutual fund, make sure that you read the prospectus. A mutual fund company is required to send this to you. You also can do research from Web resources, such as Morningstar.com. This site has a tremendous amount of information about mutual funds and even has its own rating system.

It is important to understand all the risks and fees associated with a fund before you invest in it. There's nothing worse than finding out about additional fees or costs later, once you've already committed your fund.

BENEFITS

Besides professional management, there are some other benefits to owning mutual funds:

- *Diversification.* A fund will invest in a variety of wireless stocks. Thus, if some go down, hopefully there will be others that go up—by more! This protects you from placing too much of your money in any one company and balances the risk.
- *Liquidity.* On any business day you can sell your shares.
- *Reasonable amounts.* To invest in a mutual fund, the initial amount is reasonable, ranging from $1,000 to $5,000. Also, you can set up periodic investment programs, in which a certain amount is transferred from your bank account on a monthly basis into a mutual fund.
- *Reinvestment.* Any dividends or gains from the fund can be reinvested back into the mutual fund.

SOME BACKGROUND

With the surge in high-tech stocks during the late 1990s, we saw a number of new types of sector funds to take advantage of the high rates of return. One particularly strong sector, of course, was the so-called Internet funds. Billions of investor dollars went into these funds. In some cases, funds had to close their doors to new investors. From 1999 to 2000, the number of Internet funds went from 4 to 40. After the downturn in late 2000, there were about 28 Internet funds left in mid-2001.

This trend also affected wireless, as several new funds specialized in this area. However, when the high-tech market collapsed, so did these specialized funds. One of the funds, Turner Wireless and Communications, was merged into the broader equity fund New Enterprise. In the fourth quarter of 2000, the fund fell a stunning 44.3 percent, which was pretty much in line with the performance of most technology funds at the time.

Now there are only a handful of wireless funds. They have small amounts of assets under management, and most have only short track records.

FIDELITY SELECT WIRELESS (FWRLX)

Portfolio manager Shep Perkins focuses on wireless service providers and equipment makers. He likes to see companies with strong unit growth and moderate debt.

A big advantage to this fund is the backing of Fidelity. It has an incredible pool of talented portfolio managers. Also, the research staff is top-notch.

Some of the top holdings in 2001 include ALLTEL, Vodafone Group, QUALCOMM, and Triton PCS. Assets under management are $153 million. Minimum investment is $2,500. The expense ratio cannot be determined because the fund has been in existence less than a year. There is a 3 percent load. Returns during the first 6 months of 2001 were –22.8 percent.

WIRELESS FUND (WIREX)

This fund focuses on component suppliers and software developers. At any given time, the fund will hold about 40 stocks, although not all are necessarily wireless. For example, one of the holdings was Cisco in 2001.

Malcolm Forbes and Jeff Provenance comanage the Wireless Fund. Some of the top holdings in 2001 include Openwave, Sprint PCS, AT&T Wireless, and QUALCOMM. Assets under management total $12 million. Minimum investment is $5,000. The expense ratio cannot be determined because the fund has been in existence less than a year. There is no load, nor a 12b-1 fee. Returns during the first 6 months of 2001 were –40.3 percent.

INVESTEC WIRELESS WORLD (IWWDX)

This fund focuses its investments in four areas, which include operators, software developers, content, and infrastructure. On average, there are about 40 stocks in the portfolio. The comanagers Adrian Brass, Nigel Dutson, and Seth Kirkham look for top-quality companies that have high barriers to entry. They also invest in some overseas wireless firms, such as Brokat (a German wireless software firm).

Some of the top holdings in 2001 include TTI Team Telecom, China Mobile, and Nordea. Assets under management total $15 million. Minimum investment is $2,500. The expense ratio cannot be determined because the fund has been in existence less than a year. There is no load, nor 12b-1 fee. Returns during the first 6 months of 2001 were –34.2 percent.

WIRELESS ULTRASECTOR (WCPIX)

Unfortunately, there is very little information available about this fund. Some of the top holdings in 2001 include Western Wireless, AT&T Wireless, Leap Wireless, and TeleCorp. Assets under management total $4 million. Minimum investment is $5,000. The expense ratio cannot be determined because the fund has been in existence less than a year. There is no load, nor 12b-1 fee. Returns during the first 6 months of 2001 were –15.3 percent.

While all these funds showed poor performance in early 2001, this should not alarm investors. Many technology funds experienced negative returns in this time period after years of stunning growth, so it is not too far out of line. As a matter of fact, the best time to invest in funds is often after a correction in the market. While there are no guarantees, investors can expect better results when the overall market improves at some point in the future.

Some investors may prefer other types of funds that do not have such a narrow scope as wireless funds. After all, if the wireless sector turns downward, the returns will be poor for the specialized funds in that time period.

Another option for investors would be to look into general telecom funds, which have much more flexibility in what stocks to select for their portfolios. They often include wireless stocks but may be more diversified in other areas as well.

This does not mean that these funds are not volatile. In fact, they are quite volatile. Here's a look at some top telecommunications funds.

GABELLI (GABTX)

Mario Gabelli and his son, Marc, as well as Ivan Arteaga, manage this fund. It seems like a crowd, but the teamwork has paid off.

The guiding philosophy is definitely from the father, Mario. He founded Gabelli Funds in 1977 and since then has grown the firm into a major financial powerhouse.

Gabelli is a believer in the so-called Graham & Dodd school of stock picking. That is, he looks for companies that are severely undervalued. In fact, he thinks that there are many telecom stocks that are undervalued overseas.

Gabelli focuses on cash flow, strong asset values, and companies with significant franchises. He also has developed innovative valuation techniques. One is called *private market value*, which has led him to uncover many buyout opportunities.

When Gabelli cannot find cheap telecom stocks, he lets his investment funds stay in cash. Gabelli does not only look at financials. He will visit the companies and even the customers and competitors.

About two-thirds of the assets are in U.S. stocks. There is about 16 percent in European stocks, 6.6 percent in Asian stocks, and 2.6 percent in Latin American stocks. Some of the top holdings in 2001 include Deutsche Telekom, Nextel, CenturyTel, Telephone & Data Systems, and Verizon. Assets under management total $290 million. Minimum investment is $1,000. The expense ratio is 1 percent. There are no loads or redemption fees, but there is a 12b-3 fee of 0.25 percent. Returns are as follows:

1998:   34.8 percent
1999:   80.3 percent
2000: −24.1 percent

INVESCO TELECOMMUNICATIONS (ISWCX)

The manager of this fund, Brian Hayward, focuses on high-growth, high-price-earnings-ratio telecom stocks. The emphasis is on the market leaders with improving margins.

Actually, Hayward has even done venture-capital-stage investing with the fund, such as with Corvis (which did go public). However, the fund may have no more than 15 percent of assets in such illiquid securities.

Some of the top holdings in 2001 include Comverse Technology, Nokia, Qwest, and Amdocs. Assets under management total $1.4 billion. Minimum investment is $1,000. The expense ratio is 1 percent. There are no loads or redemption fees, but there is a 12b-3 fee of 0.25 percent. Returns include the following:

1998:   41.0 percent
1999: 144.3 percent
2000: −26.9 percent

CS WARBURG PINCUS GLOBAL TELECOM COMMUNICATIONS (WPGTX)

The comanagers, Scott Lewis and Vincent McBride, look for opportunities that have strong growth rates at reasonable prices. They look for opportunities in emerging markets that are undergoing deregulation. A particularly useful investment approach is cross-border valuation. In other words, the comanagers will identify foreign companies that have similar characteristics to U.S. companies but are trading at deep discounts.

Before managing this fund, McBride managed the Pincus Emerging Markets Fund. As for Scott Lewis, he focuses on U.S. companies.

About two-thirds of the assets are invested in U.S. securities, with about 12.55 percent in Europe, 8.89 percent in the Far East, 4.53 percent in Latin America, and 1.52 percent in Australia.

Some of the top holdings in 2001 include NTT DoCoMo, Vodafone AirTouch, and Western Wireless. Assets under management total $208 million. Minimum investment is $2,500. The expense ratio is 1.66 percent. There are no loads or redemption fees, but there is a 12b-3 fee of 0.25 percent. Returns include the following:

1998:   66.8 percent
1999: 156.8 percent
2000: −38.2 percent

T. ROWE PRICE MEDIA & TELECOM (PRMTX)

Robert Gensler runs this fund and has been an analyst in the telecom sector since 1995. Not only does he look for strong telecoms but also media companies that will benefit from telecommunications. However, he focuses on trying to find companies selling at discounts to the industry. He also looks for opportunities overseas (about 20 percent of assets as of the end of 2000).

Some of the top holdings in 2001 include Allegiance Telecom, Partner Communications, and Millicom International Cellular. Assets under management total $764 million. Minimum investment is $2,500. The expense ratio is 0.93 percent. There are no loads, redemption fees, or 12b-1 fees. Returns include the following:

1998:   35.1 percent
1999:   93.1 percent
2000: −25.1 percent

ICON TELECOMMUNICATIONS & UTILITIES (ICTUX)

There is very little information about this fund. However, it tends to focus more on utility companies than on pure telecommunications companies. As a result, while the upside has not been strong, the fund did not suffer much when the markets plunged. In fact, during 2000, the fund was up 11.8 percent.

Some of the top holdings in 2001 include Telephone & Data Systems, SBC Communications, and Verizon. Assets under management total $13 million. Minimum investment is $1,000. The expense ratio is 1.59 percent. There are no loads, redemption fees, or 12b-1 fees. Returns include the following:

1998:   30.0 percent
1999:   6.9 percent
2000:   11.8 percent

As wireless continues to gain the attention of investors, more mutual funds are likely to appear. As the market develops, we may even start to see more specialized funds within the wireless sector, such as a wireless applications fund or a wireless service provider fund. Also, with the global appeal of wireless, it would not be surprising to see funds offered that contain wireless companies in certain parts of the world. For instance, an Asia wireless fund could invest in major corporations in Korea, China, and Japan, where the market may be particularly hot.

However you choose to invest your money, make sure that you understand what you're buying. If you own a mutual fund, periodically check up on its progress and top holdings to make sure that it is aligned with your goals. Keep your expectations realistic, though. There's going to be some bad years with the good.

11

Private Equity

A next-door neighbor has been working at AT&T for 20 years. He has been a successful engineer and involved in a variety of successful projects. Often you see him in the garage tinkering with new technologies. He tells you that he just quit his job and plans to start a new venture to create a wireless technology. Actually, he has a prototype of it (of course, in his garage). He is going to use credit cards and savings to start the business, but he still needs more money. At least another $25,000. You are intrigued with his idea, but you have never invested in a start-up.

This is a common occurrence, especially in the United States, which has a thriving entrepreneurial culture. Chances are you will run into people like this who have great ideas but need some start-up capital. What's more, there is also a good chance that the start-up will involve some type of wireless technology. In this chapter we'll take a look at some strategies for success in what is known as *private equity investing*.

RISKS VERSUS REWARDS

One of the interesting aspects of the private equity world is the vocabulary. For example, if you decide to invest in an early-stage private company, then you are considered an *angel investor*. And this makes sense. For the entrepreneur who is starving for cash, you certainly appear to be an angel.

Keep in mind that when you talk to an entrepreneur, he or she usually will be very persuasive. He or she will make such claims as "The technology is revolutionary" or "This is the next Microsoft" or "We will hit $1 billion in revenues in 2005." Unfortunately, in most situations these claims fall very short. Unfortunately, the death rate for start-up companies is extremely high. A general rule of thumb is that about 80 percent will fail within the first 2 years of existence.

So unless you are comfortable with high-risk investments, you likely should not put a significant amount of your net worth in such investments. Instead, perhaps set aside only about 5 to 10 percent of your wealth.

Even if a private equity investment is successful, do not expect it to happen overnight. It probably will take many years. True, during the dot-com craze, this was not the case. However, that was an abnormal time—more the exception than the rule. Do not count on a fast return. Expect more than 5 years. After all, look at Microsoft. It took 10 years for the company to go public.

However, despite all the risks, the upside can be tremendous. If you are an early investor in a company that hits it big, you probably will be in a position for easy retirement. To better understand the private equity process, let's continue the preceding example.

Your friend from AT&T, Jack, has put together about $50,000 of his own money for his new wireless venture, ABC Wireless. You are definitely interested in the venture. He says to you, "I currently own 100 percent of the company. I will sell you 10 percent of the company for $25,000."

Basically, this means that Jack is putting a $250,000 value on his business. How can you figure this out? The formula is

$$\frac{\text{your investment}}{\text{your equity percentage}}$$

$$\frac{\$25,000}{10 \text{ percent}} = \$250,000$$

Now, you should never take the first valuation. As with anything, negotiate. Chances are that he does not have many offers on the table. Let's suppose that after several months you both agree that the $25,000 investment will give you 20 percent of the company. Thus the valuation of ABC Wireless is $125,000.

Currently, Jack owns 1 million shares. In the deal, you will get 20 percent, or 200,000 shares. This translates into a stock price of

$$\frac{\text{valuation}}{\text{shares outstanding}}$$

$$\frac{\$125,000}{1,000,000} = 12.5 \text{ cents}$$

However, before making the investment, you should receive an extensive business plan. You do not want Jack to take your hard-earned $25,000 and spend it willy-nilly. A business plan needs to show how the company's cash will be budgeted. There also should be extensive discussions of the industry trends, product development, marketing, and sales.

There are three ways to make money from your private equity investment:

- *Profit.* If ABC Wireless generates profits, some of the cash may be distributed back to you as a dividend. Suppose that ABC makes $100,000, you might be able to get $20,000 or 20 percent (based on your ownership position). This is rare indeed. There are only a handful of profitable early-stage companies. And in most cases, profits are reinvested back into the operations of the company rather than distributed to investors.

- *Buyout.* Let's say that several years go by and the company has grown nicely. AT&T notices the progress and realizes that it would be a good fit. AT&T offers to pay $1 per share for the company. Wow! Your $25,000 investment is now worth $200,000 ($1 × 200,000 shares). In this situation, if you get all cash, then this is the ideal situation. With your cash, you can do whatever you want—say, buy a car or a new house or make other investments. However, all-cash deals are extremely rare. The more likely scenario is that you get part cash and the rest in stock of the acquirer. The acquirer's stock probably will have resale restrictions, such as you cannot sell it for 6 months or more. The reason is

that the acquirer does not want shareholders to dump stock
and tank the stock price.

■ *Initial public offering (IPO).* This process is explained in more
detail in Chapter 7. However, IPOs for start-ups are very rare.
In other words, in terms of private equity investments, it is
more reasonable to expect returns to come from buyouts. But
let's say ABC Wireless does go public. By that time, it is
inevitable that there will have been other investors in the
deal. Unless you have a clause in your investment agreement
with Jack, your ownership will be diluted (i.e., the percentage
of ownership will fall). Suppose that after 5 years, investors
have invested $20 million. Instead of owning 20 percent, you
now own about 5 percent. Although, the stock price of the
company has gone to $10 per share. Keep in mind that
despite the dilution, you still own 200,000 shares, which have
a value of about $2 million ($10 × 200,000 shares). The company goes public at $10, and excitement ensues. Interestingly
enough, you will not be able to sell your shares. Rather, the
underwriter of the IPO will require you to sign a lockup
agreement. In most cases, you will be prevented from selling
the stock for about 6 months after the IPO.

PROTECTIONS

Remember the golden rule: "He or she who has the gold makes the
rules." This is certainly true for private investors. It is not easy for
entrepreneurs to raise money—especially in the early stages. Therefore,
do not be afraid to negotiate hard. In fact, it is a good idea to hire an
experienced attorney to look at the proposed terms of the deal.
Unfortunately, most shareholder documents are very complex, dealing with such strange legal ideas as representations and warranties,
conditions and covenants, and so on. A trained attorney—who spe-
cializes in these matters—can help to protect your legal interests.

Also, make sure that everything you want is put in writing. As
the saying goes, "Spoken promises are as good as the paper they are
written on."

Although there are literally hundreds of things to look at when
structuring a private equity deal, we'll point out some major protections for the angel investor.

PREFERRED STOCK

As the name implies, this has more advantages than common stock. First of all, in the event of liquidation, preferred shareholders get money before common holders. Also, preferred shareholders typically have more voting control over such matters as changing management or approving new financing or a merger.

You should ask for *supercharged* preferred stock (this is explained in more detail in Chapter 8). Another strong feature of preferred stock is the so-called living dead clause. For example, suppose the company is not meeting its objectives and is likely not to do so in the foreseeable future. In this case, shareholders can demand that the company return all cash to the preferred stockholders. If there were no living dead clause, a company's management could continue running the company, pay themselves salaries, and most likely run out of money—leaving nothing for shareholders.

FULL-RATCHET ANTIDILUTION CLAUSE

Basically, this means that if in the next round of financing the valuation is lower than what you invested at (known as *down round*), then the value of your original investment will not fall. Essentially, you wind up getting many more shares.

Let's continue with the ABC Wireless example. Jack needs another $10,000 investment, but the new investor wants a $100,000 valuation, not a $125,000 valuation. This means that the ABC stock price is 10 cents per share and your $25,000 investment is now worth $20,000. With a full ratchet, you will get $5,000 more stock (from Jack), or 50,000 shares.

DISCLOSURE

Make sure you get quarterly financials and updates on any news of the company. There also should be a right to inspect the company's books at any time.

BOARD

All companies legally must have a board of directors. It is this group that represents the interests of all shareholders. It is not uncommon for private investors—at least in the early stages—to have board seats. This can give you more control over the company, as well as make you privy to what is happening.

If you become a board member, you should be compensated for your work, such as by being granted stock options in the company. The younger the company, the more options you should be able to negotiate.

If you do not become a board member, then get observer rights. This allows you to attend all board meetings.

REGISTRATION RIGHTS

In order to sell your shares after a buyout or IPO, they must be registered. When making your investment, you can include a clause that requires the company to register your shares for these liquidity events (a *liquidity event* is either a buyout or an IPO).

PUT OPTION

This gives you the right to sell back your shares to the company after a certain date (perhaps after a year) at a set price (which is negotiable). Actually, this can be very useful for putting pressure on management to go in another direction or even to sell the company. For example, suppose that another company wants to buy the company you invested in, but management is resistant. Yet you think that this is a great deal. Besides, you have been invested in the company for 10 years and want to put your money in other investments. Thus you threaten to exercise your put option. True, this is hardball, but sometimes it is necessary.

RIGHT OF FIRST REFUSAL

This gives you the right to invest in the next round of financing before other new investors do. This can help block investors who you think would be detrimental to the company.

VALUATION

As stated earlier, all entrepreneurs are optimistic and usually very convincing. Moreover, their company is, in a sense, their baby, and they usually think that it is worth a lot of money. However, do not fall into the trap of accepting an entrepreneur's initial valuation. Negotiate it. After all, early-stage companies involve high risk because the market is new, the product's undeveloped, and there are no revenues. Thus you should get a good deal on valuation.

A good way to understand current valuations is to talk to other entrepreneurs. After a few months of research, you will get a feel for the fair market value of early-stage companies (also, later we talk about how to get dealflow).

BACKGROUND CHECKS

Get the résumés from the founders, and then call their prior employers. In some cases a founder may lie about his or her background. If this is the case, you should be very skeptical of the venture. Is this really a scheme? New ventures can be attractive for frauds looking to bilk unsuspecting investors.

NONDISCLOSURE AGREEMENTS (NDAs)

When looking at a new venture, the chief executive officer (CEO) may require you to sign an NDA. Don't do it. Why? You want to look at as many ventures as possible. Signing an NDA might prevent you from doing this. Some NDAs not only require that you not disclose any information about a company you look at but also forbid you from even looking at competitive companies.

THINKING LIKE A VENTURE CAPITALIST

If you are looking seriously at investing in a start-up, there are a couple of good sources to check out:

Venturewire.com

VCbuzz.com

These sources will show all the significant venture capitalist (VC) deals being funded. By reading the newsletters, you can get an idea of where the smart money is being placed. This can help you anticipate some of the macro trends of the wireless marketplace. Moreover, you will learn quickly about which VCs tend to do wireless deals. You can then visit their sites as well. Typically, a VC site will show the investment portfolio. Also, there may even be articles about the vision of the VCs. It can be very useful information.

One firm that has invested in emerging wireless companies is Olympic Venture Partners (OVP). The firm has been in existence since 1983 and has about $300 million under management.

At the firm's site (*http://www.ovp.com/history.html*), there is a screening process for finding the next big companies.

TEAM

An old saying in the VC industry is that a VC will want five things from a company: "the people, the people, the people, the product, and the market." Heading into unexplored territory is not for amateurs, but instead, it is the domain for seasoned businesspeople.

When looking at the management team for an emerging wireless company, it is critical to look for domain experience. Why? Suppose that a new wireless company has a top-notch management team—but from industries outside wireless. In this case, the team will need to spend much time getting the necessary contacts to propel growth of the company. On the other hand, if the senior management already has a deep background in the industry, getting such contacts will be much easier. Moreover, look for a management team that has had prior success in taking companies public or selling them.

One of the emerging wireless companies that OVP invested in was SignalSoft, which develops technologies for location-based wireless services. A critical element of the decision to invest in the company was the management team. Here are some of the key players (you usually can find this information on a company's Web site or in the filings with the Securities and Exchange Commission):

- David Hose, CEO and cofounder, was the vice president of engineering at SCC Communications, where he designed location-based applications for public safety command and control systems. Before this, he worked in management positions at GeoBased Systems and J&D Software.
- Mark Flolid, executive vice president of corporate development and cofounder, was the senior vice president of sales and marketing at SCC Communications. Before this, he had

senior-level experience at Thomas Bros. Maps and GeoBased Systems.

- Donald Winters, senior vice president and chief operating officer, was the vice president of business development for Coral Systems, which develops fraud-management and churn-management software for wireless carriers. He also worked for AirTouch Communications and Pacific Telesis.

- Roy Kligfield, senior vice president of engineering, was the general manager of the Geological Development Center at CogniSeis Development, which develops geophysical processing software for the oil and gas industry. He also was an associate professor of structural geology at the University of Colorado. He has written more than 130 technical papers on mapping software technologies and theories.

As you can see, the management team consists of players that have extensive industry experience, especially with location-based systems. Developing such systems is extremely difficult, but the team certainly has the technical and engineering prowess to pull it off. However, the team is not only technical. There are senior managers who have sales and business-development capabilities in the industry as well.

FOCUS

Looking at emerging wireless companies is definitely exciting. After all, there are so many possibilities. However, this can be a trap. Too often emerging companies will try to do everything when trying to do one thing is hard enough.

According to OVP, the focus of the business must be crystal clear for OVP to invest in it. OVP uses the "elevator pitch" analogy. That is, if you cannot explain the business concept during an elevator ride, then the business is probably in trouble. In other words, the business model should be very simple.

For example, look at the underlying idea behind one of the most successful online companies, eBay: "to help practically anyone trade practically anything on earth." Simple and yet still informative.

If an organization does not have a laserlike focus, the customers and employees—and even investors—will become confused. Of course, competitors who are focused probably will eat the company for lunch.

GOT TO HAVE IT

The technology the start-up offers serves a real, sustained, compelling need in the marketplace. The technology should not serve a want. Rather, it should be so compelling that customers *need* to buy it.

An illustration of this is the e-tailing business. Look at Pets.com. Do people really need to buy dog food over the Internet? The results show that buying pet supplies online really is not compelling. Rather, it serves a *want*.

On the other hand, millions of people have flocked to eBay. This popular Web site does serve a compelling need for both buyers and sellers. The sellers cannot afford to advertise in the newspapers, and flea markets and garage sales do not reach large audiences. The buyers want to get a good deal (through an auction) and also want selection. It's a perfect fit.

In the enterprise marketplace, the idea of *compelling need* is vitally important. New technologies in the workplace mean that employees will need to change their work habits—sometimes radically. For the most part, people are resistant to change. However, if the change means incredible results (such as return on investment or lower costs), then the technology has a strong chance of being profitable.

DEALFLOW

Dealflow is the number of prospects that approach you for funding. Obviously, the more deals you see, the better your chances are of finding one that makes sense. However, generating dealflow is not an easy task. However, there are some tips, including the following:

- *Networking.* Go to industry conferences (such as for wireless) and forums. You will see many new companies.
- *Resources.* In the Appendix we talk about the myriad wireless resources. These will talk about emerging companies. If you are interested, contact the company directly and see what it is doing in terms of financing. The odds are great that the company is, in fact, looking for new capital.
- *Professionals.* Talk to lawyers, CPAs, and attorneys. They often provide services to emerging companies.
- *Angel group.* Check with your local chamber of commerce to see if there is an angel group. Actually, there are thou-

sands across America. Typically, an angel group meets every month, and several companies will present. If the angels like a deal, they will coinvest.

- *Online services.* There are a number of Web sites that provide matching services for emerging companies and angel investors. A few of the top sites are Garage.com and OffRoad Capital.

SUMMARY

Angel investors have been crucial to the formation of the wireless business. This will continue to be the case. Actually, the angel industry is quite large, with about $20 billion in investments every year. This represents about 60,000 start-ups every year.

Of course, angel investors are looking for high rates of return. And some have done extremely well over the years. But angels also invest for intangible reasons. For example, an angel will become part of the excitement of a new venture. An angel can provide advice and guidance to young entrepreneurs. The process can be fun.

CONCLUSION

Few products have crossed international borders successfully to be adopted widely by consumers of many nations. Few products have seen adoption rates grow at over 40 percent annually for years at a time. Even fewer products hold the capability to connect people to real-time information and each other from almost any point on the earth. Wireless succeeds in all these areas.

The stunning growth and continued proliferation of mobile communications enabled through a variety of wireless products and services have captivated the world. Mobile communications are becoming a way of life, and people everywhere are learning the unique benefits that a small handheld device can bring. These are exactly the types of markets that investors dream about: worldwide appeal, plenty of growth potential, and unlimited niche possibilities developing over time.

The unfortunate side of such a tantalizing opportunity is that many investors have already seen this light and have pushed the stocks of some promising companies beyond the point of rationality. As with many other industries, surges in mainstream optimism tend to temporarily turn really great companies into poor investments simply because the price to buy is far out of line with the near-term prospects for a decent return. Fortunately, this same inefficiency in the market can work the other way as well, with the mainstream investment community overlooking some great opportunities.

Hence making money by investing in the wireless industry is not as simple as buying that hot company that everyone is talking about. It takes a little objectivity and patience and a good understanding of the unique aspects of the market. The objectivity and patience have to come from you, the investor. Understanding the unique aspects of the wireless industry comes from books such as this. Hopefully, this book has helped you come a long way in this regard. If you lacked confidence in your knowledge of wireless before reading this book, hopefully you've come to a point where you're comfortable with the variety of terms and ideas often seen in press releases and news articles.

This book is intended to get you into the ground floor of the wireless building. There are many stories still far above that can be explored. While no single book or source of information can provide you with a complete summary of investing in wireless, we recognize that it is most important to have a strong, broad understanding of the basics.

This understanding encompasses both financial aspects of the market and investing and technical aspects of wireless products and services. Competence in the financial aspects of the wireless market is necessary to make investments that have a good potential for sizable returns within the time frame you prefer. Adequate understanding of the technical aspects of the wireless industry is important to properly evaluate the potential of any one company's product or service. Having basic knowledge in both these areas is the ideal toolkit for investors going forward.

As you continue to pursue your investment goals, revisit the concepts outlined in this book frequently. Avoid focusing on any one area too much—rather, take a balanced approach. For instance, try to contain the magical allure of cool technology—too much emphasis here can be costly. Make sure that all your wireless investments make good business sense—the "new economy" will not save a fundamentally bad business. Stick to the basics, and you should do well.

A P P E N D I X

Resources

WEB SITES

BULLMARKET.COM
www.bullmarket.com

BullMarket.com is a good source of information for investors look-ing in high-growth areas, such as high-tech, biotechnology, and wire-less. The site offers various newsletters (some free and some sub-scription-based) and daily content covering significant news in the market. The wireless newsletter is one of its free offerings, and the newsletter includes performance monitoring of its own stock picks. The focus of the site is to help you pick solid, high-growth stocks through in-depth analysis of companies and industries.

BUSINESS2.0
www.business2.com

Business2.0 is a popular tool for navigating the hoards of news items in the digital world, particularly in the Internet, wireless, and other technologies. The site offers daily editorial features and columns in addition to resources that give readers an opportunity to research issues and network with people who have similar interests. Features of the site include

- A guide to more than 11,000 business and technology topics
- A searchable database of 35,000 articles from Business2.0, eCompany, Fortune, Money, FSB, and C/Net
- "What Works," an interactive feature that allows readers to tell their experiences in e-business
- "Talent Pool," a networking spot for businesspeople inter-ested in expanding their contacts

CDMA DEVELOPMENT GROUP (CDG)

www.cdg.org

The CDG Web site is a great resource for everything about cdmaOne and cdma2000. It is a nonprofit organization that is funded by QUAL-COMM and other corporations to promote these technologies ahead of all others—so it tends to be very biased. It contains news and background information on these technologies and provides information on the standards efforts of the member companies.

CELLULAR TELECOMMUNICATIONS INDUSTRY ASSOCIATION

www.wow-com.com

This is the premier cellular organization in the United States. It is the "voice of the industry" and often works closely with the Federal Communications Commission (FCC) and other regulatory bodies to promote growth in the wireless industry. It also puts on two major conventions every year, bringing together wireless companies from the world over. It also offers lots of resources, such as reports on various aspects of industry development in the United States.

FEDERAL COMMUNICATIONS COMMISSION (FCC)

www.fcc.gov

The official FCC site contains a massive amount of information on just about every issue and proceeding in which it is involved. Most of the information is contained in publicly accessible "dockets" and is organized by functional groups. It is often difficult to navigate the site and read some of the reports (after all, it's a government organization), but there's lots of good information here. Of particular interest are the yearly updates on the state of the wireless industry.

FINANCIAL TIMES

www.ft.com

This site is a popular source for global financial news and information. It has a particularly extensive area dedicated to telecommunications and wireless as well. To keep abreast of news occurring with the largest companies in the world, this is probably the best place. The site also has several partner sites with which it works, including Hoover's Online and Business.com. The newsprint publication is renowned for its international perspective on world business, economics, and politics.

GSM ASSOCIATION
www.gsmworld.com

This site is a good resource for worldwide progress on the proliferation of GSM networks. It includes statistics on most of the major cellular technologies and breaks them down on a regional basis as well. The site also includes information on industry events such as the GSM plenary meetings and other conferences.

HOW STUFF WORKS
www.howstuffworks.com

This is a great site for easy-to-understand explanations of just about any gadget or technical system. Of course, there's plenty of information about cellular systems and how phones work. This is a great place to start if you want to get a handle on the basics.

INFOWORLD
www.infoworld.com

In addition to being an extensive source for market news, InfoWorld provides in-depth technical analysis on key products, solutions, and technologies for businesses. It has a lot of content related to testing products that run in enterprise environments, making it a good source of information for information technology (IT) professionals and those looking at various business tools. InfoWorld.com also features interactive discussion forums and e-newsletters as well.

INTERNATIONAL TELECOMMUNICATIONS UNION (ITU)
www.itu.int

This is the official Web site of the United Nation's chartered group. The site offers some basic information on the activities of the ITU as well as information on the implementation of wireless technologies around the world. Visitors can learn about the history of the ITU, its involvement in standardizing third-generation (3G) networks and information on various meetings and conferences.

MBUSINESSDAILY
www.mbizcentral.com

This is the companion online publication to M-Business magazine. It includes online copies of all back-issue stories as well as several online resources and information. It offers daily or weekly e-mail newsletters with up-to-the-minute news in the wireless market. It also has a sizable database of white papers published by individual players in the market discussing everything from business solutions to mobile security. The site also tracks a wireless index of 50 public companies serving all areas of the wireless market. This index is tracked against other common indexes to get a sense of the state of the industry.

MOBILE COMPUTING
www.mobilecomputing.com

As the name implies, this site has everything to do with mobile technologies. This online site accompanies a print magazine as well. In addition to a news desk, three major sections on the site break down its resources:

- "Perspectives." Insight into the world of mobility.
- "MCC Forums." The Mobile Computing forums are where mobile users go to discuss topics of interest.
- "Mobile Links." Information on mobile computing products and links to supplier companies.

RED HERRING
www.redherring.com

Red Herring is another Web site that accompanies a popular print publication. The site prides itself on providing timely market information, and strategic insight to young markets. It has a column called "Communications Watch" in its "Technology" section that is filled by a popular writer, Dan Briody. This column, plus many other feature stories, takes a close look at emerging trends in the wireless industry. Like many other sites, Red Herring offers e-newsletters. Investors can sign up to have any one of several newsletters sent to them covering a wide range of investing topics.

TELECOM WRITING

www.telecomwriting.com

This site has several sections dedicated to telecommunications history. The author, Tom Farley, has spent years building hundreds of pages of information in the areas of telephone history, wireless basics, and digital wireless technology. He routinely adds new information as well as contributions from other popular authors and industry sources.

THE FEATURE

www.thefeature.com

This site has contributions from a number of writers exploring all aspects of mobile communications. It is more of a visionary publication, looking at cutting-edge applications and trends in various parts of the world. The articles are divided into four sections: "In Depth," "Viewpoints," "Reports," and "Analysis." The site also contains discussion forums and other resources for those exploring the mobile world.

THESTREET.COM

www.thestreet.com

This is another financial site that covers various industries. It has a few writers currently dedicated to wireless and telecommunications events. Tish Williams covers many of the day-to-day stories in the wireless world and provides insight as to the impact of events. In a special section, Tero Kuittinen (aka the Wireless Wiz) takes in-depth looks at the global wireless industry and offers insight on emerging trends.

In addition to the news and commentary on the wireless market, there are a number of other tools and sections of information on the Web site for investors.

UNSTRUNG
www.unstrung.com

This Web site offers unique commentary and analysis on the wireless industry. With most of the focus on younger companies in the wireless enterprise market, the contributors to the site tend to have a "cut to the chase" approach to telling it like it is. Opinions tend to be strong, and interviews with senior management include lots of difficult yet relevant questions.

WIRELESS WEEK
www.wirelessweek.com

This is the companion Web site to the *Wireless Week* publication. Anything that makes news in the wireless industry can be found here. There's also an extensive database of individual companies working in various segments of the industry. In addition, a wireless stock portfolio is tracked on the site with links to the companies that make up the index.

WR HAMBRECHT + CO
www.wrhambrecht.com

WR Hambrecht + Co is a financial services firm that offers a large amount of research and analysis in several industries, including wireless. Extensive information is made public on the Web site, including earnings commentaries and industry reports. The senior wireless analyst, Peter C. Friedland, is well respected in the industry and provides frequent guidance for the sector.

MAGAZINES

M-BUSINESS
The motto for *M-Business* magazine is "The Voice of the Mobile Economy." A division of CMP Media, *M-Business* follows global trends in wireless and digs into almost every significant event going on around the world, whether it's a new service launch or cool new applications. The magazine is broken down into the following sections:

- "Features." The biggest stories and events for the month.
- "Currents." Quick briefs on key developments and trends overseas, snapshots of the alliances and deals shaping the mobile world, and an update on start-ups powering the mobile economy.
- "M-World." Short stories from around the world relating to wireless applications and services.
- "Opinion." Plenty of viewpoints expressed about technologies, services, and prospects of new offerings. Includes commentary from editors and writers and feedback from readers.
- "Reports." In-depth analysis from a diverse team of reporters.

WIRELESS WEEK

Wireless Week often is regarded as the industry standard for wireless companies. A publication of Cahners, this magazine is full of statistics provided by its research arm. Most of the articles are centered around general news events in the industry, but there are also several sections dedicated to specific areas, such as

- Business/finance
- Wireless Internet
- Broadband
- Paging/messaging
- Cellular/PCS
- News extra: accessories
- Classifieds
- Industry stocks
- Guest opinion

This resource generally is regarded as the most diverse and complete publication in the industry. An avid reader of *Wireless Week* will know just about everything that has anything to do with wireless technology and markets. Due to its popularity, the company also has started a separate companion publication called *Wireless Internet* magazine.

NEWSLETTERS AND OTHER MEDIA

Many of the sources for news, analysis, and perspective on the wireless market have gone to publishing e-mail newsletters. Very few continue to send out traditional newsletters through the mail due to the expense and delay in timely reporting. Virtually all the Web resources mentioned here offer e-mail newsletters at various intervals—daily, weekly, or monthly. If your e-mail box gets lonely occasionally, just sign up for a few of these, and let the information come to you.

BullMarket.com (www.bullmarket.com)—Free wireless newsletter via e-mail

Business2.0 (www.business2.com)—Dozens of e-mail newsletters

CDMA Development Group (www.cdg.org)—Periodic online video presentations called "Digevents"

CTIA (www.wow-com.com)—Daily e-mail newsletter

Financial Times (www.ft.com)—E-mail news and alerts for members

GSM Association (www.gsmworld.com)—Extensive database of archived presentations

MbusinessDaily (www.mbizcentral.com)—Two e-mail newsletters, one daily and one weekly

Red Herring (www.redherring.com)—Several daily and weekly e-newsletters

TheStreet.com (www.thestreet.com)—One free and several subscription e-mail newsletters

Unstrung (www.unstrung.com)—Unstrung Stringer e-mail newsletter twice weekly

Wireless Week (www.wirelessweek.com)—Daily e-mail newsletter and moderated online events

WR Hambrecht + Co (www.wrhambrecht.com)—Numerous audio/video presentations

GLOSSARY

1G (First Generation) Refers to analog cellular systems that were deployed in the 1970s.

1xEV-DO An evolution of 1xRTT for data only (DO). This protocol augments 1xRTT or other voice systems with a band set a side for wireless data.

1xEV-DV The next evolutionary stage of 1xRTT that includes both data and voice (DV) services.

1xRTT The first-generation (phase) radio transmission technology that applies to IS-95 CDMA-based systems. This is considered by many to be the first step into the third generation (3G) for CDMA with data rates of up to 144 kbps.

2G (Second Generation) Refers to newer digital cellular systems that were deployed in the 1990s. These systems included a more efficient method for voice services and added limited data services.

3G (Third Generation) The next generation of wireless technology. 3G networks should be able to transmit wireless data at speeds of at least 144 kbps for mobile users and up to 2 Mbps in fixed locations. The ITU-2000 specification is the coordination effort for 3G networks.

3xRTT The next-phase radio transmission technology that is built on CDMA-based systems. The 3x refers to using three carrier channels 1.25 MHz wide to get transmission speeds of up to 2 Mbps.

802.11 A standard specification for a wireless network technology in the ISM band. Variations of the standard (802.11a and 802.11b) give different data speeds in the megabits per second range and are meant for use as a wireless local area network (LAN).

Air interface The method a wireless network employs to communicate between portable units and base stations. Air interface technologies include AMPS, TDMA, CDMA, and GSM, to name a few.

American Depositary Shares (ADSs) Shares of foreign companies sold on U.S. stock exchanges. The receipts for these shares (the certificates) are called American depositary receipts (ADRs). These shares constitute ownership of a foreign company but are exposed to currency fluctuation.

AMPS (Advanced Mobile Phone System) This is one of the earliest protocols developed in the late 1970s and is often referred to simply as *analog cellular*. While it is old, it is still very popular and is the basis for many of the newer protocols.

Analog When used in the context of wireless, analog usually refers to older wireless communications systems that sent voice signals over the air in analog format. The analog format of voice simply would travel along with a carrier wave that would be stripped away at the receiving end to reproduce the original voice content. While this is the most direct method of transmitting wireless signals, it is less efficient than digital methods.

Angel Investor An early-stage investor in a start-up company. An angel investor provides early financing to an entrepreneur or small team to develop prototypes or conduct feasibility studies in new technologies or services.

ARIB (Association of Radio Industries and Businesses) The Japanese organization set up to address standards.

ARPU (average revenue per user) A service provider measure to gauge the average income from the base of users.

ATM (Asynchronous Transfer Mode) A high-speed network transmission technology that seeks an optimal method to transfer information with minimal delay. There are efforts underway to develop wireless ATM networks.

Backhaul Connections from a cellular base station to the mobile switching center.

Bandwidth A range of frequencies or channels that can carry a signal. Analogous to a pipe or conduit for information flow.

Bluetooth An emerging wireless technology that connects electronic devices such as wireless phones, computers, printers, and personal digital assistants (PDAs) at a frequency of 2.4 GHz over short distances (generally less than 100 feet). The idea is to replace short-wired connections and infrared communication.

bps (bits per second) The unit of measurement for the rate at which data are transmitted.

BSC (Base Station Controller) The electronics portion of a wireless base station that controls the radio equipment in the transmitter and receiver sections.

BTS (Base Transceiver Station) Sometimes simply called the *base station*, this infrastructure equipment is responsible for sending and receiving the actual radio signals over the air. This device takes radio signals from subscribers' phones and connects them to land-based telephone networks.

Calling party pays This term refers to the practice of billing only the originator of a call to a wireless device as opposed to the receiver or both. Network operators in most countries use this method of billing, but service providers in the United States bill both the caller and receiver. However, many U.S. carriers are pushing for calling party pays because it probably would increase minutes of use.

CDMA (Code Division Multiple Access) A technology that uses digital spread-spectrum techniques in communication between wireless devices. Developed originally for the military, QUALCOMM pioneered this air interface protocol for use in cellular and other wireless networks.

cdma2000 A 3G wireless technology that evolved from the current-generation CDMA (IS-95, or cdmaOne) standard.

cdmaOne The IS-95 CDMA standard developed by QUALCOMM. This term was created by the CDMA Development Group to better brand and market CDMA throughout the world.

CDPD (Cellular Digital Packet Data) An overlay protocol that is used to transmit low levels of data over wireless networks.

Cellular This term describes the concept of dividing a wireless network in a large geographic area into smaller coverage areas called *cells*. Each cell can handle calls on certain frequencies while providing for a method of handing off calls to adjacent cells. The cellular concept greatly increases capacity on a wireless network because more channels can be reused in a given area.

Churn A measure of the number of subscribers that terminate services with a provider. The canceling customers simply may want to discontinue use of the service or move to another provider for a better deal.

Circuit-switched data Data that are transmitted over a dedicated channel. The circuit is set up to the destination and is kept open until terminated, regardless of the flow of data.

Convertible Debt Offering This is a bond sold to public investors to raise money for a company. The bond will carry an annual interest rate. Moreover, the bond will have to be paid off in the future (say, 10 or 20 years from the offering). However, bondholders have the option of converting part or all the bonds into common stock of the company. This is done if the stock price increases in value.

CPGA (Cost per Gross Addition) Sometimes referred to as *customer acquisition cost*, this is the average cost to a service provider of signing up a customer. Some of the components of this cost are handset subsidies, marketing, advertising, and promotion expenses.

DCS 1800 (Digital Cellular System) A global system for mobile communications operated around 1,800 MHz. This is the PCS network for everywhere but the United States, where the PCS networks are operated around 1,900 MHz.

Dealflow The number of business prospects that approach you for funding. Typically, deals will not come looking for private investors until they take measures to network and increase their exposure to companies in an industry.

DECT (Digital European Cordless Telephone) A wireless system in Europe that uses a cordless phone for office communications systems.

Digital In terms of wireless, digital refers to the newest form of communications, where voice signals are converted to a binary pattern of zeros and ones before transmission. The code is then reconstructed to reproduce the original voice information at the mobile unit. This method of breaking down and transmitting signals is far more efficient and robust than analog communications, where the original signal is transmitted without coding.

Dropped call When a phone call over a wireless network is unintentionally disconnected due to a system problem, lack of capacity, or poor signal reception in areas that have inferior coverage.

DSP (Digital Signal Processor) A specialized microprocessor that is specifically designed to perform mathematical operations on a data stream at high speed. A DSP chip is central to many communications functions that require filtering and conversion.

Dual band A wireless device that operates on two different frequency bands. For instance, in the United States, most dual-band phones work on 800-MHz cellular and 1,900-MHz PCS frequencies.

Dual mode A wireless device is dual mode if it works on two different network technologies. Today, many phones operate on both analog and digital networks such as AMPS and TDMA. In the future, there will be many types of dual-mode phones such as GSM/GPRS or GSM/CDMA. Multimode phone also will appear eventually, handling three or more modes of operation.

Due diligence The process of evaluating a company for its chances of success in any given market. It usually involves thorough examination of the company's finances as well as the prospects of markets the company is going after. This also can apply to the evaluation of a stock to see if the price of the security is in line to the value of the company.

Dutch auction system A new type of online system, called *OpenIPO*, uses the Dutch auction to distribute IPOs. That is, a company will indicate that it wants to raise a minimum amount of money. Investors will then make bids on the stock price for the IPO. A computer system optimizes the bids, coming up with a price. All bidders who bid this price or higher get the optimized price.

E911 (Enhanced 911) A service that provides automatic number identification and automatic location information to the 911 emergency operator. E911 services are mandated to be phased into U.S. wireless networks by the FCC.

EBITDA (Earnings Before Interest, Taxes, Depreciation, and Amortization) A corporate income statement that measures a company's earnings performance by excluding certain items. This statement tends to paint a more accurate picture of the operational success of a wireless company because it removes debt obligations from the figure.

EDGE (Enhanced Data Rates for Global Evolution) An advanced technology for GSM and TDMA networks that supports high-speed modulation. Using existing infrastructure, EDGE technology enables data transmission speeds of up to 384 kbps.

ESN (Electronic Serial Number) A unique identification number embedded in a wireless phone by the manufacturer. Each time a call is placed, the ESN is sent to the base station so that the service provider can validate the call. The ESN cannot be altered or changed once it is placed in the phone. The ESN helps prevent fraudulent use of cellular phones.

Expense ratio This is a mutual fund expense composed of a variety of fees. It includes administrative costs, such as for keeping records, mailings to shareholders, and customer support. It also includes a management fee and a general fee (12b-1 fee) to help with marketing and distribution of the fund.

FCC (Federal Communications Commission) The U.S. federal agency responsible for commercial and private spectrum management.

FLEX A data transmission protocol developed by Motorola that is used in many paging systems. The family of FLEX technologies also includes InFLEXion and ReFLEX for more advanced paging services such as two-way paging and guaranteed messaging.

Frequency reuse The ability to use the same frequencies in two cells that are located far enough apart so that they do not interfere with each other. This technique came about with the cellular concept of a wireless system and is the principal reason for increased capacity in these systems.

Full-ratchet antidilution clause A clause in an investment deal that specifies how ownership changes with the company's valuation. If a following round of financing specifies a valuation that is lower than what you invested at, then your equity percentage in the company does not fall. Rather, the equity of the founders does.

GPRS (General Packet Radio Services) A 2.5-generation technology that is packet-based, offering wireless data access speeds of up to 144 kbps. This technology is currently being deployed across GSM networks.

GPS (Global Positioning System) A fleet of 24 geosynchronous satellites operated by the U.S. Department of Defense that continuously transmit their position relative to the earth. The signals from three or more satellites can be used to accurately pinpoint a position on the surface of the earth down to within a few meters in some cases.

GSM (Global System for Mobile Communications) A digital wireless protocol that is similar to TDMA. It is noted for being highly secure and reliable. It is by far the most popular protocol in Europe and the rest of the world (outside North America).

Handoff The process of passing an active call on a mobile phone from one cell to another on a wireless network. Two adjacent cells must coordinate this effort so that the call is not dropped or the signal significantly disturbed.

HDR (high data rate) A high-speed data technology based on CDMA that QUAL-COMM developed. It offers speeds up to 2.4 Mbps.

Hedge funds This is a fund from wealthy investors and institutions. Individual investors are not allowed to participate. A hedge fund can invest in virtually anything—commodities, currencies, stocks, and private companies.

HSCSD (High-Speed Circuit-Switched Data) A circuit-switched data transmission technology that can support speeds up to 38.4 kbps or higher. This technology fits into TDMA and GSM systems, using voice channels to pass data.

Hz (cycles per second) Short for hertz, a measure of radio frequency. The number of times a signal repeats in one second.

iDEN (Integrated Digital Enhanced Network) A proprietary standard developed by Motorola that is based on TDMA. It combines voice telephony, two-way radio, and short messaging features in one network.

i-Mode A popular wireless service offered by NTT DoCoMo. It enables voice services as well as wireless Internet access.

IMT-2000 The new 3G global standard for mobile communications as defined by the International Telecommunication Union. Also sometimes transposed with UMTS.

Indications of interest (IOIs) This is when you specify that you are interested in buying a certain amount of shares in an IPO. But this is not an obligation. You are only obligated to buy the shares on the day before the IPO.

IPO (Initial Public Offering) When a private company issues stock to the public for the first time. The shares are listed on a public exchange such as the New York Stock Exchange (NYSE) or Nasdaq.

ITU (International Telecommunication Union) A part of the United Nations, with headquarters in Geneva. This body attempts to promote the development and unification of all telecommunications services worldwide and mediates the global specifications for allocation of spectrum.

Junk bonds Bonds that have a higher risk of default. The bonds are rated as junk status according to two major agencies that judge the riskiness of bonds—Standard & Poor's (S&P) and Moody's.

LEO (Low-Earth Orbit) Refers to a communications satellite that orbits somewhere between 700 and 2,000 kilometers above the earth. These satellites typically can operate at lower power due to their close proximity to the earth's surface, but there must be more of them to provide global coverage.

Level loads This is a commission charged to an investor of a mutual fund. The fee is charged on an annual basis.

Load A mutual fund fee that represents a commission you pay to the broker who recommends a fund to you.

Lockup period A clause in most IPO deals, this is the period of time following an IPO (usually about 6 months) where early investors, employees, and insiders cannot sell shares.

MEO (Medium-Earth Orbit) A satellite system that orbits around 10,000 kilometers above the earth. These systems require about a dozen satellites to cover the globe.

MIN (Mobile Identification Number) A number assigned by the wireless service provider to a customer's phone. This number can be changed by the network operator depending on the area of service.

Mobitex A wireless data protocol developed by Ericsson, once known as RAM Mobile Data in the United States.

MoU (Minutes of Use) The amount of time a wireless subscriber uses on his or her portable device. The MoU is often reported by service providers in terms of the entire customer base. It gives an indication of the uptake of services and how well a company is marketing its services to users. The term *MoU* is also used to signify the GSM memorandum of understanding, which dictates the guidelines for GSM system operation.

Ni-Cd (nickel cadmium) Also called *nicads*, this is an older battery technology that is now losing favor in the wireless industry. These batteries have lower energy density than new technologies and suffer from the memory effect that weakens the battery if it is not discharged all the way down before recharging.

Ni-MH (nickel–metal hydride) A popular battery technology for wireless devices with its higher energy density and low cost. There is little memory effect in these batteries.

NMT (Nordic Mobile Telephone) An analog cellular protocol originally deployed in Europe and other areas.

Nondisclosure agreements (NDAs) A legal agreement that specifies what information an individual cannot repeat or distribute outside a meeting or event. Typically, NDAs are asked for when potential investors are given access to proprietary company information. The company wants to restrict individuals from using this privy information to compete against them or give advantage to existing competitors.

OFDM (Orthogonal Frequency Division Multiplexing) A modulation method for the transmission of high data rates in noisy environments where signals bounce off many objects before reaching the receiver.

OHG (Operators Harmonization Group) A group of wireless company representatives that wants to align the various competing wireless protocols to work on all major networks.

Online distribution With respect to an IPO, this is a method for distributing shares in a company over the Internet rather than through brokers or investment banks.

Operating margin A measurement of a company's relative profitability calculated by dividing operating profit by net sales.

Packet switching The process of transmitting information in packets over a network. Data are broken into individual strings that may be sent by different routes to the destination where they are reassembled correctly.

PC card An electronic circuit assembly card that is plugged into a motherboard to add specific functions (also known as a *PCMCIA card*). Wireless personal computer (PC) cards are used to make a normal computer into one that is capable of wireless data transmission.

PCMCIA (Personal Computer Memory Card International Association) A body that outlines specifications for PC cards.

PCS **(Personal Communications Services)** Usually refers to wireless services on the 1,900-MHz band in the United States. Several protocols such as GSM, TDMA, and CDMA have been implemented in PCS networks.

PDA (Personal Digital Assistant) A portable computing device that supports basic information management functions. The devices may perform functions such as scheduling and database management as well as such wireless functions as data messaging, e-mail, and Internet browsing.

PDC (Personal Digital Cellular) Based on TDMA technology, PDC is currently only used in Japan, where it is the dominant wireless technology.

PHS (Personal Handyphone System) A digital cordless phone system used primarily in Japan. It uses small cells to offer services similar to mobile cellular, but it is different in that it operates with the traditional home phone system to offer better economy.

PIM (Personal Information Management) A function often found in PDAs and computers, it is software that logs personal and business information, such as contacts, appointments, to-do lists, notes, and meeting reminders.

PIPE (Private Investment in Public Entities) When wealthy individuals or institutions (known as *accredited investors*) agree to invest significant amounts of capital in an existing public company.

POPs (Persons of Population) Telecommunications industry term for the number of potential subscribers within an area that could receive services.

Preferred stock A class of stock that has more advantages than common stock. In the event of liquidation, the preferred shareholders get money before common shareholders. Also, preferred shareholders typically have more voting control over such matters as changing management or approving new financing or a merger.

Prepaid cellular A service offered by network operators that allows subscribers to pay in advance for wireless service. This plan usually is used for customers with poor credit or those who would not use the services enough to warrant a monthly contract cost.

Prospectus This is a document a company files with the Securities and Exchange Commission (SEC) to issue stock to the public. The document is extensive, covering many aspects of a company's operations—such as management, the financials, product lines, and so on. The document is a very useful research tool when investing in wireless companies.

PSTN (Public Switched Telephone Network) A general term referring to the legacy voice telephone system, also called the Bell System in the United States.

Put option A clause in a private equity deal that gives you the right to sell back your shares to the company after a certain date (usually after a year) at a set price that is negotiable.

Quiet period The 25 days following an IPO during which an underwriter cannot publish a research report or make significant comments on a company. The quiet period was designed by SEC regulators to keep brokers and analysts from hyping a new IPO.

Redemption fees A fee paid when you sell shares of a mutual fund.

Registration rights This is when a company files with the SEC to allow investors to sell its stock in the open market.

Repeater An electronic subsystem that retransmits a weak signal at a higher power level. Cheaper than installing complete base stations, repeaters are used to extend the range of base station signals around areas that are difficult to cover.

Right of first refusal A clause in a private equity deal that gives you the right to invest in the next round of financing before other new investors do.

Roaming Using wireless services outside a service provider's designated local area. This usually incurs additional charges.

Satellite phone Sometimes called a *sat phone*, this handset uses connections to satellites to send and receive voice and data. Satellite phones are capable of providing service in areas where cellular does not reach.

Secondary offering This is when a company offers additional stock to the public after there has been an IPO.

Self-underwritten IPOs (also known as direct IPOs) When a company does not use an investment bank for its IPO. This is often because a company is unable to get an investment bank to believe in the prospects of the company enough to risk its own capital.

SID (System Identification Number) A unique number that is assigned to every wireless service provider. The number is programmed into the phones of all subscribers for network identification purposes.

SIM (Subscriber Identity Module) A smart card that is inserted into a wireless phone to store subscriber information such as phone number, personal feature settings, and messages. The SIM can be ported to multiple phones so that the user's service is transferable.

Smart antenna systems Also called *adaptive array antennas*, this technology tracks a received signal and dynamically adapts the antenna configuration to optimize wireless system performance. Special antennas are used with advanced signal-processing software to focus a signal on a subscriber rather than broadcasting the signal in all directions.

Smart card An electronic card containing data about a person's identity to allow access to a corporate network or building. In the wireless industry, this card contains subscriber information so that it can be used in roaming to different countries.

Smart phone A type of wireless phone that also includes some advanced data capabilities and other forms of input, such as a stylus or keyboard. The display is typically more advanced as well, capable of higher-resolution graphics.

SMS (Short Messaging Service) Short text messages that are sent across wireless networks. SMS is very popular in many countries and can account for a substantial amount of revenue for carrier companies.

Spectrum A range of frequencies. Also referred to as a *frequency band*. For wireless transmission, much of the electromagnetic spectrum is divided up into sections and allocated for use by government bodies in various countries.

Spectrum allocation The designation of the use of a band of frequencies by a government body. The allocation typically will specify the frequencies open for use and the types of services that can be offered on them.

Spectrum assignment Permission granted by a government body to make use of certain portions of allocated spectrum. The assignment usually will specify the range of frequencies permitted for use and the geographic area that they can be used in.

Spread spectrum A radio transmission technology that literally "spreads" information over greater bandwidth than necessary to make it tolerant to various forms of interference.

Standby time The amount of time a battery will supply to a handset turned on to receive incoming calls before it dies and turns the device off.

Talk time The length of time one can talk on a portable wireless device on a single battery charge. The battery capacity of a phone is usually expressed in terms of talk time and standby time, with talk time being much lower due to the higher power required when using the device.

TDMA (Time Division Multiple Access) A digital wireless technology that splits a channel into multiple time slots. This offers increases in capacity for a given bandwidth. TDMA systems are largely deployed in the Americas.

Telematics Adding wireless communications and location technology to vehicle monitoring systems to offer advanced services to vehicle drivers and passengers.

Tracking stock An issued security that merely tracks the financial performance of a certain part of a large company. The owner of a tracking stock actually has no ownership of the company, and he or she may not have any voting rights either.

Trimode Usually refers to a cellular phone that will work on 800-MHz analog, 800-MHz digital, and 1,900-MHz digital systems.

UMTS (Universal Mobile Telecommunication System) Refers to the effort to standardize 3G cellular systems. The UMTS Forum is composed of hundreds of companies in the wireless industry to promote a unified vision for the IMT-2000 standard.

Underwritten IPO When an investment bank backs a company's IPO with its own capital. In this type of IPO, the company raises cash regardless of public demand. Underwritten IPOs usually incur hefty fees from the investment bank.

UWCC (Universal Wireless Communications Consortium) An industry group supporting IS-136 TDMA and IS-41 wireless intelligent network technology.

Venture capital (VC) A venture capital firm raises money from wealthy individuals and institutions. The money is then invested in emerging private companies. Many top wireless companies had some type of venture capital funding.

WAP (Wireless Application Protocol) A protocol that specifies the structure of data signals such as Internet content and how they are transmitted to microbrowsers built into the portable device. WAP communications take place through special portals.

WARC (World Administrative Radio Conference) Biannual meetings of ITU member nations to discuss and resolve global spectrum allocation issues. Recent meetings have specified bands for offering 3G services.

W-CDMA (Wideband Code Division Multiple Access) The 3G network and air interface standard offered to the ITU by GSM proponents. This protocol is largely compatible with current GSM- and TDMA-based systems.

Wireless LAN Performing the functions of a local area network using wireless technologies, such as radio or infrared instead of phone lines or fiber-optic cable to connect devices.

WTO (World Trade Organization) A global organization set up in 1995 to oversee the rules of international trade. The Geneva-based group in 1997 negotiated the agreement to open trade and investment in basic telecommunications and information technology products.

SOURCES

INTRODUCTION

James M. Dorsey, "Think the New Economy Is Dead? It Hasn't Even Started," *Wall Street Journal*, June 25, 2001.

Thomas H. White, "United States Early Radio History"; available at *www.ipass.net/~whitetho/index.html* (Multipart series, 1998).

CHAPTER 1

O. Casey Corr, *Money from Thin Air* (New York: Crown Publishing, 2000).

Tom Farley, "Mobile Telephone History"; available at *www.telecomwriting.com*.

Tom Farley, "Telephone History Series"; available at *www.telecomwriting.com* (Adobe PDF, 2001).

Frant Fayant, "Fools and Their Money," *Success Magazine*, January 1907.

Melinda Patterson Grenier, "Boom and Bust," *Wall Street Journal*, November 7, 2000.

GSM Association (*www.gsmworld.com*).

Richard R. John, *The Significance of Postal Telegraphy: Toward an Alternative Genealogy of the Information Age* (Chicago: University of Illinois, 2001).

James Lardner, "Ask Radio Historians About the Internet," *U.S. News*, January 25, 1999.

J. Munro, "Heroes of the Telegraph"; available at *digital.library. upenn.edu/webbin/gutbook/lookus?num=979* (North Carolina: Project Gutenberg, Ibiblio, July 1997).

Tom Standage, *The Victorian Internet* (New York: Berkeley Publishing, 1999).

Kenneth P. Todd, Jr., edited by David Massey, "A Capsule History of the Bell System" (2001); available at *www.navyrelics.com/tribute/bellsys/ capsule_history_of_the_bell_system.html*.

Robert C. Ward, Jr., *The Chaos of Convergence: A Study of the Process of Decay, Change, and Transformation within the Telephone Policy Subsystem of the United States,* dissertation; available at *scholar.lib.vt.edu/theses/available/etd-0698-91234/* (Virginia Tech, Blacksburg, Virginia, 1997).

"Western Union Telegraph Company Collection 1848–1963," Archives Center, National Museum of American History, Smithsonian Institution, Washington, DC, 1990.

Thomas H. White, "United States Early Radio History" available at *www.ipass.net/~whitetho/index.html* (Multipart series, 1998).

CHAPTER 2

David Cassel, "Anthropologists Study Wireless Users," *M-Business,* January 12, 2001.

Nikhil Deogun and Steven Lipin, "Alcatel-Lucent Deal: Flowback May Net Foreign-Stock Selloff," *Wall Street Journal,* May 29, 2001.

Peter Lauria, "Vivendi Takes Manhattan," *The Deal,* June 1, 2001.

Dave Mock, *Wireless 201: An Investors Guide to Understanding 3G Technology and Markets,* May 2001, available at *www.MightyWords.com.*

Allyson Vaughan, "FCC Chair Speaks Mind on Fostering Competition," *Wireless Week,* May 28, 2001.

Allyson Vaughan, "Jury Out On Local Laws," *Wireless Week,* May 28, 2001.

CHAPTER 3

Phillip Ames and John Gabor, "The Evolution of Third-Generation Cellular Standards," *Intel Technology Journal,* 2Q2000.

Andy Dornan, "CDMA and 3G Cellular Networks," *Network Magazine,* September 5, 2000.

Dave Mock, *Wireless 201: An Investors Guide to Understanding 3G Technology and Markets,* May 2001; available at *www.MightyWords.com.*

Lisa Modisette, "Milking Wireless Churn for Profit," *Telecommunications Online,* February 1999.

Ramjee Prasad and Tero Ojanperä, "An Overview of CDMA Evolution toward Wideband CDMA," *IEEE Communications Surveys,* 1998.

Edward Warner, "The Great Negotiation: Searching for a 3G Standard," *Rural Telecommunications,* July-August 1999.

CHAPTER 4

Gil Bassak, "DSPs for Next-Generation Cell Phones Balance Performance and Power," *EDN Magazine*, November 23, 2000.

Anthony Cataldo, "3G Spawns 'Application Processor,'" *Electronic Engineering Times*, September 25, 2000.

Dave Mock, *Wireless 201: An Investors Guide to Understanding 3G Technology and Markets*, May 2001; available at *www.MightyWords.com*.

Dave Mock, *Wireless 350a: Emerging Wireless Technologies*, May 2001; available at *www.MightyWords.com*.

CHAPTER 5

David Lipschultz, "Security Issues Tether Wireless," *Red Herring*, June 11, 2001.

Dave Mock, "Cut Through the Wireless Noise," Presentation, Bellevue, Washington, March 2001.

CHAPTER 6

Stephen Blust and David Murotake, "Software-Defined Radio Moves Into Base-Station Designs," *Wireless Systems Design*, November 1999.

James Flanigan, "Superconducting Filter Firms Get Hot," *Los Angeles Times*, February 18, 2000.

Maeve McKenna, "Motorola Researchers Report Progress in Miniaturizing Fuel Cell Power Source," *Wireless Design Online*, September 27, 2000.

Dave Mock, *Wireless 101: A Guide to Wireless Investing for Newbies and Non-Techies*, May 2001; available at *www.MightyWords.com*.

Dave Mock, *Wireless 350a: Emerging Wireless Technologies*, May 2001; available at *www.MightyWords.com*.

Janine Sullivan, "Superconductor Filters Benefit 1, 2 and 3G Nets," *Wireless Design Online*, November 13, 2000.

John C. Tanner, "Disposable Batteries: A Surprising Turn in the Future of Portable Power," *America's Network*, November 1, 2000.

Peter Watson and Bettina Zapfe, "Telecommunications Services Using High-Altitude Platforms," Research Paper, University of Bath, Bath, United Kingdom; available at *www.bath.ac.uk/elec-eng/pages/research/rsrs/high_altitude_platforms.htm*.

CHAPTER 7

"World Wide Wireless Risk Factor," quoted from its public Edgar filings, Form 10-Q filed February 2001, available at *www.sec.gov*.

"o2Wireless Risk Factors," quoted from its public Edgar filings, Form S-1 files May 2000; available at *www.sec.gov*.

CHAPTER 8

Mara Der Hovanesian, "Junk Bonds: Pick 'em When They're Down," *BusinessWeek*, November 6, 2000.

Charles Gasparino, "Research Analysts Feel Increasing Heat over Their Ratings, Conflict of Interest," *Wall Street Journal*, June 13, 2001.

Bethany McLean, "Hear No Risk, See No Risk, Speak No Risk," *Fortune*, May 14, 2001.

J. P. Vicente, "Behind the Metricom Meltdown," *Red Herring*, July 4, 2001.

The Peter Friedland quote is found at *www.wrhambrecht.com*.

The Matthew Adams quote is found at *www.epoch.com*.

CHAPTER 9

Moon Ihlwan, "Asia Gets Hooked on Wireless," *BusinessWeek*, June 19, 2000.

CHAPTER 10

Sam Jaffee, "Street Wise," *BusinessWeek*, March 6, 2000,

Christopher J. Traulsen, "Turner B2B, Wireless Funds to Disappear," *Morningstar.com*, July 6, 2001.

Euro, 213
Europe:
  cellular standard in, 22, 24–25, 48, 49
  network operators in, 58
  (See also Finland; Nokia; Ericsson)
European Economic and Monetary Union (EMU), 213
European Telecommunications Standards Institute (ETSI), 45
European Union (EU), regulation in, 43
Everypath, 131
Expense ratios, 225–226
Extended Systems, 35–36

Faraday, Michael, 4
Fashion, 51–52
The Feature Web site, 253
Federal Bureau of Investigation (FBI), 43
Federal Communications Commission (FCC), 17–18, 19, 21, 22, 40, 41–42, 147, 250
Federal Radio Commission, 17
Federal Trade Commission (FTC), 38, 42
Fidelity Select Wireless, 228
Field service, enterprise solutions and, 121
Financial Times Web site, 250–251
Finland, 218, 220–222
  (See also Ericsson; Nokia)
Firewall systems, 133
Fixed networks, 61
Flipping, 171
Flolid, Mark, 242–243
Focus of business, 243
Forbes, Malcolm, 228
Forced churn, 78
Ford, Gerald, 42
Foreign investing, 209–224
  in ADSs, 215–217
  in Asia, 223–224
  in emerging markets, 210–211
  in Finland, 220–222
  liquidity and, 215
  privatization and, 211–212
  risks of, 212–215
  U.S. market significance and, 217–220
Frequency reuse, 20
Friedland, Peter, 202
Full-ratchet antidilution clauses, 239

Gabelli Fund, 230
Gabelli, Marc, 230
Gabelli, Mario, 230
Garmin Ltd., 89
Gates, Bill, 31
General Cellular, 36
General Electric (GE), 17, 21
General Instrument, 194
General Motors, 188
General Packet Radio System (GPRS), 67–68, 101
Gensler, Robert, 232

GeoBased Systems, 242, 243
Geological Development Center, 243
Global depositary receipts (GDRs), 216
Global markets, political issues in, 39–40
Global positioning systems (GPSs), 39–40, 88–89
Global System for Mobile Communications (GSM) standard, 22, 24–25, 37, 48, 49, 61–62, 63, 69, 108, 150, 217
Globalstar, 59–60, 142
GoAmerica, 80, 165, 171
Going concerns, 181
Goldman Sachs, 183
go2 Systems, 157
Gould, Jay, 12–13
Gray, Elisha, 10
Grubman, Jack, 203
GSM Alliance, 46
GSM Association Web site, 251
GTE, 135
Gulfstream, 194

Hambrecht, William, 171–172
Hambrecht & Quist, 171–172
Handie-talkies, 18
Handspring, 99, 102, 176, 181, 203
Havas, 52–53
Hayward, Brian, 230–231
Henry, Joseph, 4
Hertz, Heinrich, 13
Hewlett-Packard, 221
Hicks, Muse, Tate & Furst, 194
High Data Rate (HDR), 68
High-altitude platform systems (HAPSs), 152–155
High-Speed Circuit-Switched Data (HSCSD), 66–67
High-temperature superconducting (HTS) materials, 151
Hold/sell decisions, 191–207
  building wireless networks and, 199–200
  chat boards and, 206
  cockroach theory and, 205
  convertible financing and, 194–197
  hot markets and, 206–207
  insider selling and, 197–198
  with junk bonds, 192–194
  penny stocks and, 201–202
  price fluctuations and, 200–201
  research analysts and, 202–205
Hollings, Ernest, 38
HomeRF, 60
Hose, David, 242
Hot markets, 206–207
Houghton Mifflin Company, 53
How Stuff Works Web site, 251
Hubbard, Gardiner, 11
Hutchison 3G UK, 224
Hybrid phones, 99

i-Appli, 159–160
IBM, 34, 129

ICG, 195
Icon Telecommunications & Utilities Fund, 232
iDEN technology, 47–48
IEEE 802.11, 60
i-Mode service, 32, 68, 159
Incisent, 169
Incumbent local exchange carriers (ILECs), 177–178
Information risk, 214
Information technology (IT) spending, enterprise
    solutions and, 129
Informix, 132
InfoSpace, 202, 203
Infoworld Web site, 251
Infrastructure equipment, 105–108
Initial public offerings (IPOs), 163–190, 238
    for individual investors, 170–172
    prospectus and, 179–181
    risks with, 172–179
    spin-offs and, 184–187
    tips and strategies for, 182–184
    tracking stocks and, 187–188
Insider buying, 136–138
Insider selling, 197–198
Institute of Electrical and Electronic Engineers
    (IEEE) 802.11b standard, 132
Intel, 33–34
Intellectual property (IP), 70, 90, 95–98, 109–110
International Telecommunications Union (ITU), 46,
    251–252
Internet Security Systems, 133
InterVoice-Brite, 138
Intuit, 176
Inventory management, 110–111, 120
Invesco Telecommunications, 230–231
Investec Wireless World, 229
Investment banks, 166–167
Iridium, 59, 142
i3 Mobile, 178–179
ITT, 212

Jacobs, Irwin, 163, 164
Japan, 224
    consumer applications in, 159–160
    wireless security in, 132–133
J&D Software, 242
Jeremy's Microbatch Ice Cream, 165
Johnston, Stephen, 174, 175, 176
Jphone, 32
Junk bonds, 192–194

Kaston, Mark, 203
Kertzman, Mitchell, 181
KG Telecom, 224
Kirkham, Seth, 229
Klein, Andrew, 170–171
Kligfield, Roy, 243
Kohlberg Kravis Roberts, 194
KPN Mobile, 222, 224
Kyocera, 99

Land-based technology, 60–61
Latin America, 211
Lazaridis, Mike, 33
Leap Wireless, 77, 229
Level loads, 226
Lewis, Scott, 231
Licensed POPs, 74
Lightbridge, 135–136
Liquidity, 215
Liquidity events, 240
Litigation involving IPOs, 173–174
Loads, 226
Location services, 157
Location-based services, 82–83
Lockup periods, 170
LocusOne, 169
Los Alamos National Laboratory, 150
Low-earth-orbiting (LEO) satellite systems, 142
Lucent, 107, 194, 203

MacFarlane, John, 158
Magazines, 254–255
Management compensation, 180–181
Manhattan Scientifics, 150
Marconi, Guglielmo, 13–14
Marconi Wireless, 16
Market orders, 182
Market penetration, 218
Market risk, 214
MarketClip, 167
M-Business magazine, 254–255
Mbusinessdaily Web site, 252
McBride, Vincent, 231
McCaw Cellular, 36, 192
MCI, 192
McLeodUSA, 195
M-commerce, 121–122
Mechanical Technology, 150
Mergers and acquisitions (M&As), 34–38
    approval of, 42
    convergence and, 52–53
    enterprise solutions and, 128
Merrill Lynch, 167, 168
Messier, Jean-Marie, 52–53
Metawave, 151
Metricom, 100, 142, 199–200, 202
Metromedia, 192
Micro Cellular Data Network, 142
Micro-fuel cell technology, 148–150
Microprocessors, 89–90
Microsoft, 30–31, 34, 91–92, 98, 129–130, 132, 203,
    236
Microsoft Mobility, 31
Microtune, 183
Miliken, Mike, 192
Military, radio use by, 14
Millicom International Cellular, 232
Minutes of use (MoU), 77–78
Mobeo, 167, 168
Mobile Commuting Web site, 252

Mobile Internet software solutions, 157–158
Mobile Switching Centers (MSCs), 105–106
Mobile telephone systems (MTSs), early, 18, 19–20
MobileSys, 126
Mobitex, 66
Momentum investing, 134–136
Moore, Gordon, 119
Moore's law, 119
Morgan Stanley, 167
Morphics, 147
Morse, Samuel, 7–8
Morse code, 7–8
Motley Fool.com, 206
Motorola, 18, 21, 47, 48, 88, 89, 99, 100, 103, 106, 107, 108, 110, 150, 223
MP3.com, 53
Murdock, Rupert, 52
Mustonen, Panu, 222
Mutual funds, 225–233
    background of, 227–233
    benefits of, 227
    expense ratios of, 225–226
    fees and, 226

Netscape, 176
Net2phone, 65
Network operators, 55–84
    circuits versus packets and, 64–67
    coverage of, 75
    2.5G and 3G, 67–73
    1G/2G, 61–63
    investment themes for, 79–83
    metrics for, 73–79
    relationship with equipment suppliers, 102–103
    role in industry, 57–58
    technology and, 58–61
Network protection companies, 133
Network-level equipment suppliers, 89
News Corp, 52, 192
Newsletters, 256
Nextel Communications, 47–48, 57, 76, 158, 202, 230
Nextel Partners, 165
NEXTLINK, 177
NextWave, 41
Niche markets, 89
Nokia, 88, 89, 99, 101, 102, 106, 107, 108, 210, 213, 220, 221, 222, 231
Nondisclosure agreements (NDAs), 241
Nordea, 229
Nordic Mobile Telephone (NMT), 23, 63
Nortel Networks, 107, 175, 176, 194
Novatel Wireless, 165
Novell, 129
NTT DoCoMo, 30, 32, 132–133, 159–160, 217, 220, 224, 231

Olympic Venture Partners (OVP), 242
Omnipoint, 37, 178

OmniSky, 165, 167, 169, 177
Onebox.com, 158
Online distribution, 170–171
OpenIPO, 172
Openwave Services OS, 158
Openwave Systems, 157–158, 202, 203, 228
Operators Harmonization Group (OHG), 71
Oracle, 31–32, 34, 123, 125, 129, 130–131, 132
Orange, 222
Original Equipment Manufacturer (OEM) companies, 47
Original Equipment Manufacturer (OEM) modules, 87
Oros, David, 167, 169, 176–177
Orton, William, 11
o2wireless Solutions, 80, 165, 174–176
Overlay, 66

Pacific Bell, 178
Pacific Northwest Cellular, 36
Pacific Telegraph Company, 9, 10
Pacific Telesis, 243
Packet-based networks, 64–65
Pagers, 99
Palm, 35–36, 51, 99, 102, 111, 156, 182, 203
PaperWhite LCD display, 95
Parent companies, 81–82
Partner Communications, 232
Pena, Patricia, 43
Penetration rates, 218
Penny stocks, 201–202
Personal Communications Service (PCS), 37, 150
Personal digital assistants (PDAs), 86, 99, 156
Personal Digital Communications (PDC), 62, 63, 108
Personal Handyphone System (PHS), 64
Personal information management (PIM), enterprise solutions and, 121
Pets.com, 165
Phone.com, 158–159
Picocell environments, 59
Pincus Emerging Markets Fund, 231
Platforms Wireless, 155
Pocket PCs, 99
PocketNet service, 102
Political issues, 38–40
Political risk, 212
Portable equipment, 98–100
    suppliers of, 88–89
Potential customers (POPs), 73–74
Powertel, 37
Preferred stock, 239
PrimeCo PCS, 178
Private equity investing, 235–245
    approach for, 241–244
    dealflow and, 244–245
    protections for, 238–241
    risks versus rewards of, 235–238
Private investment in public entities (PIPE), 194–197

Private market value, 230
Privatization, 211–212
Product line mix, 111
Profit margins, 110
Profits, 178–179, 237
Prospectus, 168, 179–181
Provenance, Jeff, 228
Pump-and-dump schemes, 183–184
Put options, 240

QUALCOMM, 39, 50, 51, 69, 70–71, 97–98, 134,
      163–164, 174, 206, 212, 228
Quality of service (QoS), 78–79
QuickSilver Technology, 147–148
QuoteAlertService, 178
Qwest Communications, 177, 231

Radio:
   early development of, 13–17
   in World War II, 18
Radio access network (RAN), 106
Radio Corporation of America (RCA), 17, 21
Radio frequency (RF) circuits, 90
Radio frequency (RF) components, 94
Ragingbull.com, 206
Rambus Inc., 71, 96–97
RCN Corp., 195
Red Herring Web site, 252–253
Redemption fees, 226
Registration of stock, 213
Registration rights, 240
Regulation:
   in United States, 39, 40–44
   outside United States, 43
Research analysts, 202–205
Research In Motion (RIM), 33, 34, 35, 88, 99, 102,
      142, 171, 203
Reuters, 167, 169
RF Micro devices, 87
Rhythms Net Connections, 195
Ricochet, 199
Right of first refusal, 240
Riverbed Technologies, 169
RJR Nabisco, 194
Road shows, 168
Rose, Mark, 204
Rossman, Alain, 158

S-1 filing, 168
Safeway, 194
Salomon Smith Barney, 204
Sanyo Fashion House, 51
SAP, 32–33
Satellite technology, 59–60
SBC Communications, 178, 232
Scanners, 88
SCC Communications, 242
Schiffer, Claudia, 51

Security, 132–133
Sell decisions (see Hold/sell decisions)
Service providers (see Network operators)
Seven Up, 194
SG Cowen, 183
Shamrock Capital Advisors, 222
Shareholder rights, 215
Short Messaging Service (SMS), 102, 219
Short-range technology, 60
Siebel Systems, 123–125, 130
Siemens, 99
Sierra Wireless, 100
Sievel, Tom, 123
SignalSoft, 242
Single Carrier Radio Transmission Technology
      (1xRTT), 68
SK Telecom, 216–217
Sky Station, 154
Smart antenna systems, 150–152
Smartphones, 99
Smith, Alan, 37
Softbank, 65
Software.com, 158–159
Software-defined radio (SDR), 145–148
Sommer, Ron, 38
Sonera, 222
Sony, 98
South Africa, 211
Southwestern Bell, 19
Spin-offs, 185–187
Spring Street, 170
Springtoys, 222
Sprint, 57, 175, 176
Sprint PCS, 48, 57, 75, 76, 100, 103, 131, 157, 158,
      188, 199, 202, 228
Stability of network operators, 79–80
Standards, 22–23, 24–25, 37, 44–51, 48, 49
Standards development organizations (SDOs),
      44–45
Stanton, John, 36–37, 43
State laws, 43
Stock exchange rules, 215
Stop losses, 200–201
Strigl, Dennis, 146
StrongARM processor, 33, 92
Subsidiaries, 81–82
Sun Microsystems, 34
Supercharged preferred stock, 239
Superconducting filter technologies, 151
Superconductor Technologies, 151
Symantec, 133
Symbol Technologies, 88, 104

T. Rowe Price Media and Telecom Fund, 232
Tawell, John, 5
Telebras, 211
Telecom Italia, 220
Telecom Writing Web site, 253
Telecommunication Technology Committee, The
      (TTC), 45

Telecommunications Industry Association (TIA), 45
Telecommunications Technology Association
    (TTA), 45
TeleCorp, 135, 229
Telegraph, 4–10
Telephone & Data Systems, 230, 232
Telephones, 90–91, 99
    early development of, 10–13, 15
    mobile, early, 18, 19–20
TeleSpeed, 177
Telespree Communications, 155
Teligent, 195
Telsim, 108
Terra Mobile, 222
Texas Instruments (TI), 87, 88, 93
Thestreet.com, 253
Thomas Bros. Maps, 243
Three-Five Systems, 95
3G Partnership Project (3GPP), 46
3G Partnership Project 2 (3GPP2), 46
Time Division Multiple Access (TDMA), 62, 63,
    147–148
Time Warner, 52, 192
Total Access Communications Systems (TACSs),
    23, 63
Total cost of ownership (TCO), 126
Toys"R"Us, 117
Tracking stocks, 187–188
Trans-Atlantic cable, 6–7
Transistors, 20
Trend Micro, 133
Triton PCS, 228
TTI Team Telecom, 229
Turner, 192
Turner Wireless and Communication, 228
Two-way pagers, 88

Underwriting, 165
Uninitiated churn, 78
United Parcel Service (UPS), 118–119
United Wireless, 16
Universal, 53
Universal servers, 132
Universal Wireless Communications Consortium
    (UWCC), 45
Unstrung Web site, 254
US Cellular, 178
USS Squalus, sinking of, 8

Vail, Theodore, 12
Valuation, 240–241
Vendor financing, 107
Venture capitalists, 134
    (See also Private equity investing)
VeriSign, 133

Verizon Communications, 76, 81–82, 151, 230, 232
Verizon Wireless, 48, 57–58, 103, 146, 158
Viacom, 192
Vicinity, 203
Videos, 256
Vivendi, 52
Vizzavi, 53
Vodafone, 57, 228
Vodafone AirTouch plc, 219, 231
Voice communications, 60, 62–64
Voice over Internet Protocol (VoIP), 65
VoiceStream, 37, 38, 57
Voluntary churn, 78
Vyyo, 165

Walkie-talkies, 18
Watson, Thomas, 11
Web sites as resources, 249–254
Wellington partners, 222
Western Union, 6, 7, 9–10, 11–13
Western Wireless, 36, 37, 229, 231
Westinghouse Electric, 167
Wheatstone, Charles, 5
White, Abraham, 16
Wideband Code Division Multiple Access
    (W-CDMA), 50, 69, 72, 146, 150
Wilmer, Cutler & Pickering, 168
Winstar, 195, 203–204
Winters, Donald, 243
Wired Equivalent Privacy (WEP), 132
Wireless Application Protocol (WAP), 68
Wireless communicators, 99
Wireless consortiums, 45–46
Wireless Fund, 228
Wireless PC cards, 100
Wireless Ultrasector, 229–230
Wireless Week magazine, 255
Wireless Week Web site, 254
Wit Capital, 171
WorldCom, 57, 199
WR Hambrecht, 172, 202
WR Hambrecht + Co Web site, 254

Xilinx, 147
XO Communications, 195

Yahoo.com, 206
Young, Owen D., 17

Ziff-Davis Publishing, 194

ABOUT THE AUTHORS

Tom Taulli is an analyst with NetCap Ventures, an investment banking firm in Newport Beach, California. The author of *Investing in IPOs* and *Stock Options*, Taulli also is a regular contributor to print and online resources including *Bloomberg Personal Finance*, CBS Market-Watch, and others. He has been a guest commentator on CNBC, CNN, and Bloomberg TV.

Dave Mock is a syndicated columnist. Mock's in-depth reports on wireless technologies and the wireless industry have appeared in online resources including MotleyFool.com, unstrung.com, and others and are distributed to a variety of corporations and associations. Among his most popular reports are the investors' guides *Wireless 101* and *Wireless 201*.